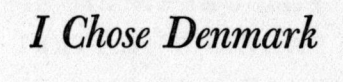

I Chose Denmark

BOOKS BY
FRANCIS HACKETT

I CHOSE DENMARK
QUEEN ANNE BOLEYN
THE GREEN LION
FRANCIS THE FIRST
HENRY THE EIGHTH
THE STORY OF THE IRISH NATION
THAT NICE YOUNG COUPLE
THE INVISIBLE CENSOR
HORIZONS: A BOOK OF CRITICISM
IRELAND: A STUDY IN NATIONALISM

FRANCIS HACKETT

I Chose Denmark

NEW YORK
Doubleday, Doran & Company, Inc.
1941

COPYRIGHT, 1940
BY FRANCIS HACKETT
ALL RIGHTS RESERVED
PRINTED IN THE UNITED STATES OF AMERICA
AMERICAN BOOK—STRATFORD PRESS, INC., NEW YORK

To My Dear Friends in Denmark
Better Unnamed

In the realm of the spirit Denmark is a great power.
                                    ULRICH VON WILAMOWITZ

Foreword

WE ARE BORN for a purpose. That purpose, it seems to me, is to revolt and to reshape. This book, in consequence, is an attempt to describe the reshaping of a nonconformity. And by saying, "I chose Denmark," my object is to underline the word "chose."

Let me spell this out. Those of us who live at all under the surface do not come lightly by our preferences. At the first they are the very core of our revolt. One of the worst agonies of our youth—and here, of course, I think of my own youth—is to fight out the duel between what was given to us as essential and what we are driven to prefer. The primeval slime is nothing to the platitude we are born into. To clean ourselves of it, our hands caked with custom, is the painful experience of our growing years. We cannot avoid the revolt. We must revolt, if we are worth our salt. And this is all the more forced on us if we are capable of ideals.

But our desire to consult our preferences, when these preferences are so often dilated by demagogues, is one of the most treacherous impulses we have. The heralds of revolt are often specialists in maladjustment who perpetuate maladjustment with the same zeal as that with which pickpockets recruit pickpockets. The leaders of youth are often misleaders. It is a point that scarcely has to be argued in 1940. The technique for misleading youth is, you might say, patented.

The time must come, then, when we who revolted have to try to become freshly and fully aware of ourselves.

At such a time we choose our community, if it be in our power. Our nonconformity, in a word, has prepared for a positive attitude. We may only move from Chicago to Washington, or, indeed, from Washington to Chicago. But we stop winding around; we settle down.

The degree to which a rebel settles down, admitting he is satisfied without being ossified, is the degree to which he has reshaped the existence that life gave him as plastic. He may be ashamed to settle down at all, of course—some men are like those sea gulls who always keep on the go, greedy to escort a new ship as far as the harbor and then off to meet the new one. (What has happened to them, I wonder, since the liners ceased to sail?) But these wander-birds are the exception. Even if it be only arthritis that anchors us, most of us end by being anchored. But on what terms? Are we cornered or are we contented; that is the big question.

When I say, "on the terms of Denmark, all things considered," I answer it with the war flaming before me and with Germany pushing its empire over the world. That empire, I know, has something in it so terrible and so imposing that fickle creatures only want to be sure that it has been achieved to take off their hats to it. Such creatures, the instant a small country is invaded, blame it for being small; and if it strove to be neutral, they blame it for that. In these matters, however, one should not be fickle. A small neutral country can always be overrun by a great belligerent. A small child, by the same token, can always be overrun by a bully. A small child, in fact, is regarded as fair political game by the very men who regard a small nation as fair game. But to protest against this, to assert one's choice against this and one's experience against this, is to arrive back at Denmark by another route. For the reason that there is an upheaval in the world masquerading as a "revolution," Denmark lives in my mind as the abiding argument against upheaval. And this in view of the downfall of Denmark. There have been such downfalls before. They need not be fatal.

A true choice is highly personal. I do not say, "I prefer Denmark for you." I say, "I prefer Denmark for me." Were I a messianic type, I'd believe in it so much that I'd willingly put tanks and bombers behind my choice. But ardent as my belief is, I propose to spread it before you on its merits and to leave conclusions to yourself. I do this believing that Denmark's independence is of inestimable importance in the world at large.

That such an independence was not imbedded in a military union, that it could be shattered overnight, does not for one moment shake my argument. An idiot can destroy a masterpiece in a second, and man himself is the most fragile of masterpieces, killed while you wink. Man's fragility in the flesh, however, does not impair man's claim to consideration. Lincoln dead by a bullet is no less Lincoln. The mortality of Lincoln, Garfield and McKinley creates a police problem; it does not touch the majesty of the office or its indispensability.

Denmark in a barbed-wire cage is no less Denmark, the spiritual being. For if the State be a being, and it can be asserted, then Denmark goes on, whether imprisoned or not. The history of mankind is too long, and too full of irony, to let us suppose that the accidents of April 1940 are decisive forever.

This is not to minimize the German will to dominate, which has now kept Europe boiling for a century and which made Bismarck say that it might have been better if he had never been born. In a period of such upheaval, when the human will is whipped to fury, there can be no doubt that new conditions, perhaps almost insurmountable conditions, are about to be imposed on man's immediate destiny. No Irishman, I assure you, is prone to forget what it has meant to himself to have been one of a conquered people. But while the very air we breathe is now laden with war, so that it is in our pores, our blood and our heart, while we cannot live without inhaling it or draw a breath without a stab, yet we remain creatures of our free past, which is so rich with our mature choice that we must revive it to be just to our being.

And this persistence of the past is inescapable. How weak, after all, the Catholic Church was in the fury of the Reformation. But how strong the Counter Reformation was! That degenerate Papacy became a Papacy with iron in it, and then the Catholic choice was to a degree restated and reinstated, feeble as it seemed in the days of Luther and Calvin.

We, the Democrats, have not supposed that we must assert ourselves aggressively. Our faith has been sapped because of that. But it is a faith, and in Denmark so living a faith that I chose to live there. As a faith, in my opinion, it can no more be extinguished than the eohippus was. The specialists in maladjustment to the contrary.

Why I chose to live in Denmark makes me refer from time to time to conditions in Ireland and England. If these comparisons are wounding, I regret it. By pointing to these two other homogeneous countries familiar to me I hope to make Denmark clearer; and it is necessarily myself, drawing on my wife Signe Toksvig at every turn, that I have to offer as a witness to Denmark—Denmark before April 9, 1940.

Contents

CHAPTER		PAGE
	Foreword	ix
One	We Make a Visit	1
Two	Frame of the Picture	23
Three	We Go to a Farm	38
Four	Farmers at School	57
Five	Is Man a Machine?	74
Six	In Search of a Social Faith	84
Seven	Government Goes to School	91
Eight	Soul Planning	100
Nine	Have Danes Got Souls?	115
Ten	Danish Modesty	125
Eleven	Danish Compassion	137
Twelve	Danish Curiosity	150
Thirteen	We Leave Ireland	164
Fourteen	The Capital	174
Fifteen	We Rent a Flat	190

CHAPTER		PAGE
Sixteen	Guardian Aesthete	201
Seventeen	We Eat and Drink	216
Eighteen	Fighting Dane	228
Nineteen	Class Spiral	242
Twenty	I Find Grandfather	252
Twenty-one	Noble Lady	266
Twenty-two	*Danmark* Ahoy!	279

I Chose Denmark

CHAPTER ONE

We Make a Visit

DIVINATION is a rare thing. When Signe Toksvig took her degree at Cornell she came to New York to a monthly called *Vogue*. It was Frank Crowninshield who divined her. He said, "My dear, you ought to be on the *New Republic*," and he sent her to Herbert Croly.

In those days the *New Republic's* little house on Twenty-first Street centered about two people whose names were not in the box. They were Martin and Marie, and they were from Savoy. Martin served the incomparable lunches that Marie cooked, and we, the staff, were thereby mellowed into the superiority for which we were justly famous.

The young Danish guest who was seated at Herbert Croly's right hand was not daunted by our solemnity. For the first time she was with the editors of a weekly that she had devoured at college, and as the daughter of a Danish editor it was a tingling excitement to be among men of the craft, one of whom, Alvin Johnson, had a Danish name. She wore a simple gray dress; she was pastel; her laughter had a fresh sparkle. As I took her to the door she smiled and shook hands firmly. "I'm coming back," she said with an animation that was a little tremulous. And she ran down the steps.

That was a strange announcement. I looked after her, hoping it was true; but what was to bring her back?

Herbert Croly was. He had made her assistant editor. She was soon back, in a room next to my own, and doing tons of work. Everyone was to discover this room: Walter Weyl, Walter Lippmann, Alvin, Phil Littell, Charlie Merz, even contributors like Harold Stearns and Harold Laski. That room on the top floor was the most living in Twenty-first Street.

On a Tuesday in 1918, before we put the paper to press, I told my colleagues they were asked to a wedding on Thursday. Signe and I were both supporters of the Lucy Stone League, by which Heywood Broun and Ruth Hale were to keep their names separate, and we proposed to keep our own names separate however our lives were joined. And we were also "modern" enough not to want much ceremony or any presents. But it was a marriage in the bosom of the family, so to speak. I met Norman Angell on the street as I went to it and asked him to come with me. But at that time it was equally modern to have all your teeth out, and I had to excuse him for this prior engagement, as you cannot have that done by proxy. In Sixty-fifth Street, in a house lent by a good friend from the earliest *New Republic* days, we stood with the long windows opening to the little green outside, and there, with friends close around us, we were married.

We then supposed we had left the paper for a week end. We stole to the roof of the Ritz to have dinner. As we sat by shaded light at a little table two men came over.

"We are going to throw you off the roof," said one of them.

I looked at them; two novelists I had reviewed, Winston Churchill and Ernest Poole. I faced Winston Churchill.

"Kamarad!" I pleaded. "You can't do it. We've just been married."

They spared a critic. And then Dorothy Straight, who was dining with them, came over to the bride. Two members of the staff! She, who had brought the *New Republic* into existence,

We Make a Visit

was visibly and deliciously astonished. She glowed. She was as excited as a child. And when later on she asked, new silver or old silver, we were no longer so fiercely modern. We said Georgian.

Once the war was over we took leave to go to Europe. In 1920 we set out for a Denmark that Signe had not seen for fourteen years. "It had been withdrawn from me," she said, "as a low, dark cloud at the gray water's end." She was to see it again from the deck of the Harwich-Esbjerg boat on which we crossed the North Sea. The sea shimmered in soft blues, bluer than her gayest illusions, and in this shimmer came a sudden silver line, the flat low sandy coast of Jutland.

Esbjerg is a new town, like a pair of white cuffs that Jutland has attached to itself. Signe saw it in a haze of joy. "I went around smiling fatuously at children," she said afterward, "because they were pink and white and gold and wore wooden shoes that went *click-click* on the pavement. I nodded to women in tiny houses because they sat behind sparklingly clean windows, with snow-white curtains and gay flowerpots. I loved the windows because they opened outward, as it seemed to me that windows should, instead of sliding up and down. I pointed out with swelling pride to my non-Danish companion"—that's me—"the spotless streets, the immaculate shops, the large handsome schools, the various co-operatives, the new post office—which, although new, was clearly in the best of taste, and the order and despatch inside filled me with more rapture."

And in spite of all this, in spite of the slight constraint between myself and this spotless, sparkling Esbjerg to which Signe was introducing me while Esbjerg looked a little sheepish and even winked at me behind her back, in spite of this handicap of perfection under which Denmark seemed to be laboring, I was nobly reserving judgment.

"You're all right, Esbjerg," I said. "Don't mind poor Signe. She hasn't seen a co-operative that she has really been in love with for fourteen years. After a while we'll calm down. But meanwhile hadn't we better push on to Copenhagen?"

2

In Copenhagen we had the luck to meet Per Faber, attached to the Foreign Office.

Per Faber was like a host in his home. The benign curve of his figure increased the kind impression he made; he opened his arms to us from the first, to assure us of welcome and to spread Denmark at our feet. It was no literal hospitality like taking us to lunch. It was Denmark itself he invited us to, and we felt we had a beneficent friend.

So completely did we rely on him that we threw ourselves on his guidance for a place to stay. Signe, after all, had not been running around everywhere in Denmark fourteen years before. She was a stranger in Copenhagen. And we were tired; we had been living between the Second and Third Avenue els in New York, so that we had been pounded, triturated, for several years. We wanted that ideal place for rest: an inn near the sea, not far from the city, perfectly comfortable, with linen sheets if possible, good walks in the neighborhood, utterly quiet and very cheap.

All I asked was to be taken care of.

Per Faber, one of those Copenhageners not in the least informed about summer hotels, plucked his lip a little, looking at us with a round eye. He suggested Køge.

It would have been like a New Yorker suggesting Perth Amboy. We leaped at it. We went in perfect faith, which is said to move mountains. There was actually a hotel, right on the water.

"Wonderful!" we said in chorus.

It was a summer hotel. Someone sneezed in a remote room. It was no secret to anyone in the building.

"It is just a summer hotel, of course," said Signe.

We Make a Visit

"Built of wood, I presume?" said I.

We shared each other's joys and sorrows in that building.

At our first meal I was next the wife of a Danish schoolteacher. She was one of those bright-eyed, russet little women who twinkle and peck through life. She was English. She had been fifteen years in Denmark and much attached to it, but not enough to learn Danish.

"Look," she said to me when a big platter of lobster was brought in. I looked, and with an ineffable smile she said, "They call that *hummer.*"

"It is very wrong of them," I said. "They know it is lobster."

"Of course they do," she agreed, "but they call it *hummer.*"

"Then God help them," said I.

We could swim at Køge, in clear water that was astonishingly warm, far warmer than the waters of Long Island. We ambled to Vallø Slot, a castle in a forest, where, as at Hampton Court, there were quarters for privileged noblewomen. As my norm for all castles is Kilkenny castle, within sight of which I was reared, the mere antiquity of Vallø and even the drawbridge and the moat did not overwhelm me; but we walked in the grounds, we saw the swans, and grave-eyed, simply dressed ladies passed us with that porcelain refinement in their features which is the effect of breeding, but a breeding that in Denmark, curiously enough, is at home on a bicycle, in a bus or at a market, a breeding that demands no glass case, that is in fact currency in daily life and with the plain accent of good Danish, however much there is feeling for things ancient and honorable.

We listened to about a hundred bakers and cakemakers, one night at the hotel, who had driven there in wagonettes and sat at long tables in a shed, clinking glasses and singing. They sang long ballads that Signe knew and loved. We stood there, gazing in, and all the bakers singing.

We walked into Køge itself, along a shore at that time not yet quite certain whether to be a promenade or a dump heap. Køge was an old town with long houses that had become bandy-walled, red of complexion, with casement windows and beams in the walls.

But that ideal vacation we were seeking, that inn into whose arms we could sink, that blend of country house and nursing home—it was not to be wheedled out of the breezy, cheerful wayside hotel where dishes and tongues were clattering.

It was many years before we were to find the place that Per Faber did not know about. It was Hornbækhus at Hornbæk, and, considering its taste, what it cost, its setting and its meals, the best-run small hotel in the world. Yet in spite of our errors and our trials we came back to Copenhagen blaming only ourselves for our ignorance. And it was then we were told that, if we liked, we might join the journalists who were going to South Jutland for the Reunion Festivities.

3

When I knew that we were to be present at the reunion of South Jutland to Denmark, actually see King Christian X cross the border to resume Danish sovereignty, my heart was moved. This, under the Versailles Treaty, was an act of pure justice, carrying out a pledge that Bismarck had broken and carrying it out with a scrupulousness that no nationalism had tainted, despite the mood of Europe after the 1914–18 war when Irredentists were everywhere and grabbing everything.

South Jutland, otherwise known as Slesvig, was part of that long-disputed territory in Europe known as Schleswig-Holstein. It is the neck by which the head of Jutland fits into the German shoulders. And when Germany had swelled its neck in 1864 it had flushed up into Denmark, absorbing South Jutland.

It was under the Versailles Treaty that Denmark was given the chance to recover its lost territory.

There were militant Danes who wished to see Germanized Slesvig carved out of Germany and restored to Denmark. But here is where a country with vigorous public opinion could assert itself against excessive nationalism. True as it was that the Germans had taken a big slice of territory after 1864, with 430,000 people in it, it was equally true that Holstein was a dukedom brought into Denmark by intermarriages. The people in it were not Danes by true affiliation. And in the southern part of Slesvig, where the people were Danes, many had been unchangeably Germanized.

The fighting type of Dane took the territorial rather than the social view of Slesvig. They wanted it reclaimed down to Kiel under the Versailles Treaty, and the junker was stirred in some as if old hunters pricked up their ears at the sound of the horn. There was sympathy for them in high places, and French and English diplomats whose object was to weaken Germany were only too happy to have Denmark go in deep.

The radicals in Denmark said NO. They were vehement. They marched to the king's palace to demonstrate against the militants.

It came in the end to a plebiscite in two zones, each zone a social unit.

After 1864, it must be said, the Germans on top in Schleswig-Holstein had done everything to root out Danish loyalty. They brought pressure on the people with that rule-or-ruin thoroughness that the centuries have not mellowed. They favored their own race. They conscripted the Danes or else deprived them of civic rights. They showed prejudice in the courts. They colonized methodically. They put police everywhere, using spies to detect nonconformity and the whip to punish it. They were detestable, as imperialists so often contrive to be without knowing it.

The defense of Denmark in 1864 had been magnificent in courage and audacity, steadiness and endurance. It compares to the defense of Finland in 1940. The submerged Danes had the possession of self that German methods intensify. The methods that make for conquest, indeed, seldom make for absorption. If they did, Europe would not bristle with differences, grievances, misunderstandings, antagonisms, hatreds, assassinations, murders, repressions, slaughter, bluster and the constant threat of "annihilation." It is remarkable how the most strenuous nationalists have tried to crush other nationalists time after time. And the ones who were down usually are the worst when they come up.

The Germans did not win hearts in North Slesvig. The Danes remained as Danish as their songs. Had they been as viciously handled as, say, the Armenians by the Turks, or had they been as inflexible as the Red Indians, they could not have come through. But against demoralization they had the inner resources of a people that had never been broken, that had matured a culture and made community into an organism. To root out a memory that has once been organized, a sentiment that has been cultivated, to break down human interrelations that have become trusting, sensitive and scrupulous, can't be accomplished easily. The Danes in North Slesvig held together like woven willows.

But for the Folk High School influence, it is doubtful whether the 165,000 Danes who occupied fifteen hundred square miles could ever have been kept permanently Danish. But the leaders were men who had come under Grundtvigian influence, who had a social and democratic outlook, who both yielded and held fast, urging the constitutional method, staying inside the law, incessantly defending the Danes in North Slesvig. They did not go far enough to suit the militant. They went altogether too far to suit the Germans.

Denmark itself, goaded by Bismarck's aggression in 1864, might have thrown in its lot with France in the Franco-Prussian War. It could thus have made a bid for victory at the risk of irreparable harm. Its restraint, by no means unanimous, was wise. With Germany thrust into it Denmark had to make the best of it without war.

But while the Allies took away this clamp in 1919, the source of the Reunion was not the Allies. It was the plebiscite that had

We Make a Visit

been promised to them by Germany in 1866. In the southern zone the Danes lost, and a Danish minority had to remain in Germany. In the northern zone a corresponding Germanized minority, about thirty thousand, had to stay with the Danes.

These accomplishments, to my mind, were democratic, not overweeningly nationalist. It was the will of the people in the northern zone to return to the land of their fathers, Denmark, and they returned, not to join a Greater Denmark, to swell an imperialist aggregation, but to function as citizens whose existence had been balked for years.

4

Stranger as I was, there were moments of this Reunion that overcame me.

A tall man on a horse is a tall man on a horse. A glance could tell you that King Christian X was a soldier. He rode on his white horse under a portal of green branches. Blossoms were strewn in his path for miles.

But there was a multitude to greet him, women and children with the men. They could breathe. They could talk and sing. A relief and an exaltation poured from them so that they hardly knew whether to laugh or to cry. If ever I saw people transfigured, it was the people in this multitude. To keep themselves from breaking down they launched on songs with quivering voices, and then the songs carried them into the deep so that they could let their voices fill like buoyant sails. The sun shone on them, spilled on their gala clothes, their fair hair, their bright cheeks dewed by tears. They hummed with sound, while the King's Own Royal Guard from Copenhagen played over and over, "Den Gang jeg drog afsted," that song the Germans had banned, and written by Per Faber's father.

It was a vast crowd around the green portal. There was no parade of tens of thousands of troops in full war equipment, each with nine different kinds of deadly weapon. There was no assertion of power, except the tall guards in busbies. There was no threat to process a minority with the whip and scourge. All that proclaimed itself was the Moment, the moment about to come. It would be more than Peace. The conscription of men to go against their own Allies would be over. The oath of office to an alien State would be over. The policing would be over. Petty tyrannies to which men submitted so they could earn their keep and eat their daily bread—they would be a thing of the past. It was a release of the innocent from prison, after six and fifty years. And they crowded to hail the messenger of it. They pushed so close that a little blonde girl fell in the path of his horse. He stooped, and for the rest of the ride he carried the child in his arms.

He was so little absorbed in himself that this Reunion swept over him from time to time like a blessed miracle, and tears rolled down his cheeks. Emotions chased through him like sun and shower. He watered the new border with tears of joy and lit it with his smiles.

It was better than salvo of cannon to hear the *hurra, hurra, hurra,* as the king followed the new line of Danish fellowship. In his person there was the discipline of the soldier, the dignity of a simple man, but more than that, the humanity of a compatriot among compatriots. Dürer himself could have done something with that figure. He would have seen him as a knight.

5

Our headquarters during the days of the Reunion was an ice cutter. We lived on board the *Stærkodder,* "Strong Otter," a craft that in the wintertime served to break the ice in Danish waters and in summer was a ferry. This boat was crammed with almost fifty journalists from all the country. I was the one overseas journalist on board.

It was by no means the rest cure we were dreaming of. The *Stærkodder,* all things considered, was an admirable little vessel,

We Make a Visit

but there had to be about twelve journalists to each cabin. (We were the icemen.) Of the forty-odd men and women on board there were, I think, two teetotalers (*Afholdsmænd*)—one a tripping, elderly gentleman with a perpetual smile and the other myself. The memorable fact about us two was not so much our odious sobriety as our hopeless infirmity compared to the accompanying Vikings of both sexes. We, the models of virtue, would slink to bed about midnight, utterly fatigued, while the human siphons could not come below till two. Then at five, when the famous reformer and myself were just beginning to relax, the jocund brethren would roll out, look for shaving water and their morning cigars. After the third day, I thought to myself, they'll collapse. On the third day they arranged a banquet. It began, solidly speaking, at nine-thirty, and at ten the speechmaking commenced.

They had great practice in short, snappy, impromptu speeches, full of neat personal allusions and ironic compliments. The turns were so funny and they looked so easy I even tried one myself. I recollect speeches in ringing voices that had the true nationalist clang in them—"Flensborg Avis" and so on, the Irredentist bark—while others were as bland as Danish sauce. The old ice cutter became thick with smoke, drowsy with good food; the guests became rumpled and a little voluble; the speeches were innumerable.

I was outside it, trying like a deaf-and-dumb man to read it with my eyes and marveling at the concord of it, the wells of good laughter, the quickness of the faces, the zest and the immense fraternity. Here were provincial editors, Copenhagen critics, a handsome matron smoking a cigar, a hot Tory, a broad liberal, a radical, all of them confederated by ink. At about one they began to be really mellow. For days I had been noticing a polite Swede with a student cap who, no matter how glorious the weather, wore a raincoat. This night he disclosed the reason. Under the raincoat, since he had to come on a bicycle, he wore a dinner jacket. It was no better for its days of confinement, but it was a correct dinner jacket and a saddened white shirt. He now had the floor. He was discoursing at great length on Scandinavian solidarity, and they were giving him a kind of warm, brooding attention such as he never had before or since. They applauded him with the gravest affection. The party went on till two. Then a number of them went swimming. At six, when I woke from a broken slumber, I was almost the only man not dressing, except for the famous reformer.

6

All over the unregenerate world you'll find men celebrating rather than cerebrating if they get a chance. But to imagine from this that the *Stærkodder* was full of provincials on a bean feast would be a prim mistake.

I kept probing as well as I could. They knew much about the U.S.A. where a number of them had traveled, and I discovered that most of the fervid speeches about regaining every inch of Slesvig, Germany or no, did not deprive the majority of flexibility, imagination and hard sense. These dwelt on the debt that Denmark owed to the principles of Woodrow Wilson, sanely applied to Slesvig, and they lamented his loss of popular favor. They talked cheerfully enough about Denmark's place in the world as a small and powerless nation. It had tried imperialism long ago, they said, and it had been cured.

Only a little special group insisted on the ignominiousness of being small and powerless, on the torpor of being merely prosperous and merely comfortable. The men in this group had fretted at not being in the war. With this in one way I felt drawn to sympathize. When conscription came in the U.S.A., just before the Armistice, I discovered I could not object conscientiously. The thought of the Germans at Calais was enough for me, and I chose to be a private in the infantry, one of the cheapest choices a myopic ever made. Everything is not settled when the inner problems of a State are settled, even to the narrowing of poverty, the solution of unemployment, pensions for the sick and the old. So I reasoned. But there was neurotic chauvinism, I believe, in most of these few young Conservatives I talked with. The older men were quite able to show that the Danish State still presented deep problems, even as regards "syndicalism" and republicanism and the humble necessity of getting England to sell coal.

The word bolshevism had no terrors in 1920.

"If we are not proof against the propaganda of bolshevism because we are democratic," said one, "we might as well give in."

So these small editors talked. And accustomed though I was to the *New Republic* talk, this was on the same topics, with the same grasp of significance, the same searching of the mind. There are, unique and startling fact, a total of about three hundred independent *daily* newspapers in Denmark, and here were the liveliest of the newspapermen responsible for them, most of them moderately well off, many of them poorly off, but masters of their own ways, close to the people, racy, thirsty for life, aware of Europe, intelligent. I was later to have book reviews from all over Denmark. The standard was high, no more searching than Swedish reviews, perhaps, but quicker and at times almost French in felicity. French, that is to say, in the good tradition, not in the tradition of the rubbish called criticism in ordinary French journalism, which is not paid for unless—well, unless it is paid for. Where France has a literary Jockey Club and then a riffraff, a horde of touts and pimps and incredibly squalid literary ambulance chasers, Denmark presents neither extreme. Its best critics lack only a final flick to rank with the best in Europe, and some of the Danish critics have ranked with the best in Europe. (I say this, who have never read nine tenths of European languages or one hundredth of European critics.) I much prefer Danish critics of the 1930's to the corresponding English critics. They were on the whole better poised, better educated, more responsible and more sensitive; I have never, for example, seen the death of an English actor followed by such an honest press as Denmark devoted to the Swedish actor, Gösta Ekman. Such criticism held in itself a comprehension of the theater as an art, of the actor as an artist and a personage, and of life itself, of which the artist is one of the supreme instruments, to experience, to dominate and to create it. Ekman's failures were as delicately indicated as the subtlety of his triumphs. A respect for this significance of the free artist one finds in the whole Danish press.

The *Stærkodder* was, in its own way, a consummation, and I was eager for it. The pace was hard and I missed much, but there were amusing byplays. On deck there sauntered a Dane in a kind of pajama suit. It was, I think, aubergine and green, with a pattern of skunk cabbage and eggplant. He was back from Russia, rather pale and slim, with a wry, jaded smile and a supercilious tongue. This was Henning Kehler. He wrote excellent, cutting short stories about the Russian Revolution, during which he had been either with the Legation or the Red Cross. His mode was paradox, and later he was to become a singular paradox himself, one of the most venomous of Christians—not a Hound of Heaven, a serpent of heaven, serving God with his fangs. Anti-Semitic, antirationalist and very, very nationalist, he should have become a Catholic and quarreled with the Pope.

There was a trig premier lieutenant with a flashing smile. He was in charge of our party. "Follow me!" he cried, and we all gladly followed Lieutenant Hammerich. He was later, poor man, to be shattered in a naval explosion, to suffer terrible facial injuries and, after his recovery, to become a leader in the Blue Cross, a salvationist movement.

I enjoyed this group, and when one has been around with many groups, as most of us have, it is good to catch the flow of spirit that sparkles as it goes, the kind and alert tone and the easy camaraderie that makes warming company. In serious groups there is a double danger: that the talk will have too much purpose and that the merest hint of human inconsequence will make the great men shy. I've seen Herbert Croly settle like a stone crab in the middle of a lively company, and I've seen another great man like a fig leaf among nudes. Even W. B. Yeats, superb talker as he was, could become so altitudinous that one froze. Better a hilarious death with a brass band in your ear than to be frozen stiff. Felix Frankfurter sometimes breaks up a Quaker meeting with a war whoop of laughter. Herbert Swope sometimes shakes the chandelier with his foghorn. But no party has ever died of overstimulation that didn't have a weak heart. A lack of nimbleness in company implies no lack of authority or of faculty in a man, but there is a lack of facility in him that lesser men may be rich in, and this richness helps in the human circus. The Danes appreciate this; and while there is such a thing as shy innate superiority, a good wine that won't go with convivial gin, it is still a great relief to be with people who are not tortuous, who have no complicated idea of themselves and no habit of disdain.

So I enjoyed this group for its sheer vitality. When you reflect that even the small towns—towns of five thousand—may have four daily newspapers, you see that the local editor must keep his end up. Within a few hours the Copenhagen dailies are on his heels, and he has to be a good international as well as a good national and local politician. He can't be a necromantic poet or an editorial Simon Stylites. It is in other ways that Denmark favors these private figures; the editors delve among the people. They cultivate public opinion.

At table, with conviviality so endless, or on deck where everyone effervesced, these Danes of all groups showed the highest social trait: they were not contentious. They left their swords at home.

One of them, A. J. Poulsen, a portly man with a little tuft of beard, I was to know for many years. He had studied theology but became a journalist on the Left and then was made head of the Foreign Office press bureau. He luckily died in 1938, yet not before he had realized the trend of Europe. This was an ample, sagacious human being. I never went to Denmark without seeing him, and in him I saw the good man, the ponderable Dane. He was laden with cares yet always accessible, till he died worn out. I mourned that man. So, no doubt, did his confreres of the *Stærkodder*.

7

We were kept moving by day. If the king took as much as an aspirin, I was there to see it. In fact I did see it. All I missed was the reason for the aspirin, the kick the brown horse gave him, and that wasn't on the agenda.

The Reunion itself took four days. We drove from town to town, flowers thrown to our humble selves as well as the king. At first I had followed on foot, along this new border traced not by a barricade of soldiers but by a lane of flowers. A burly attendant kept saying to me, "to the right, to the right," whenever I was actually thrown in against the queen's carriage. She sat in this open carriage, a German princess, smiling radiantly at this crowd. Some queens are public women. Queen Alexandra in London was really confected as a queen, as regal as a wedding cake, nodding to the crowd with a perfect fulfillment of their expectations, so perfect that if the mask had stayed there, and the real Alexandra escaped from it, it would have sufficed. But Queen Alexandrine, in Slesvig, remained somehow private—not the least effort to dramatize herself, leaving the day to her husband. It was his day, and the Danes'.

At each town there was a bravely festive council hall, or a church resplendent with candles, or a hotel bursting with food to rejoice the visitors. One group of the Germanic burghers, in a historic Danish chamber, rather prodded the cavalry king to be tart with them. They were, after all, to have high guarantees of their culture that no Danes had ever had in Slesvig. Well, of course, but Germans! The umbilical cord! The parturition of Germans is somehow never quite pulled off. I rather think the

We Make a Visit

soldier felt like drawing his sword and performing the operation. But his heart was given to something else—to the homecoming, to the exiles returning to free speech and the Danish tongue to speak in. That tongue, with the flag in sight, was music enough for those days of feast and song. And there was no talk of supremacy or of Nordic blonds, though these were as blond as the cornfields.

The great moment of the Reunion was on the site of Denmark's battle in 1864. This was at Dybbøl where for sixteen days the Danes, with some Swedish and Norwegian volunteers, held back four times as many Prussians. They withstood terrific bombardment, resisting until two thirds were gone. A very few of the survivors still lived to climb to the platform that day, to greet their king.

A hundred thousand flowed over the grass-grown hill where the earthworks had been, and as we waited—this immense assembly carpeting all space except that islanded platform—the national songs went in waves of soblike sound, not in perfect unison but in succeeding ripples that inundate the heart more drenchingly, as if the burden of memory were too heavy for the multitude to bear. The heart of Denmark was exposed in those moments. There was a stillness in the crowd, lest it might be injured if one moved.

It was in the early days of flying. We were startled by an airplane that passed over the platform and let a flag fall at the king's feet—*Dannebrog* from Heaven, as the legend told. But there was another flag. An old man, small and humble, had hidden a Danish flag in 1864. He had now brought it to give to the king. In the light of day, at Dybbøl, this treasure of his life was handed over, and he stood there, just a little old man, in the center of the hundred thousand. And as he was too small to be kissed on the cheek, too near the earth, the king bent over and kissed him on the head. That salute, from the younger to the older, was the seal on the Reunion.

8

Premier Lieutenant Hammerich saw us off. I had bought a seven-foot-long African boat, with figures in it, that looked like a mammoth cigar in its wrappings. This was in Haderslev. In his politeness the naval officer wished to help us, so I gave him the boat to carry. He was an unhappy man, his sword in one hand and the mammoth idiocy in the other. It took me years to get rid of that aberration. It had no beauty. It had no meaning. And I doubt if it was African.

Back in Copenhagen we went to stay at the *Kongen af Danmark,* the King of Denmark. This was an old hotel. At this time it was in the early October of its fortunes; quiet had descended on it, and acquiescence. It had a courtyard that resounded, and its echoes held my ear. I found myself listening for horses and the grind of wheels, for a baronial coach to arrive, so that I longed for the North in winter, with lanterns and the snow. It was the first time I conceived of the nearness of Russia—that immense-hearted Russia of which Tolstoy and Turgeniev had made me a citizen, in those passionate assignations with Russia which for years had been the richest hours in Europe's fictive life.

When we asked for a bath in this old hotel the chambermaid prepared it like a ceremony. She was a brisk, almost martial person, in a crisp white dress with pink stripes, with fresh cheeks and hair a little the color of brass. The bathtub itself was long enough for a long grand duke. I rather hoped that the firm chambermaid intended to give me my bath, as I was told this was a Northern custom, but while she conducted me in person into the bathroom, where I ascended into the tub as onto a throne, she made no offer to scrub me. I was regretful. I don't think she liked me. And when I finally swam out of the tub I was even more regretful that I was not eight feet tall and able to do full justice to the bath towel, one of those fundamental bath towels that you feel you have not used enough and yet must leave behind you, conspicuously wasted, in the language of Thorstein Veblen, like a ham of which you have only taken a slice.

We were in a quarter of Copenhagen that nothing profaned. Two years ago, walking through it with Salvador de Madariaga, he stopped and said, with his Spanish eyes on fire, "Think what has gone to make it, all this, this Europe, this civilization!" He waved his hand toward the Bourse, toward the houses of parliament, toward the statues, the canals. He felt, and I myself felt, that it was a presence, molded with intention, with deference to every artist who had worked in it, with that superintendence which would no more jostle the past than a sensitive man would jostle Château Lafitte. Thorvaldsen was in that embracing sweep of Salvador's arm, and Hans Christian Andersen who had looked out on the same scene, the fishwives from Skovshoved, the East Asiatic Company's offices and that government office of the Chancery whose name he vainly asked me to translate. Many of these buildings had been made over in recent times. A whole street, in fact, had been torn out, or a complex of streets. The past had not been allowed to impose itself. But to stand there, to see the church where Lutheran songs could be heard, to know that Palestrina could be sung there in a country entirely Lutheran, was to respire free air.

A year later the English minister to Denmark went to hear one of the free concerts, which happened to be German church music. The German minister's wife listened to the same concert. It was still Europe.

Could it remain Europe? Had Versailles proved irreparable?

We came from Slesvig in 1920 in the mood of people who, whether knowing it or not, had been affected for their whole lives.

We had seen Denmark put to the test. Was it moved by nationality, that self-possession of a National Being, or was it moved by nationalism, a greedy and unscrupulous egoism?

Before our own eyes we had seen the proof of Denmark's spiritual clarity. It had not fallen into the trap that nationalism set for it. It had risen above Versailles.

Ever since it had been framed we had discussed the Versailles Treaty. The *New Republic,* in spite of itself, was going against the League of Nations and yielding to isolation. Whatever hope there was in the world, it seemed to me to be along the lines of democracy, which had to be international and anti-isolation. Here, in this little area, one small nation had resorted to democratic method, had gone to the people, honestly taken a vote, followed the line with beautiful solicitude and sealed it fairly and openly. There was no use of force, no hatred, no "revanche." If the world were to see it through, like Mr Britling, this would be the only way to follow.

But Versailles!

It was no credulity about the Germans that moved me. What the Germans themselves would have done, had they come out on top in 1918, was not in the least left to idle fancy. The terms they had dictated at Brest-Litovsk to the defeated Russians gave an exact notion of "peace through victory" and the German imperialist state of grace. Many as might be the sobs, the shrieks and the quavers in diatribes about Versailles, no mood of pity and fraternity, no humane feeling, no live-and-help-live existed in the Bismarck tradition. Whatever Herbert Croly could glean for the new nationalism, German nationalism was pure egoism. They were ready to trade on the whole range of sentiment implied by the word "democracy" that Woodrow Wilson used, but the professional beggar who peels off his make-up has no more contempt for the gullible than a Pan-Germanist for the democrat. Germany had woes, plenty of them, and the Danes were ready to nurse back many thousands of German and Austrian starvelings into well-being; but nothing on earth, not the mildest treaty imaginable, not the Fourteen Points down to the last tip, could alter Pan-Germania. To carry out that philosophy the leaders would willingly kill their best friends.

We Make a Visit

We, who objected to Versailles, were well aware of the German imperialists, whose "world power or downfall" had been written plain in the sky. We critics of Versailles did believe, however, that there were other Germans, social-democrat Germans, and we aimed to favor the elements in Germany that were socialist rather than nationalist. We were not helped by the excesses of Red Russia. Winston Churchill was busy magnifying the excesses of Red Russia and striving for its extinction.

Instead of appealing to those socialist Germans, however, instead of strengthening and protecting them, the French victors deemed it utterly useless. They set about weakening Germany in every vital way, in order to fortify the non-Germanic on strictly nationalist lines. They deliberately whipped up nationalism. This opposition between nationalisms was the potent animus in the Versailles Treaty and recklessly undemocratic. It forced Germany to counternationalism. It defeated the social democrats in Germany. It whetted the least balanced and the most nationalistic critics of Versailles, the German demagogues. And Germany was full of ex-soldiers to be played upon, home to misery, balked ambition and humiliation.

In this choice of terrain in the peace treaties, the terrain of nationalism, on which the social-democratic cause has never secured its footing, a terrain on which foreign offices feel at home, the democracies must always lose. A nationalist democracy is in fact a boobocracy—H. L. Mencken's word. The German boobocracy was to become the most gulled in creation.

Versailles was bad, not because it sought to punish the German imperialists. It was bad because it presented a winning cause to the German imperialists. We ourselves suspected this in 1919, but who was interested? I went to hear Jane Addams speak in Chicago late in 1918 to a prosperous woman's club. There were no unfashionable ideas under those fashionable hats. They whispered, hat to hat, that Miss Addams was pro-German if not pro-Lenin. It should have been clear to me then that the French politicians had won, that Europe was in for military nationalism, that the new war was certain and Versailles a mere interlude.

9

Had the Reunion festivities made less impression on me—and it is twenty years ago, after all, that we went to them—I daresay I should have left Slesvig rather amicable but still an outsider, like the rationalist who goes to Lourdes. But here was a miracle, a people so patriotic that every inch of territory regained was as dear to them as their own flesh and yet rigorously just about the wishes of residents who, as a matter of fact, had been planted in Slesvig to oust the original Danes. Had the *Stærkodder* been less full of vitality, I should have put it down to political indifference. But here were the most vigorous and the best-informed political animals you could possibly meet! Behind the sanguine humor of the *Stærkodder* and the inherent good will there was a vibrant political life, the most formative you could possibly imagine.

This little Denmark, was it such an open book as people told me? Good rural schools and all that? Good co-operatives, just like bees; read the *Life of the Bee,* by Maurice Maeterlinck. Yes, I looked at the Danes. They could sting all right. But why were they not wasps? As an Irishman, I asked myself that. Even if Signe had not been a Dane, I'd now have been interested in Denmark.

CHAPTER TWO

Frame of the Picture

IT IS A PITY, of course, that Denmark is such an old story. I once knew a man who went to Tibet that has the same number of inhabitants but is twenty times as big and not as easy to get to. Owing to what is termed as "the inhospitable attitude of its people," my friend bumped into the border. There was, in fact, a marked difference of attitude, and whatever happened to the Tibetans, Edmund Candler certainly lost an arm.

How easy it would now be for me had Denmark been more like Tibet. I imagine myself at a cocktail party, with friends looking at an empty sleeve. "It is nothing, dear old boy. Forgive my left hand. I had a little brush with the natives at Esbjerg, and so, as you see! Another martini, old bun?"

"I chose Tibet." That would tickle any listener, especially if Tibet had returned the compliment. When I tell you that Edmund Candler rolled his dinner jacket into a bundle and packed it on his back, so that he could dress for dinner as soon as he reached Bangkok on another expedition of his, you perceive the immense distance between the romantic journey and the familiar one, even though a Swede could be equally punctilious cycling to Slesvig. Candler had the right to take on mild proprietory airs about bits of Asia, but who can appropriate Denmark? If Candler suffered and lost something in his collision with the Tibetans, he also gained something. All I lost at Esbjerg was my trunk, and all I gained was a rebuke, when I tried to tip the head porter who found it.

"I am well paid by the Company," he growled. "Why should you pay me too?"

That was twenty years before the redcaps were given a fixed rate in New York. But had he tried to spear me, with Signe by my side, how piquant, how much more the real thing!

I was downstairs, with an Italian and a Russian, while Candler died upstairs, in a house in the South of France. But before I leave the ghost of this adventurous man who tried to enter Tibet without permission, let me suggest that it would take just as brave a man in 1940 to enter Denmark without permission. Under German management Denmark is as closed today as Tibet ever was, and for a Dane to attempt to leave his own country in 1940 without official German authorization is to incur the penalty of death. We have lived to see Forbidden Denmark.

Why is this, when the most doddering old lady felt perfectly competent to take a cruise on the Lancastria in 1939 that gave her a stopover at Copenhagen? Why should ingress and egress be a matter of life and death?

That, my reader, is the mystery that removes even the most familiar country from the commonplace and invites us to go back to political A B C.

2

The first thing to put into any picture is what the Danes call the yardstick. In my account of this country that we went to in 1920 and that I have come to love, I begin with what the police term its "visible means of support." By this I do not mean to parade statistics, not being a political scientist, but in the most general way, in any love affair, we are all political scientists; we like to know what the girl has got.

Frame of the Picture

Heiresses have always thrilled me, but this vulgar passion is not gratified by Denmark. It is not for nothing that Hans Christian Andersen, who shared this passion, piled up gold in his fairy tales. He had glorious daydreams about it, not having too much of it, and in this he was far from exceptional. But he had the irony of a Dane. Denmark is modestly endowed. That's worth remembering. The cabin on the *Stærkodder* with twelve roommates in it was no bad symbol of Denmark. The fare on the ship was superb, but the room made no pretensions. Some would have thought it hard, bare and primitive.

If you go to see what automobiles Denmark makes, you'll be disappointed. It doesn't make automobiles, doesn't build skyscrapers, doesn't manufacture millionaires. The exciting and fabulous existence of, let us say, Palm Beach and Miami, without which the world would be poorer, the flashing brilliance of the show parts of New York, belong to an order of things that doesn't include Denmark. The Englishwoman who arrived in Canada and said, "You waste everything! You ought to be ashamed of yourselves," was used to scrimping and scraping. All that fine wrapping paper that goes to waste, the "package goods" that cost so much and create such a housekeeping problem for a city, the lavish heat, the thick bills, the good stamps! The vast public works all over the country! The noble highways! Denmark has no such affluence.

To draw a compliment for Copenhagen out of Alvin Owsley, the genial American minister to Denmark, I talked of the new sea road that had been so ambitiously constructed along the Sound.

"Yes," he said, "I came in that way this lovely morning, and as I saw Copenhagen in the distance it made me think of Traverse City, Michigan."

Good God, said I to myself, the city of Absalon, the city of towers, the city of Amalienborg Plads, the city of a hundred refinements, a thousand memories. A cranberry bog comes to his mind.

I later asked Paul de Kruif to tell me the truth about Traverse City. He laughed. He said it was all right, very fine!

I have still to see it for myself. It has to be admitted, of course, that breaking the sky line of Copenhagen to the south there are certain petroleum tanks. The magnificent beer bottle, brewery-man size, that Tuborg set up at a fair, now preserved in a local garage, is not so beautiful as any of the towers. And there is a tower in the brewery itself, Tuborg Cathedral, that is not so classic. I weaken in my lofty attitude toward Alvin Owsley. There are probably rapturous mornings in Michigan when Traverse City could almost suggest Copenhagen. No, I take it back. I deny it. As Lowes Dickinson said to me when I asserted that Arthur Brisbane had a style, "it is not possible."

But when it comes to a drive along the Sound, when it comes to trees in a park, when it comes to the general exterior wrappings of the package, it is useless to rebel against anyone who asserts the relative simplicity of the Danish setting. And it is not only in the region of engineering, it's in the region of luxury, all the way through until you reach the kitchen.

If polo, for example, is a necessity of your life, you'll be quietly miserable in Denmark. You wouldn't go there for the bargain-basement race horses that it buys. Not even for the trotting horses.

But Tuborg has brewery horses. There are those billowing, matronly horses that are to be seen in the country, with foamy manes and tails, not so heavy as Percherons or so stocky as the Suffolk Punch; you could make a trip for them and not be disappointed. Once, on crossing from Germany, I saw one of those gentle beasts clop-clopping into Gedser under a lambent sun on a country road. It was placidity itself. The farmer had been up since five. Now he was taking his ease. Denmark was intact, untouched and very near. It was an honest symbol.

But Denmark does not flaunt big-scale achievements in general. When it tries to create according to the world pattern such things as motion pictures, the result is seldom happy. The manifestations of life that directly depend on an immense market, that is to say, on an immense endowment, on rich and deep resources that are at hand, on the things that spring out of owning coal, oil, iron, water power, forests, the mining of diamonds or gold itself—these are not the Danish manifestations.

Even the most eminent Dane may equip himself with an absurd little bag and go off into the world like a schoolgirl going to a picnic. We met the most discriminating and penetrating of art directors in Denmark—Frederik Poulsen—who was traveling to England in precisely this manner. His lectures and articles are of the rarest texture. He smiled when we noticed the single suitcase he took. We had about fourteen.

"Yes," he said, "I was going to a ducal castle in England the last time to examine its art collection. They sent two Rolls Royces to meet me. One was for myself. The other was for my luggage. I started off in the first. The other came behind with this object and two men to take care of it."

No one has written so understandingly about the civilization he has found in these same English establishments.

But judged by its possessions, its minerals, its raw materials, Denmark is a Cinderella. The sobering absence of great wealth is never to be forgotten. There are surprises, but there is nothing of that lordly, profuse and marvelously heartening endowment by nature that makes America an heiress beyond compare. If you look for this, you might as well look for a Niagara or a Grand Canyon. In this respect Denmark is poor.

3

Denmark is poor. But in the same breath I say, Denmark is rich.

Poor as it is in the great deposits of coal that started one country ahead of all the others in industrial revolution, poor as it is in the oil that gushes wealth in Pennsylvania, poor in the forests that endow Finland or the ore that is Sweden's bounty, this relative impoverishment has not meant that on that account Denmark must lead a wretched and melancholy existence, sitting in the shadow and sucking its paw. One of the most audacious bits of bunk that has gone round the world in the last quarter of a century is the bunk of empire builders who demand a place in the sun. The essence of this argument is that there is not enough sun to go round, or enough coal or oil to go round, or enough gold, diamonds and the rest; and therefore if nature has not provided you with these bounties, it is your duty to yourselves and the unborn generations that are to come after you to go out with your knife and carve these bounties out of your neighbor. The "pressure of population" is to be your best excuse. On the one hand you are to urge your mothers to have all the babies they can. You are to pin a medal on any brood mother that has had more than five children, a gold star for her, and at the same time you are to point out how terrible the "pressure of population" is and to use these children for gun fodder. By such an argument—your unendowment on one hand, and your pressure from within on the other—you build up a great case for the irresistible necessity of being a holdup man.

Such an argument, in its crudest form, reduces life to economic determinism, putting self-interest in the first place, removing free choice and eliminating guilt, so that "life goes on," and that's all the philosophy you need for it.

Girls who become prostitutes are occasionally excused on some such ground as this. The bad factory conditions on the one hand, and the vital need for silk stockings on the other, results in a bighearted break with the conventions.

And even the Catholic Irish-American businessman, who'd frown on such determinism in sex life, embraces it with both arms in the business world. Not long ago one of these New Men, on the ground that war is the enemy of democracy, urged that a peace should be "compelled." This fight, he said, has nothing to do with democracy. It is a clash between two sets of self-interest. The flow of foodstuffs to Germany, Germany's raw material, Germany's trade, are choked by England. And naturally Germany wants a New Order in which no hand stronger than her own can touch her life lines.

Germany rearmed, therefore, "at great sacrifice to her people," to procure a new "world setup." And who is to argue with anyone who wants a new setup so badly?

The same sort of argument, oddly enough, was to be found in that distressingly sentimental book, *The American Tragedy*, by Theodore Dreiser. There it was the poor boy who wanted a new setup. Where in his earlier books Dreiser had planned his story for the woman who was taken advantage of, he toned down the girl's tragedy in this particular story till it was dove gray, but he laid the greatest stress on the inescapability of the young man's plight. A cruel society was to hold him guilty of murder, when it was society's own fault, making him want that new setup.

One sentimental Danish novelist, Martin Andersen Nexø, made out the case against cruel society with great eloquence, and although he was a Communist in the end, greatly read in Russia and admired in Germany for years, the Danes held him in such respect that they gave him an annual stipend. There was something, they felt, in Nexø's heart-rending indictment.

Of course there is something in it. Of course we are in the grip of economic forces. But suppose it were Denmark that demanded that there be no hand stronger than her own on her life lines, would not the businessman smile? There is one law, he feels, for the strong and another for the weak. So he feels, and yet he calls himself a democrat.

Denmark has not put forward its plight in the same manner as these determinists. Handicapped in many ways, with no raw materials to speak of, deprived of innumerable advantages, at the mercy of tariff laws, living on sufferance between Russia and Germany, Denmark has still been far from taking the lachrymose tone about its poverty that Germany has, or that

Italy has, or that Japan has. The various direct ways out of poverty, either by prostitution or by crime—and nations try both ways—did not illude it into making no effort of another kind. By such effort it has become enriched.

This is not to say that Denmark has found any golden recipe for avoiding the predatory, either in itself or in its neighbors. Denmark was predatory for centuries. It had to be beaten out of Sweden and pulled off Norway's back. Its military class was at one time formidable and merciless. But faced with the first need of all, the need to escape the kind of misery that Nexø described, a debased life in Denmark itself, it can be said that Denmark, for all its disadvantages, did go about the task without flourishing a gun. That it did not combine this economy with a strong military development may now, in 1940, seem a radical defect. But when you look back far enough over the history of Europe it is still a question whether military nations do not, in the end, generate infinitely greater misery than they remedy. If the mothers are willing to pump out babies for the slaughterhouse in sufficient numbers, and if a victory is in the end achieved which can be maintained by a sufficiently vigilant police, with spying, imprisonment, torture and summary execution, as the commonplace of daily life in the conquered countries, then the argument in favor of the conqueror is a good one. But as an Irishman, to whom the Massacre of Mullaghmast, the Battle of Vinegar Hill and the story of the Manchester Martyrs were the meat and drink of my childhood, I venture to believe that you can no more eradicate the thumbprint of such unjust conquest than you can keep grass from growing in the fields. Plough it down, pull it up, smother it in sand, asphalt it, and yet, with the least softening of vigilance, the seeds that the wind bears or that the birds sow come sprouting from the earth as if never forbidden. The human heart is no less fertile in its dream of justice than the earth in its grass, and so long as conquest prepares fury, so long will protest throb. No one who has so much as glanced at the northern sagas can suppose that outrage is ever forgotten. If out of the rancors of the Versailles Treaty the Germans themselves fermented such smarting pain, so deep an outrage, such ruthlessness, what do they think the rest of humanity is made of? Leaving their foe aside, do the Germans think that they can trample down refugees in their mad eagerness to pursue a plan without bruising from the heart its bitterest juices? Every smashed face they trod on, every broken child in their path, every crushed mother, remains to be paid for. These choices are dyed into the fiber; out of this fiber the future is woven. It is a fact that civilizations have utterly perished, but literacy is the modern preservative of memory, and nothing is so slow to be forgiven as contempt of the innocent. If the Germans themselves talk of the Black Hole of Calcutta and of Amritsar, the words Stavanger, Bergen and Narvik will be seared into them by the same token.

The intellectuals, who were reckoned pro-German after the war of 1914–18, have now the right to raise their voices. We have seen the victims of injustice bid good-by to decent tradition, break with good will and steep themselves in the guilt that they rose against.

4

An independent Denmark did not foresee that it might have to resist "protection." Its real war was a war on poverty.

Nature, which had been grudging, did give Denmark the greatest of all boons—a good climate. Or rather, to be less man-centered, the race that has occupied the Danish region for the past ten thouand years was induced to accept privations in return for the clemency of four seasons.

Often in Florida last winter I was lured to the window to look at that vein of opulent blue in the Atlantic that we call the Gulf Stream. Few as Denmark's rivers are, the Gulf Stream makes up for them. It gives suavity to a latitude that would otherwise be harsh. It tempers winter. It keeps the harbors open. It brings an early spring. The Danish summer, bland when the continental heat is hammering down on Paris or Berlin, owes much of its serenity to the bathing moderation of the waters that sparkle in it. And the autumn, with its lingering lights, has a caress in it that the Gulf Stream makes gentle.

From the very beginning of summer, sure of a steady warmth, the young Danes, especially the Danish girls, give up as many garments as possible and live as much as possible in the sun. The Lord has so arranged it that, in view of His stringency in other respects, the Danish skin should become sunburned more quickly and more becomingly than the skin of most other races. Where the Irish fry in the sun, the Danes bake. But they bake in the heavenly oven so as to become brown all over, appetizingly. A cannibal would eat a Dane long before he'd eat an Irishman, since the eye is omnivorous. I have myself considered biting a Dane, somewhere about July.

The American visitor, straight from the swelter of Illinois, cannot understand what one means by the Danish summer. He sees girls in the lightest of summer dresses when his own flesh is curdling in the chill. The mere sight of the bundled bathrobes on their bicycles gives him heart failure. Even without having seen the Vikings break the ice to bathe on the first of January, he feels a little sick to see them go in on the first of July. But this is inexperience. To enjoy a temperate summer, you must have been kept in the half-dark for about six months and then released with the certainty that at sometime in the year, in May or in August or in October, there would be a golden spell after whatever silver or nickel or leaden days you had to put up with earlier. This halcyon spell comes to Denmark every year, almost. It is so rapturous that even on the dullest day in the dullest quarter in Copenhagen, when the clouds are thick as mattresses, you recall the rapture and forget the drab. A girl with flaxen hair and cornflower eyes, wisped in muslin and cycling in the sour afternoon to the disconsolate beach—she is not enduring the cold summer, she is merely accepting a rain check for the time being. Summer has a rendezvous with her, and she is dressed for it, not to keep it waiting.

5

It is from this Gulf Stream climate, with the ocean paled to a Copenhagen blue, that the wealth of Denmark has been conjured. What was born in the Tropics, that swirl of ocean current laden with the sun, winds up in Buckinghamshire as bacon and eggs. Denmark, after all, is in the same latitude as Labrador, and while the geographers rather sniff at the notion that it is the Gulf Stream which mellows Danish waters, take away the Gulf Stream and it would not be mellowed. The northern sun alone, at a Labrador latitude, does not allow man to subsist as a farmer. Denmark would have four thousand, not close on four million, were it not for the warmth in the sea.

But the people have grown, as everyone grows, by the exercise of their powers. They rose from this equable sea, they live on it, they work with it, they master it, fish, sail, trade, by means of it, build harbors, fashion ships and ply from island to island, from continent to continent, the most unpretentious of the maritime peoples and yet proportionately the fourth in the world.

When an island people has been cut off from the sea, as the Irish have been, the economy of the people is completely deranged. That is one of the tragedies of being conquered. But when a nation has been able to keep its independence, as the Danes have, and has developed as seagoing, a whole range of activities is opened up for it that some poor fool of a theorist would call sea-determined. It is not *determined,* any more than it is *determined* that I write this book. Had Tristan come under the influence of Matthew Arnold, let us say, he might never have kissed Isolde. It was not determined that he'd kiss her. Had she really behaved as the nuns told her to behave, he'd have found her in cellophane. Perhaps a genteel tradition, a strong reverend mother, might have kept beauty and ardor from working to its end, but only a rare beauty and a singular ardor lead to the unfolding of a great story. The story of the Danes on the sea is no inevitable story, no automatism.

Hence, while motorcars have not been invented or developed by the Danes, they have a great record in shipbuilding. Like the other Scandinavians, they were to be found in the carrying trade from one end of the earth to the other, until the blight touched them; and if anyone has any doubt whether they build ships or not, he has only to go for a quiet half-hour to the Yacht Pavilion on Copenhagen Harbor to have steel riveting across the harbor drive the fact into his head. Another shipbuilding yard is down the coast, and great liners are built there. There are four other building yards. It is not only oceangoing vessels that they lay down and build up, it is every kind of craft for the home waters. The Dane is at home on the water. Even since his navy was wiped out he has made the sea his own.

6

For a couple of years we were to live right on the Sound, just over from the Hellerup yacht basin. In that little square harbor there were a number of upstanding mahogany-finished power-boats over at one side, as if a little purse-proud and a little ashamed of themselves. Splendid places in which to eat lobster with mayonnaise. But the smørbrødpakke that would be right for the other boats could not be so voluptuous. These were owned by men who came after working hours to sail in the Sound. Some of them were professional, some traders, some were mechanics; but as I'd stand to watch any one of them, to see a square-jawed elderly man who rather needed a shave go to his job with that methodic severity that informs the labor of love, I was never jarred by the feeling that this was "sport." At Cassis, in the South of France, there is a small harbor for the fishermen, and when they come in early in the morning it is as natural as the dawn itself. They glided in as easily as the Kilkenny harvesters, when I was a boy, went off in carloads at the break of day. The Hellerup sailings are just as casual. Each boat slips in or out with a little cluck of the tackle or a swish of canvas, but no visible Strength Through Joy. Even the batches of young men from the boathouse, or young women from the neighboring boathouse, do not feel it obligatory to have high spirits. They have no formula for it, no so-called discipline.

Beside the harbor there is a long, narrow communal rose garden. We often walked through it. It was shrewdly planned for succession of display and for every possible variety, carefully labeled. It had a thirst for perfection, a thorough respect for the work in hand, knowledge of it, stubborn docility under the limits imposed and loving care. Just as these roses, lyric from the bramble, gave an intense moment to the quiet people who passed through, the small craft in the harbor met the same yearning for a moment of—not escape, but relief, translation, attainment. It was not to go anywhere in particular, or even to go, but to pass from the fathomable to the unfathomable and to do it with the laconic lightness that is Danish.

In the summer the evenings are long, and on certain evenings the whole Sound is thronged with small yachts. The spread of sail against the earlier blue is exceedingly lovely, but as the evening advances, and as the sunset light fills the white canvas with a molten glow from the boom to the top of the mainmast, one boat after another a wing on the water licked by the sun, while the Sound itself is no longer water but roses and pearls dissolved, fire and sapphire, then the variant on the routine of life for an ironmonger or a plumber does, low mechanics though they are, become quite inescapably evident. As the evening falls in and they come back to the little harbor, with green and red lights showing, there is perhaps a bottle of beer, with Christian the Ninth cheese, or red beef with onions, and even songs to be sung, and one sees that the yachtsmen are good bourgeois. The sea and the beer are in their blood.

But with the sea mastered, as Hellerup could see by a glance out the window at *Kronprins Olav,* or *Dronning Maud,* or a Greenland ship, or the boat for Aarhus, or a white P & O boat on a cruise, with the ferry for Sweden a perpetual reminder of the neighbor, it could scarcely be out of the question that import and export should become the dominant activity of Danish life.

7

To colonies? No. So long as Denmark could keep colonies and hold them down for the sake of trading with them, the gentlemen with vested interests could argue strenuously for colonies and did so. But exploited groups grew restive, they broke from the grasp that held them, and Denmark had to look to the open market, the fair field and no favor. It had to make its honest way in the world.

Having no mountains and no rivers, the obstacles to communication at home were to that extent diminished. Of all the countries in Europe, Denmark is one of the most tightly combined. It uses the telephone inordinately. It has a superb telephone service. It is one of the great radio countries. It has a big railroad mileage. It has, to an exceptional degree, urbanized the country dweller, with a postal service extraordinarily competent. By having such a good circulation, so to speak, the energy to export could be commanded and marshaled without any of those awkward impediments that hills put in the way. And once the nation found what to ship out, manipulating its economy to meet this, the imports of raw materials for manufacture simply walked into the ships.

Where was the technique to come from, to work up the raw materials? Denmark was equal to that. It had never shirked the duty of popular education.

From its conquest of the sea, from its exports over the sea, from its imports to equip a hard-working and life-loving people, Denmark rose out of the dire handicaps that a small, thin endowment imposed on it and grew into what may be termed a prosperity so sufficient that no one in the whole country has to stretch out his hand to beg and no one has to raise the cry for pity, or for hatred, or for aggression.

What is one to say for an era that, with this achievement plain before its eyes, has nothing to offer but invasion and the plunder, the systematic vitiation of this economy, that follows on invasion? And defended by American industrialists?

In Pearl Buck's *The Good Earth* one sees the locusts come. In Bromfield's novel one sees the rains come. But when the zone that a race has cultivated from time immemorial has been inhospitable and grudging, when this race has converted sand into waving fields of grain, when it has drained and tilled its folk no less assiduously than its plains, when it has reclaimed bog and heath, built bridge and highway, articulated trade with trade and town with town, asking no more than it gives and believing in law—when this is the fact, indisputable, what can any ordinary observer say for the ideology that permits the wrecking of such a system in the name of God knows what greed, what cruelty and what grandiloquence?

"If you go to a certain gallery one day," said a high-spirited friend, "and examine a Pissarro pastel there, you'll see that the elbow of my assistant, who thought it was an oil painting, has made a marvelous turbulent sunset of a clear sky."

It was funny, and we both laughed at it. But when the clear sky is smudged by a destructive gesture, when the outrage is for a purpose, when a masterpiece of social management and social sacrifice is in question, then it provokes indignation. The derangement of Denmark in 1940 is man-made. By contrast locusts are harmless and deluge a joke.

CHAPTER THREE

We Go to a Farm

WHAT the precise nature of Denmark's social management was, we could not grasp on that first visit. But, little equipped as I was to know, I was intent on knowing. So when we gave up our work with the *New Republic* in 1922 and sallied forth into the world we planned to voyage to Denmark after we had visited Ireland. I was to write articles for the McClure Syndicate. But first, in view of the crisis that had been produced in Ireland by the split on the treaty with Britain, we were to have a look at Ireland.

2

We reached Ireland in late April. It was a moonlit night when we came to Cobh. So still and so expectant was it, with the mystery of moonlight on those gentle hills and the placid water, that it was breathlessly lovely. You could have said, a bridal night for that country so often named with a woman's name.

The landing had been delayed for hours, and it was long past midnight when we went to seek a hotel. On the ship, which had started out the *Blue Hen State* and became the *President Harding,* I think it was, in the middle of the voyage, we had asked about hotels in Cobh and were told to go to the Rob Roy.

We Go to a Farm

So we followed a local guide, weary after endless passport cues and queries and barely aware of the spacious dignity of the sleeping town.

It was not so big a hotel. We passed up the stairs. The linen closet was open, and to my surprise a huge carcase was hanging in it, half a dead cow. I didn't like that. We were asked to wait in a waiting room. Enlarged photographs scrutinized us not too softly. There had been clerics in the family, and the enlargements were implacable. We felt we were intruding, but at last we were bidden to follow upstairs and into a very bright room where there was a multiplicity of beds. Four beds, if you please.

"They won't be occupied," said the maid.

When she left us, and we made our choice, my wife gave a cry. "But it has been occupied!" She was looking at the linen sheet she had turned down.

"Impossible!" I said.

No, it *was* possible. It was a fact.

"I won't stay here," she said. A kind of consternation, a horror at the cynicism of it, made her incapable of staying. We agreed to leave, went down past the picture gallery, down past the cow and out into the street. We had met no one. Our porter had not yet arrived, so we stood there with Cobh looking at us from its dropped eyelids, and it reminded me of Henning Kehler's story where a man deliberately drops a hair in the officer's soup.

Another hotel took us in. It was rather grandiose in size, and in style it resembled an elaborate frogged dressing gown that had never been cleaned.

There was only one vast bed in that room. The previous occupant had been a smoker, and a little ridge of cigarette ashes had formed where he had used the carpet for an ash tray. We decided not to undress but to lie on the bed as if it were a raft and wait till morning. By this time there was a most delicate freshness in the air, a faint breath of morning and a feeling of the country outside.

"I'll go for the suitcases. They'll be at the other hotel." So I started for the Rob Roy.

In the entrance of the Rob Roy I met the proprietor. He was a lean Iberian with a long face, hair like black wires and gimlet eyes.

"Why aren't you staying in the hotel?" he asked me.

Before I answered him I saw a portly man, wearing a raincoat to protect him, presumably, against the moonlight and pretending to be intent in the study of the masterpieces on the wall, which were beer advertisements.

"If your hotel had been clean, I'd have stayed in it," I said.

"That's enough." He turned away from me and went into the bar.

The porter arriving at that moment with my bags, I took them from him and went back to the grandiose hotel. I did not feel that Cobh was very friendly.

A short time on the raft was enough for me. "I'll find when we can go into Cork," I said. "There's a train very early." I went downstairs to ask about the train, but as I descended the broad staircase and looked into the lobby below I saw a raincoat. The portly man was there with his hat still firmly on, and with him was the Iberian, now hatted, and a third man, a man with an iron jaw, in leggings, what was then technically known as a gunman.

"There's the very man we want," said the portly man, glancing up at me. I came down. The three of them were ready for me, while the clerk in the cashier's window bent her head over her books.

"We have come to arrest you," said the proprietor. "You think because you write for the newspapers—I know all about you— you can come over here and say what you like. I'll show you whether you can or not. I'll teach you to call my hotel *dirty*." He paused. "I have thirty witnesses . . ."

He was drunk, but drunk with a kind of drilling, sizzling intensity, and his two companions stood by.

"Did I say his hotel was dirty?" I barked at the raincoat.

"No. You said . . ." and he repeated my words.

"Look here," I said to the angry man. "I am not an expert in hotel cleanliness. You have thirty witnesses. I formed my impression very quickly. It may have been wrong. I was on my feet for five hours before we landed, and we were dead tired. I left your hotel under an impression that you tell me was not correct. What do you want me to do about it?"

"Apologize," he roared.

"I am perfectly willing to apologize," I said. "If I was wrong, I was wrong."

"That won't do at all."

"What will do?"

"You must *apologize.*"

"Look here," I said to the other two. "What is the sense in all this?"

The man with the iron jaw listened, and then he turned very respectfully to the proprietor. "I'm afraid, Mr O," he said, "there's nothing we can do."

"You're quite right," I said and shook hands with him. I shook hands with the portly man, and then, to his surprise, Mr O was shaking hands with me.

"Who are they?" I asked the girl cashier.

"I never saw them before," she said dully and sourly.

It was full dawn with bird song when we went to the train. As we sat in the railway carriage a hatless man came running the length of the train. He stopped when he saw me. He had been one of the passengers on the *Blue Hen State,* a Brooklyn Irishman.

"I have heard more things tonight," he gasped. "I was in the bar. For God's sake, for Christ's sake, don't open your mouth in Ireland. When that man left you in the lobby of his hotel, when you were waiting for your bags, he came in to get his revolver to shoot you. You were gone before he went out."

It made us happy when the train pulled out of Cobh.

3

The day that a treaty with England had been signed, the previous December, had been the most soberly happy day I had ever experienced. The terms of 1921 made us Irish citizens. Ireland could now be a democracy. Ireland could now have its own economy, debt free, domestic, consultative. The door was not closed on total independence, but to achieve the real power for this, to build up education, to gain technique, to master resources human and physical, was all implemented by this treaty. Six counties in the North were not included, but Britain pledged a plebiscite. Those counties, in a sense, were to be a South Slesvig. I thought it wise and honest.

The day I found so glorious was a day of black humiliation for many Irishmen.

This treaty that gave Ireland the substance of self-government gave endless talking points to the opponents, especially the hagglers. Two out of the five delegates went back on their signatures. Out of 111 members of a national assembly, the majority for the treaty was three. The debates to which we listened were highly personal and politically inadequate. There was no Jefferson, no Hamilton, no Federalist. Michael Collins, Arthur Griffith, Cathal Brugha, Erskine Childers, Harry Boland, were already marked for death. This was not a constituent assembly, it was a condemned cell. And the parliamentary method had not seized on its imagination.

"It's the extremists," Harry Boland said to me. "Childers and Griffith."

"Four hundred men," said a Jesuit through his teeth, "know what is good for Ireland." A good Fascist sentiment. He was not Mrs John Jacob Astor but he was certainly one of the Four Hundred.

The Civil War, as they called it, was brewing, and everyone had a faggot to put under the pot. I felt baffled. Isn't it a devil

We Go to a Farm

of a world in which such a thing can happen! A lanky, tubercular young man, whom I'd gone to school with, thought the moment propitious for seizing the Four Courts, a stout public building. He was blown out of it by Winston Churchill's guns, accepted by Collins. He was later one of the four hostages to be executed in reprisal for a deputy's assassination. His old father walked up and down outside Mountjoy Prison, the morning of the execution, wringing his hands.

We traveled all round the South of Ireland and saw that the two parties would be at one another's throats. Civil war was certain, unless both sides got together on the Treaty. De Valera on one side, Michael Collins on the other, tried to maneuver the parties who were clashing. It was a typical case of nationalist controversy, all-or-nothing on one side and live-and-let-live on the other.

By the time I reached Dublin I learned the identity of the man in the raincoat at Cobh. He was the local commandant of the Irish Republican Army. His chiefs in Dublin did not approve of the way I had been handled, and they sent me an apology. It meant no more to me than my own apology. The "arrest," the threat of an "unknown destination," simply meant to me that the gun was in the hands of anyone with nerve enough to use it, and this gave Ireland to the killers, if they appeared in big enough number.

The "putsch" was on. And the man who seized the Four Courts was of the same Iberian type, and of the same name, as the man in the Cobh hotel.

In spite of this background, in spite of the strenuous days ahead of Ireland, in spite of the emotions that were seething in everyone, I kept thinking of the folk high schools in Denmark and the great lesson Ireland had to learn from them. So when I had a chance to meet Michael Collins I made up my mind to speak to him of this.

A spring-heeled man, thirty-two years old, burly, ruthless,

flashing, Collins has won the unwilling admiration of another of the Iberians, Michael O'Donovan who writes under the name of Frank O'Connor. *The Big Fellow,* Frank O'Connor called his book on Collins, a book in which the horse ran away with the jockey. The day we met Michael Collins he strode past us, not to loiter where the assassin's bullet could get him. Up the stairs, three steps at a time.

"Now the folk high schools." I went at him earnestly.

A smile, a smile in which kindliness, malice, irony and pity mingled for an Olympian instant, as if a man in another world had glanced down and seen a daisy. Folk high schools for the Rob Roy hotel! Yes, he smiled. And within two months the I.R.A. in Cork managed to kill Michael Collins, by far the biggest Irishman in the essentials of leadership that rose in Ireland in the troubled times.

We were at the Danish seaside when, in those local papers I spoke of, Collins' portrait and the news of his being killed were there in inexorable print, August 1922. His own countrymen, those four hundred who knew better, had felt so rich in wisdom and loyalty to their own preferences, most of them derived from one-sided history books, that they took it on themselves to destroy a fruitful intelligence, a strong will, a heroic courage, a passionate disinterestedness and a lively human spirit. Well, it's a wealthy country that can throw away a man like Michael Collins. I lived eleven years among the men who survived him, and not one of them could match him. I even believe he could have induced folk high schools.

4

Yet in Denmark, whenever I mentioned Ireland, faces lit up. Sometimes it was with dismay—"that wasps' nest," one man called it—but nearly always it was with a singular interest, a feeling that there was some dynamic spiritual quality in Ireland, a recklessness and a naturalness so alien to the North that it could not but excite envy. I have found in some Europeans—even my friend Hendrik van Loon, for example, and some good Germans—a latent hostility to the Irish, a prejudice based on the loose, slovenly and lazy characteristics of the Irish, on their boastfulness and pugnacity. This hostility I never found in Denmark. The very fact that the Danes themselves are hard-working people, good organizers, attentive to detail, systematic and on the job, might incline them to look down on the Irish. But it works the other way. Where a Dutchman has a good stout conceit in himself, fortified by success, by wealth, by a fantastic productivity and an all-round prowess in life and art—think of Rubens—the Dane is one of the least conceited of human beings; he is self-critical and tentative in a world about which he is so informed that he is not rash to judge, and he goes his way quietly and not rambunctiously. For that very reason the salient peoples delight him, and the improvident, the wayward, appeal to that element in him which his own life has perhaps not satisfied. The Irish catch his imagination. Not all the Irish, of course, but there is something disciplined in himself that hails the undisciplined instead of rushing to squelch it and hails it with not the slightest complacency or superiority—no, with a real zest for the liberation he detects in it. Professor Grønbech's interpretation of the Irish sagas is the most luminous tribute to the historic exuberance of the Gael.

5

That exuberance was put to a severe test, in my own case, when we left our hut near Vejle and went visiting my wife's relatives in Jutland.

At the first house, up near Aarhus, we sat at a hospitable table till a late hour, and among other things we ate eel. The eel was served cold, in little sections like snippets of black solid rubber tire. I ate it, along with lobster, sausage, three or four salads, hot meat balls, pickled herring, smoked herring, raw herring and all the other foods with which the Dane sustains himself in the desperate struggle to survive.

Opinions differ about eel. We had once crossed on a ship with a professor who had made a close study of its love life, pursuing the eel across the ocean and watching it, I believe, in a glass-bottomed boat. He was flown with happiness when we met him, and if ever I saw an acute case of geheimerat fever he was in the throes of it. He stepped on air and was inclined to step on everything else. Why he had chosen the eel when he might have picked the salmon I don't know, but everyone told me it was worth his while, and I tried to like it in spite of its personal appearance.

The eel alone I might have got away with, but that night I found myself in bed with a strange animal. This was a feather bed, what the Danes call a *dyne*. At first it was one of the most benign and fondling beasts I had ever become introduced to. It warmed me up so gratefully and rubbed against me so softly that I thought the *dyne* and I were going to be lifelong friends. It had all the qualities one demands—pliability, gentleness, insinuating warmth, passivity and devotion. Safe in the arms of this comforting monster I fell asleep. Perhaps an hour went by, or two hours, and then I began a terrible struggle that nearly ended me. I was in hell-fire. I could feel hot breath on my face. Determined not to be annihilated without a blow, I lunged out with all my might, but instead of making an impression on the enemy I wasted my efforts and was borne down by a suffocating, overwhelming mass that tried to asphyxiate me without uttering a sound. The battle was all the more fierce because it was wordless. I was dumb. At last, summoning all my strength, gritting my teeth, purple in the face with effort, I decided either to die or conquer, and I woke up, gripping the *dyne* by the throat.

It was then three in the morning, and we had to catch a train to other relatives by five. As I looked at myself in the glass I realized that all was not well. I was in a state that is no less

We Go to a Farm

distressing because it provokes derision. My cheeks sagged, my eyes were round and bulging, I looked woebegone. In that no man's land of time, somewhere after five and before seven, when the hospitality of the night before has condensed from a glowing vapor into a lump of lead, when the word "darling" seems an insincerity and the word "hurry" is a poke with a pointed stick, we packed to go to these new relatives, and by a slow train.

There was one amelioration, we had a pass on the train. We stepped high up into a coupé that was padded and carpeted. It had everything a first-class compartment should have, including a little washroom. It was so clean, so fresh in its light fawn upholstery and so evidently exclusive.

Several other passengers sat across from us. One was a sand-colored man in a high starched collar, frail and thin-nosed. There was a somewhat broad lady with faded light blue eyes and a severe aspect, but as candidly, transparently a lady as pebbles are clear in a brook. There was a third, but who it was, or what, never came to me, for by that time, either due to the vibration of the train, or the battle with the *dyne,* or the antipathetic eel, waves of heat, succeeded by clammy cold, were passing through me, as though I were a third party and had gone into the hands of the receivers. Yes, my palm told me, my brow is beaded with beads of sweat. I could see my wife eying me with a steadiness that was not exactly incriminating but that bordered on the supervisory. I gathered into myself, and yet I knew that outside I was taking on the hue of an unripe lemon.

Students of will power hold out great prospects for self-mastery even in the most critical situations. If you slip on the waxed floor, they say, just as you are about to genuflect, control yourself and all will be well. I had never taken a course with the Pelman Institute, and I wished I had, but I doubt very much whether the original Pelman himself could have carried it off. One extra little kangaroo hop—it was a strictly local train

—and I knew what was going to happen. Like a shot from a catapult I cleared the thin, outstretched legs of the elderly gentleman, the laced boots of the lady and the space between myself and the washroom.

Once in the washroom, with the door closed, all should have been secret. I had never been seasick in my life, and my difficulties in going into reverse were considerable. Still, they were my private difficulties, and a man has a right to his privacy. The partition between myself and the rest of the world, however, had been designed for the eye rather than the ear. Even before the somewhat lengthy performance I had embarked on was concluded, it was apparent to me that the world's a stage and the first thing you have is an audience. I saw it through, I wiped my bleary eyes, I flushed and flooded and demonstrated my cleanly habits, but as I had no ticket for this compartment the moment came when I had to join the ladies. Still green, but now more like a lime than a lemon, I stepped out, and as I did so all the feet were tucked icily away from contact with me. I sat down.

The cad! The self-indulgent brute! The drunkard! Oof! Surges of disapproval told me that just as my movements had been involuntary so had complementary movements been suggested, in defiance of self-control but in obedience to the way we're made. The odium of this, of which I was aware, was too much for the company. Had they been able to get out, all would have been well, but we were traveling at thirty miles an hour, and they were cooped up with me.

We parted as if we had never been together. They were oblivious of me.

When I reached the cousin's farm, and it turned out that I had a temperature of 102, I felt vindicated. No man was ever so grateful for a temperature. I'd have preferred 104.

6

This farm was on the Jutland heath, but all I knew of it was a large dark bedroom, until late in the evening. Then I was told that Mette had cooked a dish for me. It was extremely light, a fricassee of chicken, and I still remember that it had a green sauce. It was not much to judge by, but that fricassee in a farmhouse told everything. It bore out a remark that Christian Brinton had made to me in 1902, when we both lived at Mrs Meagher's boardinghouse, 73 Madison Avenue, New York. "You do not have to see the girl," he said. "She need only stick her leg out of the cab." The power of inference is man's highest gift, and the Danish folk high schools dawned for me in this fricassee of chicken.

Jutland is swept by west winds off the ocean, and like the west of Ireland it is, or was, impoverished and waste.

This farm, Overgaard, belonging to my wife's uncle, had been long in the family. Her own name, Toksvig, was the name of a small place near by, and her own father as a boy had worked on this very farm. She knew it well. She returned to it with the poignant emotion of the exile. The family living there was gentle and affectionate, and as she reunited with them and with the house she shimmered between laughter and tears. The precise manner in which her husband had made his entry, after the battle with the *dyne*, was scarcely as heroic as we could have wished. But if you can't be heroic it is best to be pathetic, and my collapse was complete enough to throw me on the mercy of Overgaard, a quality in which it was both strong and dry. I felt at home; and I was in bed, where I feel most at home, while Signe, back from America with an author-husband, could tell the family's saga.

No mariner home from strange coasts could have been more eagerly followed. It was a story of hurricanes, of blizzard, of pure and simple hearts, and through the prism of their love of P. K.

Toksvig, Signe's father, they watched the little bark that he navigated through all its storms. It had been an inland story, from New York to Colorado, from Colorado to Alabama, from Alabama to Tennessee. It was not for its successes or its failures, but for its inner meaning, its adventure, its pain and its wonder, that Overgaard heard the tale. Something that is in the symphonies of Sibelius may be experienced on the Jutland heath, and these Jutland farmers, with their insight into character, could live into that struggle of which Signe gave them her word. The narrative and the narrator united, I do not doubt, to leave an impression that stays unaltered, since it satisfied their three inherent needs—their love of truth, their family loyalty and their pride in P. K. Toksvig.

Life, by the way, has to be lived to be appreciated, and one of the great jokes it plays on the urban is to convince them of their superiority to the rural. H. L. Mencken has taken many a whack at the yokels. H. G. Wells writes bitter pages about the peasants in his book *Wealth and Happiness*. Cockney authors satirize the ladies who plod in Thomas Hardy's furrow, and Somerset Maugham has not spared Hardy himself.

Well, to test any art you must find at what point it loses contagion. That is the object of satire. By reducing the friendly temperature you discover under what conditions it perishes, and the great books, of course, are so powerful in contagion, so capable of raising the temperature by themselves, that no satire can touch them. A comic version of the Bible falls flat. There is, in rural novels, a sort of soulfulness about the forces of nature, a kind of Millet pose, a stress on dark love and so on, that draws shouts of protest; but to go from this to vituperation of the peasant is to make one ask, Who are these city folk?

The modern city has been made possible by sewers, by garbage disposal, by subways, by bus service, by "public utilities," by marketing, by water supply and so on. This, in turn, has allowed human beings to specialize. By specializing, heights of attainment are reached that the rural have never achieved. But where the yokels are often self-sufficient in the bad sense, cut off, full of prejudice, stubborn and behind the times, the urban may be self-sufficient in another bad sense and the victims of mass delusion. Most city dwellers are veneered peasants, nothing more. They have given up the all-round handiness of the countryman to earn their living by some deft operation which has an economic value but no cultural value whatever. They read newspapers in London and New York and other capitals so demagogic that no groveling peasant could have a sillier picture of life than that which these urban folk consume.

A fining of the nerves goes with a submission to mass suggestion, and this gives the manipulator his chance to control people wholesale, to slap them into ideas as they are slapped into the train. The church has to cater for a city public in competition with the big shops, the cafeterias and the cinemas. Music, art and literature have to crawl on their bellies to win favor, and the city dweller is no sooner paid for his work than he is milked of his nickels by a thousand expert hands.

There is something warm and glittering about the ocean of humanity in which he bathes, but he is so stimulated that he becomes depleted, till he suffers in the end from chronic malnutrition—a victim of urban anemia. It is bloodless, half-developed, suggestible multitudes like these who are recruited by dictators and given a physique that is powerless to nourish a mental and moral soil that the city has exhausted. Were there a process other than mere aggregation by which cities grew big, the peasants sucked into them might be paraded as superior. In course of time, certainly, the true opportunities of the city do enable a proportion to become all-round in a new sense and more highly organized than before. But how many city dwellers live in the third dimension? Most of them are glued to their jobs, which are usually impersonal, and then glued to their entertainments, which are the equivalent of thumb-sucking. The city dweller, in short, is a new form of being who has attained not community but coagulation. The result is so abnormal, so one sided and unfamiliar, that one seeks in vain for the old-fashioned plethoric man in these spectral organisms. To kill a city dweller, indeed, has lost all the enormity that we used to associate with life and death. It is virtually an insecticide. For this reason the insects, aroused by full-blooded yokels, attack them with venom.

It should be said, perhaps, that there exists in England a rural population of a peculiar consistency. When we lived in Kent we met some troglodytes who were compounded of clay and beer. In Ireland, where the native families of a superior culture were broken into the peasant mass in the eighteenth century, you find, on the other hand, simple people of exquisite sensitiveness; and one of the hardships of these Irish has been the uncritical facility with which the English have grouped them with the serfs who clump around in rural England. These besotted serfs, and they exist, are what a strident critic means by a peasant, but when David Garnett reports that a small boy to whom he gave an orange in Connemara ate the whole fruit, skin and all, he should not infer from this that the boy was a barbarian, akin to the downtrodden English. It was the boy's first orange. He ate it as he would have eaten an apple, and Garnett might have warned him that it wasn't yet in the state where all of us eat oranges, skin and all. It wasn't yet marmalade.

7

Before I was on my feet there came a caller to Overgaard, long a friend of the family, who had heard that Signe Toksvig was home. He was one of the grand old men of Denmark, Christian Dalgas. Next day he took us driving through forests of pine and spruce. It was warm in those heavy, redolent roads, and I could scarcely believe we were on the heath in Jutland. Yes, and with the son of the founder of the society for the reclamation of the Danish heath. That, if you like, was a "public utility." He had lashed down the sands that quenched life in the fields. He had made ramparts against the winds. In this shelter the earth could be held and cultivated, and the poor farmer could win his way. But this utility was not for the sake of the Dalgas fortunes. It was a public work, for the sole benefit of the public. The force and conviction, the initiative, had sprung from Dalgas, and simple men who had become his converts were the gainers. There was a new Jutland because men like E. M. Dalgas had given their lives to an enterprise that was not for gain. And his son had continued his work.

There is a Dalgas Boulevard in Copenhagen, to commemorate this reclamation of the heath.

Men who have power in them and who use it directly for a community apart from the government nearly always have a large, massive, benignant presence, the result of their paternal role. Some, I daresay, end as unhappy as King Lear, in a world where the seasons change abruptly, but Dalgas was rounding out his years in a mood like Prospero's. We went to his home. One of his daughters was going to Copenhagen to be a nurse. A privy councilor was there. An inborn fineness in the family seemed to be grooved into a social obedience. It had an extraordinary charm. The incidents of the day are blurred and the flower of it is dead, but it remains like a pale silhouette between the leaves of a book, a wistful, enchanting souvenir.

The people of Jutland love the heath, just as the people of the Middle West love the prairie. Its great spaces wed it to the great skies. It has the loneliness that invites depth and melancholy. It has many moods. Its grim inutility made life so hard, in the old days, that Jutland was the land of gnarled and taciturn men. In the past seventy-five years, however, the economy has changed, and it needed no Mussolini to bring this about. This change came from the people under leaders who have seldom or never been shot, even by a camera. The idea that heaths cannot be reclaimed or marshes drained without batteries of cameras revealing the hairy chest of a sweating Duce is a recent aberration. Democracy was at this work just about the time that it took Benito Mussolini on its lap and gave him a free primary education. His histrionic talent would have been wasted in Jutland.

The plantation through which we drove was six thousand acres. Signe told me of the solitary tree in two parishes that stood when her father was a little boy. It was a red pine. It survived under the bank of a stream, but whenever its top shoot reached the height of the bluff the west wind smote it off. It was not till the plantations were resolutely secured that farming could grip into the sand.

"Yes," said a neighbor, speaking of Signe's father, "he was twelve, and we had him for the cows, and another boy who was ten for the sheep, and a lad of six for the lambs." It was that man's father who had treated the twelve-year-old boy like his own son, sending him to school, that protecting bank behind which he had grown.

We came to the forestry school at the other side of the plantation. Behind this school, unfortunately, there was a gooseberry garden. Up till then Signe had been communicative. I was still a little weak and not interested in gooseberries. She, on the contrary, was strong and incredibly interested in them. She went back to the age at which she had played the princess in charades with the Dalgases. There was no more conversation about forestry.

8

As I regained vigor, however, the welcome at Overgaard was so quiet and warm that the curious fineness of it was more than grateful.

It was like picking up a silver horseshoe to find so much amenity on a farm in Jutland. Had this been a luxurious, fashionable farm, I should have expected quaint latches on the doors, candles on the dining table, a stark and expensive simplicity. But here was a stern, working farm, out on the heath, with flint arrowheads that Kjaer had picked up on a shelf at one end of the room and the telephone at the other. Here was a windmill charging a battery and a belt run by a Ford. Here was electric light in the pigsty. And here was Mette's fricassee of chicken.

We went to the co-operative creamery. It had just been slewed out with water, and it had the somewhat clammy smell that is cleanliness at an early stage. Improved milk cans stood around, made in Denmark, and the machinery would have told as much to an observant man as a mound of shells to an archeologist.

The separator, to which Laval and Nielsen have attached their names, much as Wallace and Darwin to the theory of evolution, stood before my eyes as I nodded sagaciously.

Kjaer, a wiry dark man with a leaping spark of temperament in him, went from one high point to the other. Would we see storehouses of cheese? We looked into a cool dim place where ponderous shapes were ranged in stolid rows, utterly acquiescent. I was then only at the beginning of my acquaintance with Danish cheese, which is now deeper but still respectful, or even more so. The Danes have not the immortal fame of having created Brie and Camembert. But Madsen's Brie, as we later bought it in Hellerup, is a surpassingly good cheese. It knocks out most French Brie, though there is a kind that came from les Halles at three in the morning which we used to buy from an ex-sergeant in the Rue de la Glacière in Paris, and that creamy Brie, brought from the cave where he sold water cress, Brussels sprouts, pears and all the other dewy, earthy stuff that had come straight into Paris from the country, was of a quality for which there are no words. This Frenchman conferred the Brie on me like a decoration. It was Michael and George, so far as he was concerned, and he held me worthy of it. He was tall, rather brusque, with an aquiline, cruel nose and high color. The minute I entered his shop he'd take his shapely French knife and cut me a section of that melting yet stable Brie which my gastric juices were almost doglike for. In France you establish liaison. It is melancholy to think that one may never know this again, never again have unspoken accords with those highly individual people, so capable of giving you the Midi in a bottle and meadows in a bit of Brie. What a wonderful organ the stomach is, to bring people into such sympathy. The French understand it as Mozart did the flute, and since they also understand the flute, to think of them is to love them. That tall sergeant, with command in the quiver of his nostrils and a glance as querulous and sharp as if he were still under fire, could condescend to selling vegetables because they were the best, the selected best; I valued it when he gave me the Order of the Brie.

I am far from an epicure, by the way, and to crack up any small exquisiteness in this present world, where dead horses have to be eaten by people lucky to have them, does seem a lack of vision. Yet tedious as the fop and the dandy and the dilettante may be, in a crisis like 1940, they still are in an infinitely healthier frame of mind than the Nihilists who feed men on carcases. When one is young, with the body exigent and the spirit struggling to assert itself, it is right to dwell on reciprocations above and beyond the senses. Then joys may be ranked as "higher" and "lower." But to pervert the young, to exploit gallantry in them, to enlist them for death after a long and cynical indoctrination, is to disgust me with the asceticism of the power mad. I say then, suspect the disdain for the body that is in the least degree conscious and especially look out for the noble ones who are speechlessly exalted before idols, political or religious or aesthetic. The Danes have a very small proportion of these rapt beings. If anything gives them a keen pleasure, they attach a value to it.

But the rare dish at Overgaard was not just food. It was a sign that an angel had passed that way. Now where did the angel come from? If it is a silver horseshoe, find its mates, trace the horse, learn its stable, visit the castle and then discover whether or not the girl has read your books. If she has, the outlook is black, but don't stop until you see her.

CHAPTER FOUR

Farmers at School

TO the folk high school Mette sent us. It was from there she had derived that touch in cooking that is analogous to a touch in poetry. From there Kjaer had come home alert and awakened. With others who had shared the same voluntary courses he was the member of a dozen co-operative societies, but a member who knew how to consult, how to forbear and be rational. That bristling suspicion to be found in many farmers, that grim refusal to budge, all the traits of the wild goat and the stubborn mule—they were gone, washed out, replaced by a social touch, an ability to get together, be together and hold together. Something had oriented him.

The practical result of this, of course, leaped to the eye. At the co-operative dairy he had told me two facts that Peter Manniche puts in concrete figures. First, the average yield of butter per cow had increased from 110 pounds in 1880 to 200 pounds at the end of the century. And, second, the milk recording—that is to say, the day-by-day record of each cow's output in terms of butter—revealed that while it cost 5.85 kroner per kilo for the poorest cow, it cost only 1.12 kroner for the best cow. How grateful, you may infer, a member of a union may be that he is not a 5.85-kroner cow. If he were he'd be excommunicated.

But was the poor cow eliminated by ukase? I then heard of the method by which milk below standard was eliminated from another dairy. First year, a recording of unclean milk. Second year, a fine for unclean milk. Third year, when public opinion had been educated, a refusal by the co-operators to handle any milk below standard. And the weeding out of the poor farmers by the farmers themselves, in an organization where the little fellow had his vote like the big fellow, on an equal footing, was done just as methodically, as objectively and as patiently as the weeding out of the bad cows. When you know that ninety-two per cent of all Danish farmers are members of co-operative dairies, and ninety-four per cent of the butter produced by them, you are advertised that the Danish farmer has gone to school. The day of the Kentucky feud is far distant. The possibility of a Tobacco Road is nil.

As for pigs, it was another era from that of the pig buyer in the Irish hills who glances at a razorback on the horizon and says to the poor owner in the stony field, "An' what would you be askin' for the greyhound?"

Kjaer's pig looked like one of a board of directors. He reposed on clean asphalt. He honored me with an indolent, sidewise glance. I saw his electric light in the pigsty. I looked around for his shower bath.

Would Kjaer, then, have to be liquidated as a kulak? But by whom? We had tea at a farmhouse on a twenty-acre farm where a man lived who sometimes helped Kjaer. There was a tea cloth on the table, good cake, good china. The *husmand,* a small holder, had himself gone to a folk high school. He said "thou" to Kjaer. He was not asking to liquidate or be liquidated.

These were practical results. In the course of time I was to hear complaints, but at the beginning I felt as people do when they hear, We are beating tuberculosis, we have beaten diphtheria, we are going to lick pneumonia. The relapses, the failures, the half successes—they come later.

But the first view must be a view of averages. H. G. Wells

once called the nineteenth-century merchant ship "a fragment of floating slum." Farmhouses all over the world tend to be fragments of anchored slum. But here I was in a country where the farm was anchored in a garden, where there were books, flowers, friendly faces, quick minds and a wealth of living spirit. How was it done? That interested me more than the eventual wrangle about pig-export tickets.

2

In English "folk" has a slightly archaic sound. A song and dance sounds free, lively, but a folk song and a folk dance sound like Gothic restoration. Folkways, folk museum, folk costume, folklore—they do not limber the mind like Howdy, folks! That's different, in daily use. Doesn't suggest the cedar chest and fancy dress.

In Danish "folk" is a simple word. The lower house of parliament is the Folketing—folk-thing. The folk are the commons.

There is nothing archaic, therefore, about the folk high school. To go from high school to folk high school isn't going from beer to root beer or from Socialism to Christian Socialism. Even in the names Boy Scouts and Girl Guides there is an attempt to touch up virtue with Fenimore Cooper. It is hard to do this, to try to make virtue palatable, without making virtue lose its dignity and consequently its dynamic. The imperishable in Lincoln's utterance, to name one great political moralist, is largely the candor with which he makes a republic not a device for playing Indian but a test of moral being. Undisguised.

The folk high school in Denmark undertook, in its own way, the task that Lincoln undertook.

3

Well, we went to have a look at them. We saw about ten per cent of them. I was so fascinated that I tried to get the Rockefeller Foundation to give me a year in which to make a study of them. The English representative was persuaded, but New York ... but New York ... but New York ...

In the very heart of the country we stayed at one. There we saw the actual process by which the shy, isolated country girl is initiated. It was no routine institution. In the lectures we attended, the games we saw played, the songs we heard sung, it was evident that Denmark still remembered the crushing defeat of Dybbøl, out of which sprang this deep impulse to cultivate the National Self, to escape from the blind sluggishness and enslavement of farm life.

In this particular school we were surrounded by girls who seldom before had left home. For three months they were mingling together from every district, were discovering not only Danish history, Danish literature, general culture, but the feel of one another's lives.

They had been out of school since fourteen. They were now between eighteen and twenty-five, no longer children, no longer giddy, but vibrantly eager to make something of existence and giving themselves to it, faithfully giving themselves.

The program was hard, the food plain, the dormitories severe. But the buildings were handsome, well equipped in essentials. The surroundings happened to be idyllic. The temper was gay and earnest.

A week before, the graduates of this school had been asked to come to a reunion. Fourteen hundred came galloping from all Denmark. That impressed us. That showed love.

My own feeling was one of amazed admiration. It was these people themselves, not the state, who had built up the high schools. Sculptors and painters and architects and writers and teachers had contributed.

But not for profit, naturally. The courses cost five dollars a month or so and lasted during May, June and July, the five dollars a month to cover, with a little state aid to the school, not only tuition but board and lodging. There was obviously no margin for extras.

The girls sang as frequently, it seemed to me, as most people smoke cigarettes. The gymnastics were vigorous, the director being a woman who was then, almost there and then, about to have a child. One of the lectures we attended was so eloquent that the girls were breathless. It was a story of Ruth among the alien corn, related with simple passion. Most of the lectures were on the world at large and Denmark in particular, with geography as well as history and pivotal topics as well as human beings.

The leader, as he is called, is something of a shepherd. We sat under the trees with him and heard about the school. It was all, in some curious way, familiar.

4

I had myself, without knowing it, once been a teacher at a folk high school. Substitute immigrant for country girl, and I think you can compare the classes we taught at Hull House in Chicago to the classes so often taught in high schools.

Jane Addams of Hull House was the most admirable high-school "leader" you could imagine. She was of the same stuff if not the same sex, and had she run Hull House at Rockford, Illinois, had she herself given several daily lectures, had she taken a hundred students from all over the state and the country, using her theater and her gymnasium and her restaurant such as she had at Hull House, you would then have had a voluntary institution with much the same atmosphere, much the same educational tendency and much the same cast of mind as were to be found at Vallekilde. Some of her teaching staff would have been paid by state aid and they would have had full-time jobs, but the financing would have been on rather the lines of Hull House, with the school belonging either to trustees or Miss Addams.

The folk high schools were, in short, what Hearst would have called "Unsettlements" in a class country. They were the leaven in the peasant lump. Begun almost exactly a hundred years ago, they have changed the whole civilization of Denmark, and they ran into very much the same misunderstanding, hostility, opposition and animosity as Miss Addams encountered and over which she soared with that pained serenity so often visible in her beautiful countenance.

You must imagine two thousand six hundred Hull Houses, each of them in charge of a genuine leader, each of them independent, each of them processing the young people who chose to go to them between eighteen and twenty-five, to obtain some idea of the dimensions of the folk high school development in Denmark.

You must imagine, in addition, that the attendance in the United States would be about half a million students each year, sons and daughters of farmers, of artisans, of laborers, three quarters of them off the land and perhaps forty per cent receiving state aid in the payment of the fees, which in Denmark come to about a dollar a week for tuition, board and lodging.

Now, over two thousand Jane Addamses do not exist. But if you think of inspiring men and women who could possibly take hold of a school like this, building it up from a single house to a working plant such as Hull House has, never dreaming of making "graduates" of the students, not examining them, not mechanizing them, not disciplining them in any way, but leading and forming them, with a five-month course for the young men in the dead months and a shorter course for the girls in the summer months, you have something not unlike the Danish folk high schools.

5

What would you say was the gist of Hull House? Was it social revolution? When I was a resident there, in 1906, a Russian named Tchaikovsky turned up. He was a revolutionist. He believed in assassination. I remember so well the honesty with

Farmers at School

which Miss Addams, though his hostess, had to disagree with him. That same man, in 1917, was working with the Whites in Archangel.

Hull House, under her leadership, had no doctrine, no dogma. It tried, more than anything else, to create a faith in life and to link bewildered or benumbed immigrants to the American community. It tried to give meaning to the daily process, to put it in terms that in another age would have been religious, and to do this for a civic ideal. Jane Addams, Fridtjof Nansen, William James, MacLeish, Nathaniel Shaler, DuBose Heyward, Eugene Debs, Max Eastman—I can imagine any of these giving folk high school lectures to young people of that seventy-five per cent of the farming community who, in the long run, come into touch with the schools.

Out of the inflamed and anguished feelings of a defeated people it is easy to arouse the fear of a juggernaut, to see one in the economic or national conqueror. From that it is but a step to a state of war.

We have lived into an era when a state of war is chronic. Assassination is now routine. Hitler's assassinations in 1934, thorough and simplifying as they were, told Europe he was Nihilist; while the murders of anti-Fascists, the wholesale removals in Russia, the terrible crimes in Japan, show the demoralization that springs from political impatience and despair, that impatience leading to a trespass on the opponent's life. These trespasses—"forgive us our trespasses"—make the Lord's Prayer rather ironic.

Is a state of war like this really to anyone's liking? Is it unavoidable? Is it not a breach of social faith? Even the hero of *Grapes of Wrath*—how tenderly his murderings are regarded, just two little marked-down murders, while the bankers who sent out the tanks are juggernauts. War situation between the bankers and the refugee Okies. But does it have to be war?

6

The gist of the Danish answer to all this is to be found in the Danish folk high schools. The Okies are tenant farmers. Well, the Danes would still be tenant farmers had it not been for the folk high schools. They were born below sea level, just as the Okies are, but they built a dyke between themselves and the sea. That dyke was education. So long as they were ignorant, power was in the hands of the landlord class. The difference between an Okie and a Willkie is not feudal. It is not predestination. It is not capability. It is a difference in power, and knowledge is power. The Danish Okie went to school. He oriented himself in the world. All the wind that was blowing through his head, he learned to harness it to a power mill. All the torrents of spring in him, he learned to turn a wheel with them. But he became a powerhouse by no easy prescription. The state did not do it for him. The academic class did not meet him halfway. He'd still be an Okie if he had gone chasing the Apples of the Hesperides. He stayed home and minded the cow.

7

If anyone wishes to know about the folk high schools he should read Josephine Goldmark's short, cheap book, *Democracy in Denmark*. That gives you the essentials. He should also read Peter Manniche's *Denmark: A Social Laboratory*. And, having fallen into step with Manniche and Miss Goldmark, the rest takes care of itself.

My aim is not to guide your baby steps but to describe my own. In the fear, however, that my words will be inadequate, and they are bound to be, I warn you that the roots of these schools go so deep into Denmark, into the ways of the people, that my bright-eyed visit can only reveal what is above the surface. And even there I may go wrong.

Marquis W. Childs, in *Sweden the Middle Way*, goes pretty wrong on this subject of the Danish folk high school. He wishes to point up the story, for the sake of contrast, to say, "gaze on this"—Denmark before taking—"and then gaze on this"—Denmark after taking—with Bishop Grundtvig as the Happy Warrior or Joan of Arc or the Angel of Mons. It is a good patent-medicine formula. Children cry for it, and so does Mr Stout of the *Saturday Evening Post*.

Quote: "The fortunes of this small country were at the lowest ebb in the decade after 1865. The people themselves were in a state of abject misery and apathy that was close to utter despair. . . . Denmark was actually on the verge of national disintegration."

Bad case, you'll admit. Worse than arthritis. But a bottle of Grundtvig! "That extraordinary national hero, Bishop Nicholas Frederik Severin Grundtvig, had through his teaching prepared the way for a new epoch." Grundtvig is good for you.

On the state of Denmark seventy-six years ago, Miss Josephine Goldmark is a more sober witness. "The defeat of 1864 meant not only national humiliation but also the loss of two fifths of the nation's territory. But, by this time, a new spirit had emerged in the land. The defeat of 1864 did not crush Denmark as had the earlier defeat of 1814. The people rose to meet it."

"If we ask," she continues, "to what the renaissance of Denmark was due, undoubtedly no one factor or agency can be named. . . . But all observers, Danish as well as foreign, agree that the essence of recovery lay in this: that it was not a static, but a dynamic, continuous movement; not imposed from without, but fed from within; a long process of thought, as well as action, on the part of many people. Education, in its broadest sense, worked the miracle."

It was education, beyond doubt, as Grundtvig conceived it, and he knew exactly the kind of people who had to have it, as well as the kind it should be.

"Only barbarians and tyrants," he cried, "can imagine that

this root and kernel of the people—tenants and freeholders, large farmers and small, artisans of all kinds, sailors and tradesmen—does not need any more enlightenment than they can obtain behind the plow, in the workshop, on the boat and behind the counter."

Three hundred years before, it was the Bible that Erasmus wished to put into the hands of these very people. But Grundtvig, priest though he was, wanted them to be men and Danes before they were Christians. He wanted them to have the "living word," but word about social life and national institutions, about birds, animals, human beings, about Danish literature and Danish history, but, above all, Understanding, Enlightenment.

"It was in 1832," Miss Goldmark says, "when the first political concessions were being made to the people, that the leader who was destined most potently to influence Denmark's future—Bishop N. F. S. Grundtvig—seized the opportunity of putting forward his ideas on Danish recovery, based on a new liberal education for the people as a whole. They must be educated, he said, to be able to take part in the new popular assemblies. They should know enough of their country's history and social conditions to enable them to discuss intelligently, and help in advising on, the laws."

For thirty years, that is to say, Grundtvig prepared the way, and after the Prussian onslaught in 1864 the word was, now or never. The antiliberalism after the war, the recrudescence of junker spirit in the landlords and the reaction in the towns, gave incentive not only to Grundtvig but to a group of other patriotic men to start these schools which could put rungs in the farmers' ladder.

It is too much to say, as Mr Childs says, that (1) Grundtvig preached a kind of nationalism new to Europe, that (2) Grundtvig prepared the way for a strong national government that would direct the economic and social life of the country and that (3) Grundtvig taught the Danes co-operation.

Grundtvig did preach, and he did prepare the way, and he did

Farmers at School

teach, but while, as Peter Manniche says, the Grundtvig influence can be traced in all phases of Danish life, the co-operative movement, arising ten years after Grundtvig died, can in no direct way be traced to him. To put the emphasis on "strong national government" is to misplace the whole emphasis. And Grundtvig's nationalism was not "new in Europe." A great nationalistic wave was sweeping Europe in Grundtvig's period. Mazzini, Kossuth, Victor Hugo, Thomas Davis in Ireland, were all learning to intertwine a post-Revolution belief in the common people with a revolt against the academic. Mazzini as "prophet of the new Europe" can be set up by the side of Grundtvig, "prophet of the North."

But the last thing to link folk high schools with is a "strong national government."

Grundtvig did believe that the people should be prepared by education to take part in government, and in time the educated folk, the "yokels" as Mencken calls them, have done much to reshape Danish government. But self-help is the first fact about them. They owed little to government. The supreme lesson of the folk high school is a lesson of unorthodox methods to meet needs not yet heeded by authority. The assertion of these needs by Grundtvig was a great service. He oriented the farmers at a critical time, or at any rate he oriented the men who oriented the farmers. But the satisfaction of these needs by a unique process of education was accomplished by the Danish people themselves. And in doing this they proved that, among all the people in Europe, they had the firmest possible grip on the inner secret of popular government.

A German may smile at this. How can it be a good ship of state? he may ask. Didn't we scuttle it?

8

When it's all said, however, about the folk high school and the Danish farmer, there must be a few very definite reservations.

Not on the score of what the Danish farmer produces. Some may prefer the best Irish bacon, eaten in Ireland, to the kind one gets in Denmark, but bacon curing is not the same for export as for local consumption. The pig, anyway, is an animal of such sternly local excellences that he is prized all the world over for the local stamp on him. There is Bayonne ham, Westphalian ham, Virginia ham and a dozen others, including jambon de Yorck, shipped to France from Cork in the South of Ireland. The Wiltshire bacon made in Denmark may not rival Limerick bacon to my taste, but it has been a sweeping success in England for years. As for Danish butter, only the highest tariff walls can keep it out of any country that knows good butter.

Denmark has no such chicken as the poule de Bresse. The egg comes before the chicken in Denmark. And each of them is stamped, so that a bad one can be traced to the producer.

Some years ago the minister of agriculture in Ireland was P. J. Hogan, endeared to thousands as "Paddy" Hogan. He was not the sort of man who minces words. Gifted, active, clear-minded, brave, he'd just as soon quarrel with you as look at you if you crossed his path. We met him for lunch at the restaurant of the Dail in Dublin. This was no social affair, it should be said. The restaurant was run by the widow of a political comrade and nearly everyone was lunching modestly. Hogan was sustaining his labors, which were colossal, on tea and cake. I mentioned Denmark at once, and then I saw that as minister of agriculture in Ireland he was so fed up on Denmark that a chop would have choked him.

He was like a terrier at the word Denmark.

"The only place I got a bad egg when I was abroad," he said, "was in Copenhagen."

He dismissed Denmark. He scoffed at the notion that the Irish were farmers, or ought to be farmers, as the Danes were. The Irish had never been farmers in that sense. He told me about Ireland down the ages. The Irish were traders, cattlemen, cowboys, wanderers, "gay roving blades," while the Danes were evidently poor slogging slaves who stayed at home, co-operated themselves sick and produced bad eggs.

If he had had four legs he could not have planted himself more stubbornly over his contention. He barked. And I gave up. I thought of my mother's people, farmers for hundreds of years on a hill in Kilkenny. But this was not an argument. This was a temperament. It did not shake me about Danish eggs or Danish farmers. It shook me, however, about my methodistic impulse to be a lay preacher. Even Rider Haggard, author of *She* and *King Solomon's Mines,* who had traveled in Denmark much more thoroughly than I had and written a fine book about it, could get nowhere with a man who does not want to listen. I am not sure that people should be asked to listen, unless they invite you to dilate on it.

But the unfairness to Denmark is to picture it as a land of Boy Scouts and Girl Guides, a land of Sandford and Merton, a model for all others, even a "social laboratory." A reservation must be made on this score. If it couldn't be made, Denmark would be insufferable to live in.

9

Nobody has endowed the Danes. That is the basic fact to remember. The Dane who was born on the Jutland heath had to root or die. A certain number emigrated, but that solution was not open to everybody. A certain number degenerated, but that is no solution. The cards were so dealt to the Danes, in the middle of the nineteenth century, that unless some extremely quick thinking was done the most of them would have poor pickings and some would have no pickings at all.

Paddy Hogan to the contrary, it was very much the same in Denmark as in Ireland, except that the Irish, being an English-speaking people, had nothing to do but ship to America if the solution was too arduous at home. Nearly five million Irish left the Irish classroom, where the lessons were so brutally hard.

The Danes could not leave the classroom. They had to stick to it and work out the lesson. But being a free people, a true community, they buckled down and slogged away at it, and the folk high school was one of the devices by which a land-bound class managed to raise itself out of the mire and reach a decent standard of living. They did not find it a Jacob's ladder that landed them in Paradise. A Danish farm is no Paradise. But compared to a Polish farm, to an Italian farm, to a Swedish farm, an Irish farm, where similarly handicapped and undereducated people had to work out a solution, it is well worth contemplating, so far as I hear. It must always be remembered, however, that the achievement is relative to the initial poverty of Denmark, to the acceptance by Denmark of modest standards and of an irksome, inexorable discipline.

Do the Irish get up at five in the morning to begin farm work? They may stay up till five in the morning, but they don't get up. The Danes must, for the simple and unamusing reason that their life is mechanized. The Danish farmer is a success because he has submitted to a degree of organization and standardization that condemns him to machine routine. Rather than have a sob story to tell about himself or have a Demon in the cellar who is accountable for all his woes, whether that Demon is a banker or a landlord or a foreign tyrant, he gets up early, he rules his temperament, he makes the best of his neighbors, he learns to figure closely, to sweat and stew and to be on time with the milk.

No one would welcome a self-milking cow more than the Dane. That's the animal he'd adore. But he has a rendezvous with his cow, and you can't be a gay roving blade if you or your wife has to lash milk into a pail. The whole motion of his life is centered on operations that he cannot dodge. No matter how he has smoothed the way, he is a conscript. The cow and the pig and the hen, the dairy and the barn conscript him. But it is a mechanized life that enslaves only himself, that destroys nothing, that cheats nobody and that in the end liberates and enriches him, so long as the markets he has won by his standards are not shot to pieces by the adventurers.

It is *faute de mieux*. When warfare ceased to be piecework, when it got off the hand loom and went into the factory, the Danes had such a deficiency of raw materials that they were whipped out of the empire they had. The adventurer's way was closed to them. They could mechanize themselves for peace. To do it for war, under modern handicaps and on their resources, might appeal to the more adventurous among them but in the end could only so burden them with debt that not all the pigs, cows, hens, milk cans, beer barrels, cement barrels and clothespins could enable them to buy bread and herring. That shortcut to acquisition, which Germany has taken, has not been open to the Danes for several centuries. And they have had to do remarkable teamwork to break up the big holdings, multiply their independent ownerships and still industrialize their farming.

10

Having made this reservation about Danish farming, in order to insist how arduous it is, I could report grievances from manor houses, most of them with a bias against state regulation. The big landowners—they have about ten per cent of the land—do not love the Social Democrats in Copenhagen. They talk of the government very much as Long Island talks of the New Deal.

Seen from the manor house, the parceling of Denmark into small lots is not a gain all along the line. A class that gave many leaders to Denmark and that has had singularly unselfish and noble members, as well as highly individual and picturesque ones, has claims of its own to be a "social laboratory," with a power to attain delight and to contribute it which cannot be curtailed without a risk. Grundtvig owed something to the manor house. Hans Christian Andersen did. So does the small holder himself, who has nibbled away the manor.

But the social outcome for the agricultural population has

been worth the price. The Danish farmer is submitted to routine, but he is no robot. He is alive to the existence of Europe. He listens to dozens of excellent lectures on the radio. He uses his telephone as much as an American. He reads books, goes to the pictures, dances, sings, travels, takes electric treatments, keeps up with the dentist, has nervous breakdowns and operations. He is, in a word, a civilized man. And he often knocks you out by some bit of special information, some proof of special curiosity, some glimpse of a secret room in him where there is music or a field of stars.

And they laugh.

The success of the folk high school is not in technique. It is in road making. The boys and girls who come from these schools are no longer trudging in ruts and dirt tracks. They go from point to point with a firm footing.

II

After a big social shock the Irish co-operative movement folded up. The government became its receiver.

"Did you not put the cart before the horse?" I once asked Sir Horace Plunkett.

Unlike Paddy Hogan, he could talk about the Irish patient as if he were a doctor rather than a solicitor.

"A cultural movement before the agricultural movement?" he said. "That was our mistake, not to have had high schools."

His lifework was Irish co-operation. But he had not prepared the co-operators.

My temerity in speaking to him I admit, but in Peter Manniche's *Denmark: A Social Laboratory* I learn that others put the same question to him.

"When Sir Horace Plunkett, the Irish land reformer, visited Denmark to study agricultural conditions and methods he found to his surprise that the success of farmers' co-operation had its deepest root in a purely cultural institution, the folk high school. He who had come to investigate a piece of machinery remained to study a philosophy."

The essence of that philosophy is in the precedence of cultural schools over agricultural schools—Grundtvig first educated the farmer's social imagination.

CHAPTER FIVE

Is Man a Machine?

IN THE AISLE of the train an American turned to me with a friendly smile.

"Wonderful little country," he said.

I thought it imaginative of him to say so. We were going through flat Sjaelland on our way to Esbjerg. The roads run straight through Sjaelland down there. The houses are remorselessly parallel to the roads. It is not swooningly romantic.

"But"—and he gave the decimal fraction of a laugh—"I guess one of our good men could run it in two days a week."

I said nothing. (Why don't those good men take a whack at Southern Pacific? I'd have said later.)

"A country this size," he added, "hasn't any real problems. Not what we understand by problems."

Was he a high executive? He was dressed as scrupulously as an undertaker. I guessed he was an executive. Said I to myself, if your wife could hear you laying down the law like this, I wonder what she'd think. Would she regard it as justifying her charges of extreme cruelty? But I said nothing. Never provoke customs officials, traffic policemen or high executives.

"What do you do?" he asked, turning his Sulka tie to me.

"Write."

"Oh," he said hopefully; "detective stories?"
"Articles."
His interest died. He disappeared.
He was probably a sales manager and third vice-president. He was patting Denmark on the head because he was on top of the world for the first time, and if he wished to pat Denmark anywhere it had to be on the head. In a period of Boom such men come right up. Not until a Boom has passed do they pass. As the poor old world, turning from black to red in the boiling process, began to shed its third vice-presidents I venture to think that this kind of executive met the stern gaze of the Old Hand and heard a sentence beginning, "I need scarcely tell you, Mr Pitkins, that anything I personally can do, but you understand, in the present condition of the world market, the directors do not feel justified, in fact we have hung on longer . . ." Mr Pitkins is at the elevator. "Down, please."

All executives, high and low, are inclined to oversimplify the problems of the small unit. Why, with a little compression, you could fit three Denmarks into Greater New York.

2

It it no use feebly arguing that Russia is a better country than the United States just because it is bigger. A paper with a 2,000,000 circulation is not, in so far forth, ten times as good as a paper of 200,000. Just because a million dollars is better than half a million, a million people are not twice as important as half a million.

Are they not? They are if they are "territory." They are if they are circulation for advertising. They are if they have to be housed or catered for. People also are quantitative.

Not only in business, in government as well, you run into the kind of executives who feel there is no serious problem in a small unit. Why? Because they think in terms of the machine. A grouping of small units recommends itself to them, and as for small nations, I have heard bright people ask whether they should be "allowed" to exist.

The art of government, whether of a country or a corporation, suggests itself to many engineers as "rationalization"—an organization, that is to say, on scientific lines in order to eliminate waste. For hardheaded men who have listened to the behaviorists it is really the art of operating a slot machine.

Against this conception of government, "strong" government as it has to be, the Danes seem to me extraordinarily united. They cannot be understood as a people who do things by government until they are first understood as people who do things by social imagination. The government is not the master of the people. It is the creature of the people. The Danish people are not guinea pigs.

Now, while people must be dealt with as a mass in those matters where it is silly and wasteful to be qualitative, and while government has very often to treat people as sheep to get a quick collective result, the Danish method comes out of a degree of social imagination that my executive on the train had no notion of. He did not see that there is a conflict between the engineer and the democrat. This is perhaps the basic conflict of the twentieth century.

3

Pooh, say the hardheaded men. We are such stuff as guinea pigs are made of.

Well, speaking as a pig and with the courtesy native to Guineans, I admit, and most Danes I believe would agree, that certain early indentations in the emotional being do seem to sink so deep that we remain indented for the rest of our lives unless—and here I cease to be a guinea pig—unless we use brain and imagination to surmount the early impression.

Being human beings, not pigs, we are unique. Our uniqueness consists solely in this power to imagine. Where a fish goes on

Is Man a Machine? 77

being a fish, blunting its nose against the glass, blunting its nose against the place where the glass used to be, we have it in us to imagine a removal of the invisible partition and to pass through the space where our habits assure us the partition ought to be. We surmount. We not only surmount the exterior obstacle but also, in rarer cases, surmount those inner obstacles created in us by early and ungoverned experience. We learn, that is to say, to govern our own being in relation to the world outside us and to take new evidence on it; evidence that our habits, our emotional bias, our upbringing, may make repugnant to us, and yet convincing evidence about a state of reality we had not desired or suspected.

By this immense power of adaptation, this exercise of imagining, we are rather more than animal beings. We are human beings. By evil imagination, which is perfectly open to us, we are harmful, destructive and loathsome creatures. By healthy and springing imagination, we are creative creatures who unite with outside reality on terms that rise above our emotional bias. An emotional bias may be so violent and incorrigible that facts no longer can be fitted into it, even by the aid of six doctors and twelve nurses. A healthy imagination has to be corrigible, pliant.

Hugo Muensterberg to the contrary, Shakespeare was a very good amateur psychologist, pre-Freudian, of course, but feeling his way. And when he said we are such stuff as dreams are made of he was not interpreting dreams in the Freudian way either. He was saying that we, and we alone, have this supremacy of imagining. Man harnessed the horse through having this supremacy. The first day a horse harnesses a man between the shafts I'll admit I'm a guinea pig.

4

There is much that is seductive and consoling about thinking of yourself as a mechanism.

If you make the distressing discovery that you are a coward, it is pleasanter, I agree, to be told you have a phobia. I had a phobia once. I was scared of lightning. I was so scared that if I went out to make a call and I saw a flash of lightning between the rubber plants I could not go home. I had to find any excuse for spending the night. It was a phobia of disreputable dimensions. So one day I said to myself, in the best manner of the eighteenth century, either I or this phobia must cease. When the next thunderstorm came, one of those truly royal thunderstorms that Manhattan provides, I went up on the roof of 73 Madison Avenue and stayed there until lightning had taken manageable proportions. It is now thirty years since I have been a coward in this particular respect. If my life depended on it, I do not believe I could now walk on a plank from one twelfth-story level to another. The threat to my instinct of self-preservation would be stronger than my instinct of self-preservation. I'd be like the millionaire who killed himself because he lost $30,000. The poor devil had only $970,000 left!

5

What a stranger brings to Denmark is, of necessity, the emotional system we call a personality. I had not been born a Liberal. I had been born a myopic, astigmatic, fatty, apprehensive bundle of human expectancy. Out of precisely the same family environment were produced Capt. B. J. Hackett, M.C., a Tory with a complexion at which you could warm your hands and a very nimble wit, and the Rev. W. P. Hackett, S.J., a Jesuit priest who gives Retreats to edify the Prohibitionist. Three little guinea pigs were we, Born in the same societee! But not born Liberal. We could not have been tagged at birth and pushed out into the market like numbered engines.

As against one brother who wished to be in the regular army even if a doctor and another brother who wished to be an officer in the Church Militant, my bias was to be outside all regimentations and standardizations, all totalities, all absolutes. What I loved in the New Testament was the revolt in it. The tragedy of that revolt was for me, as for millions of my generation, the deepest comment on values that could be made. I did not take the Jesuits seriously; I had gone to school to them. But I took very seriously the divine being from whom they borrowed the name. That was a bias, a something innate or at least promptly suggested and absorbed. It was the one fluid culture in Ireland that I could imbibe like milk. But I assimilated it to the national protest. The fervency of politics colored the Saviour I imagined. I do not say, in any blasphemous way, that I wove Him in with Robert Emmet and Lord Edward Fitzgerald and all the other heroes in our bible of nationalist propaganda known as *Speeches from the Dock*. But they had been on the scaffold and so had He. They had been destroyed by an Empire and so had He. These similarities arrested and fed my imagination. And when I came to read Mr Robert Emmet Sherwood or to listen to the ululations of the Democratic National Convention of 1940 I was made aware that other imaginations have been fed and stimulated by ideologies not so far from this which made me an Outsider. The bias in favor of the injured and the oppressed, the defeated and crucified, was a bias that was obviously promoted by having been an immigrant. And also, perhaps, by those two great handicaps to a military career, myopia and astigmatism.

Going to Hull House was a monastic impulse. I was too enamored of the world to "leave" it, as the religious do. But I half left it, as the uplifters do. And when Theodore Roosevelt half left the Republican party I heard his war cry with a thrill in my heart. The word Armageddon was, indeed, a purely Protestant word. Franklin D. Roosevelt has too much political instinct to employ a word like this in a party where Armageddon must have a more direct relation to Tipperary. But that valiant, heady, vainglorious phrase that was flung out like a banner in Chicago, "We stand at Armageddon and battle for the Lord," caused me to get up on a chair and shout with the multitude. We were shouting against monopoly, against the trusts, against the labor crushers, against Mr Elbert Gary's two shifts, one of twelve hours and the other of fourteen hours, in the steel mills. We were breaking the bonds of judicial decisions. We were demanding their recall. They were not sacred to T. R. in those days of Armageddon. And outside, on the Lake Front, serious-faced boys were trying to master the new flying machines. We went from the Convention where we had exulted in Armageddon, to see those boys in another element risk life and limb in a proud adventure. We saw two of them die. And Richard Harding Davis was watching them, still in his nonage.

Armageddon—and again we are standing at it. But this time it is the steel mills surrounded by steel helmets. This time it is the monopoly of monopolies. This time it is mankind under the wheel and everything, including judicial decisions, turned out by the machine. The merciless "efficiency" of a trust was a thing that deeply revolted the imaginative thirty years ago. The subjection of a government to labor crushers sent T. R. into that wilderness reserved for bad Republicans. "Traitor to his class." But no one living in 1910 could have imagined a Europe so mechanized as the totalitarians desire it to be. We were luxuriating in a revolt against even mass production as such. We were not sure about electric lights, or about Fords, or about money made in Standard Oil, tainted money.

6

Once the economists became our prophets I found myself at a loss for a positive attitude. What had the economists to say that could guide us about the qualitative? Are there no *values*?

I make myself a Douanier-Rousseau picture of the economic approach, to clear this up for myself.

I conceive of a skyscraper in New York, before the bombardment of New York.

In this skyscraper there are ten floors at the top. One floor is given up to the offices of a firm that sells flower seeds. The next sells golf clubs. The next sells hats and caps. And the other seven are occupied by a lawn-mower concern, a fire-extinguisher concern, a dollmaker, a maker of dog biscuits, a maker of prayerbooks and two floors given up to the firm that makes Infants-Cry-for-It.

The government says to the lawn-mower people, to the makers of golf clubs and to the makers of dolls: Get busy. Munitions.

It says to the hat-and-cap people: Army caps.

It says to the makers of dog biscuits: Navy biscuits.

It says to the makers of prayerbooks: Swell, more prayerbooks. And to fire extinguishers, more of them.

Flower seeds? No. Make it hayseeds.

Infants-Cry-for-It must be turned into a concern for antiseptics. Wound irrigation.

Viewed from the economic angle, I cannot see myself that it makes the least intrinsic difference in employment, in turnover, in the distribution of wealth, whether these firms manufacture and sell what they were selling or the new things they are to make and sell. The economist cannot make a true discrimination about it. He can tell you whether the consumption of munitions is greater or less than the consumption of dolls, etc., in terms of cash, or persons employed, or use of machinery. He can point out whether labor is more or less secure in the munitions factory. But can he have any way of equating the benefits to labor of a steady munitions job with the irregularity of employment in making lawn mowers? Can he prove that munitions, on the whole, are more beneficial to society than dolls? Has he any business whatever to have an opinion about anything except the technical end of production, consumption and distribution?

He cannot even, in my opinion, try to direct human habits without running human risks. One evening in Ireland an English economist, Maynard Keynes, began talking on the radio. He had a big idea. Spend! Unless the world is to go bust, you must stop hoarding, you must stop crimping, you must stop stopping; you must loosen up, step out, spend.

It was a stirring talk. My wife was away. I thought, "How can I best spend? I am in debt, and I wish to put the economic system on its feet so that I shall be no longer in debt. Let me contribute by spending."

Nelson Doubleday had sent me a Christmas card of emerald green. So I went in to Dublin and ordered a carpet for a cold northeast room in this brilliant green. I ordered a rose-colored wallpaper and silk bedspreads with a cream-and-rose design. It was to be a surprise for my wife, from myself and Maynard Keynes.

She liked the room. An English friend came to stay. He stood on the threshold, blanched and said: "Rather overwhelming."

I liked the room myself. So did the decorators. I was grateful to Keynes. But about six months later, instead of the usual bill, there was a letter beginning, "In spite of repeated demands," and so on.

I went to an economist. "Keynes is not wholly orthodox," he said, "but he is unquestionably a genius. His theory is perfectly sound."

"Yes," I said, "but Anderson, Stanford and Ridgeway are asking me for forty-five pounds."

"Eh?"

There was a flaw somewhere. And while economists have every reason to be proud of themselves, proud of the concepts they work with and the way they can talk and smoke a pipe at the same time, it is better not to act too hastily on what even a genius among economists advises you to do.

7

Is a government at its best when it says, "Hay rather than azaleas"? In an emergency, yes. In an emergency it is better to have a man with a voice like a bull, since to herd is essential. But when a government takes the initiative, when it comes into a peaceful era and says, "Navy biscuits, not dog biscuits; Navy caps, not derbies," and so on, the answer must surge from the laymen: This may be convenient economics, but it is foul interference with human haphazard preference. We wish to live in a world where you can have dolls, lawn mowers, golf clubs and flowers and medicine for the baby, provided there is no emergency of life and death.

As I write these lines I hear that Germany has ordered the killing of three million pet dogs.

This is logical. The economist is working for a government so strong that no mere sentiment can be urged against its mechanizing. He, in turn, advises the government what is important and what is not important. What's a dog to him? What are church candles to him? What are these things except imponderables? He cannot deal with imponderables.

And yet he does. The very fact of not dealing with them is ruling them out, and that is dealing with them. The promise of unlimited New Architecture, unlimited Wagner, unlimited Olympic Fizz, as a substitute for the pet dogs, is based, I think, on overweening confidence in the taste of economists.

8

The economist, it is vital to observe, has not had the first word in modern Denmark. He has been invoked by a people who themselves have decreed the values. He has followed, not preceded, the molders of social imagination.

CHAPTER SIX

In Search of a Social Faith

THE WORLD I think of, when I write of Denmark, is not that amazing world of the human will that has been fabricated and exploited in my short lifetime, which is the world of the superman, or rather of the man with a super machine.

The world I am thinking of is somewhat prewar. It is a world of hit and miss, a cruelly real world of effort and failure, of calculation and miscalculation, of criticism, slow gains and many disappointments. It is, in its way, disillusioned.

Against this, since 1918, has been launched a series of experiments in a faith world that we call totalitarian. It is a New Order, a New Order in which the critic is the worst public enemy. Success is public policy in this system. The experiment is in itself sacred, no matter how many happinesses are thrown on the scrap heap or how many corpses.

An old showman like Bernard Shaw has been found to prefer the streamline efforts of dictatorship to the sprawling, less pointed and dramatic performances of the prewar world. His previous impatience with humanity sustained his comic muse and had the tinge of humanitarianism. But he gave up his tea, his coffee, his beer and his tobacco to be clear headed, and im-

In Search of a Social Faith

patience with humanity has been succeeded by patience with inhumanity.

His critical sense was once aroused by the existence of a censorship. He was up in arms against the censorship of plays. Without free criticism there is no possibility of measuring any experiment. There is no measure in an election, for instance, where the minority does not dare to vote. The failures under dictatorship cannot be known, because the voice of criticism cannot be heard. No cry can be heard above the din of self-advertising. But grant success in organizing, grant dedication to a purpose, grant the self-immolation of the masses, say nothing about the decoys and the blinds that helped the Germans to bag the game where the democracies missed, the fact does remain that a world like the totalitarian world, posed incessantly before a camera in lights that devour shadow, does offend one's lifelong habit of inference from familiar and sober existence. Let Bernard Shaw forget the slaves, in his dream of a pyramid. Let him accept human sacrifice, since the victims are willing. But how about a fixed grin on the face of life, how about a complete absence of candor, an experience that never admits an error or publishes a disillusion? Coué and Mary Baker Eddy and the Oxford Movement were orgies of critical intelligence alongside the goose-stepping of 1940. It is this wiping out of evidence that makes the faith worlds of dictatorship so offensive to a critical man.

2

This *is* a world of hit and miss. I remain astonished at the enormous proportion of misses, even in the simplest human affairs. A good cup of coffee is by no means hard to make. There is a restaurant in Copenhagen where the probability of it amounts almost to a certainty, once you grant that Brazil coffee is what you like. But how many restaurants hit this target, big as it is? Not ten per cent. Until the Jews put their minds on it there was no good coffee in a popular restaurant in London, to the best of my knowledge. And Hamburg!

At this moment I am blistered with poison ivy. Can I find a certain remedy for it? I've already tried half a dozen. Some help. I am half engaged to one, at the moment. But I am still poisoned.

And where it is no concrete little problem like this, where the requirements are many and exacting and variable—as in marriage, let us say—it is admitted that most of the experiments limp, while many blow up. The more you have to count on the human agent, the less you can count on anything. Failure, in short, is the normal human expectancy.

3

A democracy is more hit and miss than a dictatorship. It is more disobedient, looser, less disciplined. But the discipline and obedience it has, as in the case of Denmark, comes from a consensus rather than an imposition of opinion, and it allows Denmark to be at home not only with itself but all over the world. The saying of the Buddha, that it is simpler to wear shoes than to cover the world with leather, is the biggest existing argument against the efficiency of a dictatorship, which can only ship its citizens or its money or its ideas abroad on the condition that it conquers the entire globe. To be at once so powerful and so fragile is a fantastic price to pay for specialization.

No one can deny that an atmosphere of criticism is trying to the human ego. Criticism is a depressant, and democracies are full of it, much of it unjust. That is why, in the broad public, there is a yearning for the assurance that life begins at forty, that advice can help the lovelorn, that you can win friends and keep them by massaging the ego and that, if you cannot otherwise be refreshed and uplifted, you can use Sweetheart soap and chew gum. (Don't chew the soap.) But depressing as criticism is, it has to accompany the groping of individuals to adjust them-

In Search of a Social Faith

selves. When rules are finally arrived at, in a place like Denmark, they are a true adjustment and they are obeyed.

The tendency of all great institutions is to treat us as objects. For this there must be rules. It is when rules come to be formulated without consultation, without inflection, without solicitude, that the citizen is warranted in his revolt. He is then unfaithful to himself in being docile. When he complies with tyrannical rules, he is vilely, loathsomely obedient.

Democracy is no method for dispensing with rules. It is a method for devising them. A bad democracy vitiates the means of consultation; a good democracy improves them. But we are far from the day when Bernard Shaw said, "The golden rule is that there is no golden rule." Poor Shaw, a man who strained at a gnat and swallowed a Nazi.

4

Yet I can understand Shaw's committing himself to the dictators. To be a rebel, to revolt, was a negative attitude. I have found in my poor self a strong desire for a more positive attitude. The quest of a more positive attitude, however, entailed a positive faith, and where was that to come from?

One day I met Amos Pinchot on the street. He was the debonair rebel, salient, nonchalant, with a whiff of incense and a whiff of sulphur to be sniffed from him, a little touch of the fallen angel. He looked at me quizzically, the Lucifer look.

"You are a lucky man," he said.

Lucky? Was he ironical?

"I mean it," he said. "You are doing work you care for. You've married someone you care for. And you love Ireland."

Was it the Frenchman in him that commended these three positivenesses, that came not from the head but from the diaphragm? They were acceptable, at any rate, to his hard critical sense. But could not one relate them to a greater positiveness?

The League of Nations seemed to me a positiveness, but

when I went to Geneva for my newspaper syndicate I discovered that I was expected to be anti-League. I could not sell my articles with this positive attitude to any big-circulation American magazine. Was I willing to denounce the English on the question of opium, yes, that was salable. But the rest was taboo. The League was not news.

At Geneva, however, on a sweltering day, we sat lunching with a Scandinavian. This was a man who could have worn a crown had he wanted it. He was tall, with a great brow and a long chin, broad shouldered and athletic. His hair was white. His light eyes were direct in their gaze. He was unaffected but somewhat reserved, until some general European situation such as the famine in Russia or the Bulgarian prisoners or the transfer of populations excited him, and then he spoke with a frankness that showed no respect on earth for power politics but the deepest concern about human beings. He had just come down from Norway. He had sat up all night in the train, owing to some hitch at Stuttgart, but this left him undisturbed. He was not a man to spare himself or to trouble about his comfort. Geneva was not an incident in power politics for him; it was a flimsy machinery for international purposes, but still a machinery, and by its means he proposed to check that most abominable of all things, unnecessary suffering.

It was this Norwegian, Fridtjof Nansen, who had striven to avoid war in the case of his own country's separating itself from Sweden, who had brooded over the war in Europe from a Norwegian mountain with a misery that suffused his entire imagination and who, knowing the consequences of war, had left his mountain to reduce the agony of peoples whom the machine had scrapped. This love of peace was not a craven love of peace. He was no appeaser. He seemed to me wisely aware of the ruthlessness of the state, and in this sense the most remarkable of statesmen.

But he wore a negligent hat with a very broad brim. He was obliged to do this, I have no doubt, because an ordinary conventional hat would have been absurd on him. And yet this hat marked him as not exactly, you know, the true European like Apponyi or Sir Eric Drummond or Gabriel Hanotaux. Sometimes he carried his hat; "Mais, monsieur," as the French hatter, very mournful, said to me, "mais, monsieur, ce n'est pas correct!" Geneva, going up in the world, just preparing to deal with Mussolini by that famous policy of appeasement we hear about, did not quite like Nansen's hat. "Nansen, pas correct!" It was hard, in Geneva, to shape a positive attitude, except a positive attitude about leaving Geneva. It was torture to see, on every occasion, the preparation of internationalism, the perception of internationalism, the frustration of internationalism. Only in the Secretariat and the Labor Bureau was the tissue woven. In the League itself the tissue was becoming a tissue of lies. Try as the small nations would, the great nations balked them. And but for one man's compassion, one man's assiduity, one man's noble pestering, there would have been no Nansen passport, no gateway out of Hell.

5

But what positive attitude was one to assume about a League of Nations? Was this a thing to believe in? Was this a thing to lean on?

The most dazzlingly intelligent man we met at Geneva was a dark, small, thin, burning man with living eyes, a flash of the poet in those eyes and a shaft of wit, a quick devil in him.

"Forgive me," I said to this Spanish Ariel; "what great work do you perform here?"

I expected him to say, "I am working out the Greek inscription for the new building." Instead he said, "I am the head of the disarmament section."

"You are to disarm all the great powers?"

His eyes were fixed on me, luminous and aware. I burst out laughing. His eyes responded.

"You have a life job, anyway," I said to Madariaga.

It wasn't even a division all by itself. It was a piccolo in the orchestra.

6

Back in Denmark, I tried to write about Nansen, whose benevolence in a world that manufactured famine could not deal with famine at its source. How could the world be run where ideologies were so imperious that they themselves become the law, superior to everything accepted and everything established? What invites these ideologies? When they have seized on human beings, how can one combat them?

Robert Cecil was an ideologist. He was a cardinal, a cardinal not of the League of Nations but of the British Empire. But what nationalism was fit for internationalism? Internationalism cannot rise higher than its source. H. G. Wells had schemes, of course, for doing away with nationality. It was rather like deciding that all babies born with blue eyes must never let them turn hazel or black. Who could stop regionalism? And who, in the World State, could stop it from civil wars?

Famine had been devised by the Whites to destroy the Bolshies. The Bolshie ideology had led to it, but it was a boomerang policy. Boomerang policies were filling the air at Geneva.

By this time, let it be said, Massachusetts was deep in the soul-searching Sacco-Vanzetti case.

Up at Aalsgaarde, with the League articles so perfectly not selling, it succeeded in puzzling me.

CHAPTER SEVEN

Government Goes to School

WHAT had struck me, in those days in Jutland, was the evidence of voluntary association.

It wasn't the government in Copenhagen that had set things in motion. Dalgas hadn't worked through the government at first to reclaim the heath. He and the community had gone to work on their own account as a community. Theirs was self-help. When the time came to enlist the government there was already an integrated opinion, an opinion that could be brought to bear on any government agency. No bureaucracy sets out to do damage, obviously, but the indoor are prone to dogmatize. Here there was an outdoor opinion to correct that.

It struck me that the secret of Danish immunity to Bolshevism wasn't the efficacy of Famine. It was, at least in large part, the efficacy of Plenty. And the Danes had gone about procuring plenty by using their civic sense.

When we were in Ireland I had heard of a forceful man out on the far edge of Ireland who had built up a fortune. He was cock of the walk. He cashed in, stout and dictatorial, sticking out his chest and his chin. I am sure he thumped his broad chest and said to his mirror, "What in God's holy name would they be without me?" A self-made man is not a conceivable thing, any more than a self-made baby, but he was the inconceivable thing, a self-made man. And one of the things he had done was to corner cement out there. The stuff that was 100, let us say, in Dublin he sold to peasants for 225. Those peasants could not get a living in the locality. They were migrant labor. And this man of the people sucked their veins when they came back from migrating.

To prevent this sort of exploitation the Danes organized the Danish Cement Co-operative. They had to fight a trust which was both Northern and German. This trust kept them from borrowing funds to start the co-operative. They finally, through a Copenhagen bank and a loan from another co-operative, got enough to build a factory. The banks refused them operating capital. This they raised by private loan. "In the first year of operation, 1913," says Miss Josephine Goldmark, "it forced a drop of 2 kroner (then 53.6 cents) per barrel by the cement ring."

A similar story can be told about the first bacon co-operatives. The private companies put up a big fight. The banks obeyed the private companies. But by courage, by ingenuity, by sweat and toil, these Danish citizens broke through. And then they had taught the banks, the private companies and the government a lesson.

I can imagine no better type of leader than the one who is favored by the right kind of voluntary associations, and it is this kind of man who has been so admirably—not prevalent so much as evoked in Denmark.

2

What Denmark has happened to need is a kind of citizen who is less interested in building up a fortune than building up a community, and the temptations in other fields have not been so strong as to draw the suitable men away from the community. The sense of community has been so long cultivated, so favored by circumstance, so deeply understood, so associated with honor and prestige, that few men who could be drawn into its service have declined or shirked it. It is, in its way, a conscription, but a conscription by the community rather than the state. And the wealthy men who have not served the community are rather out of it. The others dominate Denmark, so that the wealthy nip into the service of Denmark in some way or other and line up with the teachers and the economically contemptible. To be just Margerine or Cement or Oil or Ships is certainly something. It is not enough. And in Jutland, where the community has had the toughest experience, it is the Dalgas type that is surest of honor.

This, in a great measure, has been due to folk education.

3

Just by revisiting Denmark, by seeing a state with almost no police, by observing a serviceable government, I began to capture a positive attitude.

It had not always been so in Denmark. The government had been autocratic and stiff necked. The governing class had been superior. But in proportion as the people had developed the power of enlightened association, had shown their ability in group after group to take care of themselves, the government had been led to offer itself not as a dictatorial power but as a superior method of association. It saw itself as the means by which society could best facilitate its common actions, and its response to the community became a solicitous response, a familial reciprocation.

A rosy picture, the industrialist would say. A rosy picture, the owner of a manor would say. A rosy picture, the landlord would say who had to sell his estates or the soldier who no longer was in service.

Yet even those who had to submit to factory inspectors, who had to submit to export regulations or the exigencies of trade unions, were by no means without the power to voice their grievances or to put pressure on the community. There was no core of privilege in Denmark, that I could find, around which the governing class had encrusted itself. If a prominent bank had a dishonest director, there was no group in the community to cluster round him and save him. The newspapers could not give him immunity. He had to go to trial. The trial had to proceed unsparingly, with the bank on the dissecting table and all its rottenness exposed. Whatever it cost, in self-criticism, in disillusion and in loss of credit, Denmark went through with it. The sense of citizenship, that remarkable fund of public virtue to which every class had contributed, was something you could be sure of, like water out of the faucet. There was no "invisible government." There was no Praetorian Guard. There was no collection of higher-up, full of higher-uppishness.

Denmark was like that incredible tank at Marineland in Florida where you see a goldfish bowl big enough to hold dolphins and sharks, turtles and rays, schools of plump little bulging-eyed fish that look like pig-tailed Sunday-school children, and tarpon whipping around and goggling bourgeois tucked into an aqueous corner. How is it done? It is done by feeding the predatory at such regular intervals that they no longer predate. They don't even bite the hand that feeds them. They wait around for the man in the diving helmet who brings them the Marineland equivalent of clam chowder. Sometimes, of course, a shark becomes antisocial. Then they put him in the reformatory. Marineland, by the way, is superintended by Tolstoy's grandson. It is a community in which the monsters of the deep go their several ways in peace. I saw one piscatory Romeo waltzing after a piscatory Juliet with the most fatuous, lovesick expression. This was a dolphin. And a young dolphin swam around, wearing a dead fish like a mustache, proud to have it but unable to swallow it. It was what the Danes would call his *mad-pakke,* his lunch basket. If one remained long enough and collected crime statistics I am sure the story would be dark enough for Erskine Caldwell and William Faulkner to feel cheerful. But at a casual glance there was nothing shameful, nothing to emphasize the sinister.

And what chance for a New Order in Marineland?

4

To account for this lack of belligerence and the deep considerateness in Danish life and the social wisdom of it, one has to ask: What are the main motives behind it?

The profit motive, it is fair to say, cannot have a dominant part in it.

Your medical man is the best-paid professional man in Denmark, on the average, but highly qualified as he is, and admirable as he is, he is not a profiteer.

In Dublin I have had occasion to pay doctors for their services. One of them was a brilliant young man with a vast practice. He'd charge fifteen dollars for the first visit and ten dollars for every subsequent visit at his office. I have seen a worker shell out his two pounds for a few minutes' service. And his physician would charge five dollars a mile for a visit down the country. A small farmer who had to have a specialist would pay a hundred pounds to bring down the specialist from Dublin, and the specialist would take it, even if the farmer did not clear a hundred pounds cash a year.

That's what I call the profit motive.

The top physicians and surgeons in Dublin live like fighting cocks and behave like fighting cocks too. They hunt, they yacht, they drive in noble cars, they wine and dine admirably and they live in the best mansions on the best squares in Dublin. To be treated by one of these experts confers lasting distinction on a small farmer. "A hundred guineas, not a penny less."

The corresponding class in Denmark ask five dollars for the first consultation from an ordinary patient. A top physician treats a prolonged ailment like sinus trouble for a dollar a visit.

Four fifths of this is recoverable if one is insured. A childbirth, with a private room in the clinic, costs an insured family—my brother-in-law's, to wit—less than twenty dollars, and this is in a suburb that has the best golf course in Denmark and is to be rated as prosperous.

One surgeon I know personally, a pupil of Harvey Cushing and now eminent in his profession, so eminent that he has been offered chairs both in English and American universities, does allow himself the luxury of playing golf. But he arrives there by train. He does not own an automobile.

The profit motive plays a very small part in the life of the Danish medical profession, which, as I say, averages the highest professional incomes in Denmark.

Is this common sense? *Mes amis,* it is social sense. The Irish doctors are still privateers, profiteers, racketeers. They are bloated with ill-gotten gains, perfectly honorable and legal in their own eyes and in the eyes of the community, but steeped in the perfidy of extortion if you compare them to their brothers in the North. As for Harley Street in London, it was a Barbary Coast.

5

The legal profession in Denmark makes less money than the medical, on the average. Mind you, it is no sinecure to obtain either a medical or legal degree. It takes even longer than it would take elsewhere. "Lawyers are plentiful," said Miss Brochner a generation ago, "and although the modesty of their charges would call forth a scornful smile on the face of an English solicitor, many of them manage to accumulate a fair competency." This has not changed. The smile would still be scornful.

And yet that instinct Thorstein Veblen wrote a book about, the instinct of workmanship, is highly developed in both these professions. When a young doctor argues his thesis it is not only in public but it is fully reported in the newspapers. It is a public event. The hospitals in Denmark, the medical research in Denmark and the medical publications in Denmark do credit to a country so little privileged. There are go-getters, of course, and the efflorescence of a shipowner's appendix attracts one of those laborers who, in the eyes of the wealthy everywhere, must be expensive to be worthy of his knife. But there are only sixty people in Denmark who pay income tax on over $50,000 a year, only ten who pay tax on over $100,000 a year, and of these I am certain that seven have lost their appendixes. The other three are now in good shape, since they must cycle to work.

They have national prestige, some of these magnates, but I venture to say that it is for workmanship, not for wealth, that the Danes esteem them. There are no exclusive night clubs, no places where they may at once segregate and display themselves, no chances for conspicuous waste. To do this they must leave Denmark. If they stay at home, much as they are respected for their power as men and their salience as human characters, they take care not to resound. All these powerful and salient men who work for modest charges that call forth a scornful smile have ways of their own of punishing ostentation.

In the government service, especially, the salaries but not the brains are nominal.

It is not so long since the Irish government gave themselves much higher salaries than Sweden provides for its ministers. The Irish cabinet is now infected by the profit motive so prevalent among the dominating Irish. In Sweden and Norway, however, as well as in Denmark the civil service as well as the cabinet ministers have another motivation.

6

The government in Denmark is not "strong" in the military sense. It is not "strong" in the sense of using compulsion. When a taxpayer who has repeatedly failed to answer summonses is at last hauled to the authorities in an unceremonious manner, every newspaper in Copenhagen is outraged and every official who had anything to do with the order is put on the defensive. The impatience of bureaucrats, who have the right to shove the citizen around, is held in check by a prompt and vigorous protest against the least sign of arbitrary or even unmannerly procedure. There is no conspiracy of silence. There is no pulling of wires. A police official who loses his temper and strikes a citizen may expect to have an investigation into his conduct, down to the last detail of the incident, reconstructed in slow motion by the most scrupulous of inquirers, and the decision will flatter neither one party nor the other. Denmark is too sane to encourage private bullies to harry the police. It is also too sane to give the police carte blanche. As a result, it is the least lawless country I know of. What the New Order can do for this nation is already made known. It can multiply policemen. It can reduce the law abiding to the law fearing.

7

Only a government that goes to school to the people, that learns to inflect itself, to give and take, to consult and defer, can hope to make the best of democracy. But, as Bishop Grundtvig enunciated, this lays on the folk the full responsibility of being worth consulting.

In the parliament we heard and saw the peasant proprietors and the agricultural laborers. Their presence was effective. As youths they had not been permitted to stagnate. Their teachers, their editors, had stirred them into active mental life. Whether male or female, the children of farm owners or of "small holders," they belong to a country where culture first, then agriculture, has been brought to the people and where the cooperative system ensures to the people the largest return on their labor.

It was not for nothing that we saw rows on rows of plows in the agricultural museum at Lyngby. To the Danish farmer this evolving plow is the symbol of his own evolution. It is a machine, but one he has guided with his own hands, to turn his own soil, and better and better. Government has become a machine like this for him.

You can perhaps imagine the feelings with which a Dane read (one hopes misquoted) Mr Ray Atherton, the U.S. minister to Denmark, on his return from a country whose neutrality had been violated. He did not have his mind, apparently, on the human values at all, only on the new rule that sweeps clean. He had no mind for the organism that had been interfered with. He had no remembrance of other occupied countries and the Schuschniggs, etc., who must either obey or pay for it. No, Mr Atherton had a compliment to pay. It was to the Germans. "The first and best thing done by the Germans was a rearrangement of the notoriously bad traffic system in Copenhagen. Within two hours the Germans had set up traffic standards."

The efficiency of the machine. It is the modern touch, to admire that above everything.

But I invite my American reader to substitute the word Washington for the word Copenhagen and see how he likes this American diplomat's tribute to the Germans in 1940.

CHAPTER EIGHT

Soul Planning

BIT BY BIT, in the many visits we were paying to Denmark, the positive attitude I spoke about began to form in me. I had had the revolt against the parent that is so normal to the human animal. Emigration was perhaps a phase of it. Leaving the Catholic Church was another phase of it. Moving from New York to Chicago was another. This strong impulse to be independent was partly emotional, partly intellectual, but it was the Ibsen impulse. "Man is strongest when he stands alone." And all the literature of emancipation, with Shaw and Wells as the emancipators of a popular kind, with Nietzsche, Samuel Butler, Amiel, Schopenhauer as more drastic critics, with Tolstoy, Ibsen himself, Dostoievsky, Kropotkin, Tchekov having their influence, made it urgent to be free from the least sign of parental authority, from the softest hint of tainted money, or a command from above, or "ukase," or conscription.

All sorts of revolts, in any event, were the order of the day. It was the day of Suffrage, of explosives in letter boxes, of *Ann Veronica,* of birth control, parlor socialism, food fads. A woman's club was called Heterodoxy, and that was the kernel of it. We were heretics.

But the time does come in life when you have to give dinners rather than accept invitations for them. The time comes when you have yourself to fire the cook, to dispute with the tax collector, to hire labor, to invest your few *sous*. When that time comes, when you have yourself to accept the positive role, what kind of authority are you prepared to commit yourself to? Or do you never intend to play the host? Are you always to be the guest?

The more I saw of authority, as wielded in Denmark, the more tolerable it seemed to me.

It was for the little people. But I was, and I wanted to be, little people in this sense. And as its solicitude for the little people became evident, that extraordinary solicitude—that civilization, in short—came more to occupy me. Here was a government that had chosen to equip little people not for subjection but for independence.

This is a question of method as well as a question of attitude. I wish I were an expert to reveal this method. But I did not study it. I came on it casually. I lived it. And, as it developed for me haphazard, I try to give it to you.

2

Last summer as we were rolling our bicycles up a hill behind Hornbaek we saw a column of smoke. It was a clear blue day with a brisk breeze. "Go on, go on," said Signe. I leaped on my bicycle, pedaled down a cart track, and as the column grew higher and blacker I actually galloped the bicycle across stubble and stone.

The fire I was headed for was more frantic than myself. By the time I reached it a whole homestead was in flames.

The wind swept the blaze in a brilliant sheet from one end of a straw thatch to the other. Its roar was so intense and its color so savage that none of the crowd already gathered—and it was a big crowd—could do anything for the first building but gaze at it. But hands were busy elsewhere. All the neighboring buildings were being deluged with water. Furniture of every kind, pictures, vases, kitchen supplies, were being stacked across the road. The cattle were being driven out of danger, and sparks and smoldering brands were being put out as they spread.

It was a fight. The fire fighters were amateurs but they had a hose from a village near by; they set to work tight lipped, without panic or flurry. So great was their phlegm, in fact, that I felt called on myself to get busy. I saved an old farm wagon that was hardly worth saving, I recruited boys to rescue a plow —the woodwork was scorched—and I dissuaded a sow from following the plow's example. By might and main the real fighters delimited the blaze. They had it in hand within an hour, though by this time the roof of the first building had fallen in. Nothing stood of it but the bare walls and a lone brick chimney. On a window sill, quite untouched, stood a flowering geranium.

How had it happened? My inquiries were met dumbly by the local people, which I set down to my halting Danish. Then I saw, standing desolated among the sticks of furniture that had been saved, three women with such stricken faces that I was driven to ask more about them. The truth was that these sisters, no longer young women, out of pity for a demented brother had kept him living under the same roof rather than send him to an asylum. He had set fire to the house. What they were gazing on so mutely, with eyes so fixed, with graven faces, was not only the destruction of all they treasured. It was also the defeat of their loving kindness. I have never seen gentle human beings so grim and so visibly wounded to the heart. Even to look at them was to see sorrow too clearly. I turned away.

Now one of the strange things about this fire was the abominable beauty of it. It was so ferocious, so powerful and so elemental that even the young tree in fresh leaf that stood in the midst of it, alive and quivering, seemed feeble and insipid. This power of destruction had drawn us all headlong to the fire. It freed something in us. It was indescribably thorough and glorious.

A few weeks after that we went back to look at the house. There was not a sign of life, nothing but desolation and a stench. The madman's work may have filled him with towering satisfaction. He had let loose the furies. For him, I did not doubt, it was the fulfillment of a magnificent dream. It was the end of a home, for the sisters.

3

Against such tenderness as these sisters had, such unwillingness to yield to a public agency the burden of caring for a brother, I don't think even Denmark would, or could, have taken steps. Unless the family had taken the initiative, and with the consent of the brother, or, failing that, with a certificate from a doctor and so on, he could not have been removed to a hospital. Denmark is extremely slow to intrude on a family. But if the family is unable for the burden, or alarmed, or anxious, the degree of solicitude that exists in Denmark surpasses any that I have knowledge of elsewhere. I am quite certain that some official in that zone must have scratched his head and shaken it. Those good women, those poor good women!

4

Before the Foundling Hospital moved from Bloomsbury to the country we went there one Sunday for religious service. I honestly don't know what kind of religious service it was. I go to Quaker services, to Catholic services, to Church of England, to Lutheran, to Christian Science. They are all solemnities, and most of them are dignified and expressive. This was a beautiful little service, with one of the most perfect little sermons I ever heard. It was not one of those mile-long sermons that make you sorry for the man in the pulpit. It was, so to speak, 440 yards and so spirited and distinguished that it left me breathlessly admiring. Then we were taken—and by this parson, as I remember—to see certain treasures, among them drawings by Raphael, and from that to see the children have their grub.

It was cold. The refectory was cold. They were small, purple-handed, clumping, blunt, blue-faced foundlings. They wore uniforms, quaint and colorful uniforms of the eighteenth century I daresay, both for the boys and the girls. I looked in their faces as hard as I could to catch a glint of the innerness. I couldn't see anything but an opaque conformity. Puppies on sale have somewhat the same absent or rather distracted expression. We went to the dormitories. They were clean and blank. Blank the way a prison is blank or an infirmary.

Well, what had the little wretches done? I couldn't see it. Here they were encased in an institution, regimented, destined to be shoveled out to menial positions and with their hair chopped off, their expressions chopped off, their imaginations chopped off, through no possible fault of their own. I left that well-meant and well-endowed Foundling Hospital with a proper gratitude for its picturesqueness and a horror of its existence.

The very first country district we visited in Denmark had a small home for children. All I'll say of it is this: each of the children had a big locker of personal belongings, of books, of implements, of playthings. They looked at us with living faces. They were gentle and a little shy and they were warmly human. Whatever talent they possessed would be evoked. They would not be lumped into life like coal into a basement. They would be treated as a gardener treats rose trees or even cabbages. They would be soul planned.

Near by this home for the children, out in the heart of this Sjaelland district, there was a home for the helpless people at the other end, very old people. And not only did they have their own rooms but these rooms were furnished with their

Soul Planning

own belongings. They were still persons, in no way institutionalized in a hectoring or heartless sense, and they were thriving on this respect for their personalities.

What creates a slum? Congestion. And what creates congestion? The presence of people in the boat who are not rowing. Two people in a room do not make a slum unless they read the Sunday newspapers. Even two people and a baby and a dog—well, the presence of the dog begins to make a slum. But when you have Grandad and Granny and three babies, then you have a slum. And a slum is a social Humpty Dumpty.

The Danes have no slums.

The people who are not able to row in the boat are given a boat in which to ride as passengers. It is these passenger boats, so to speak, that free Denmark from slums. Denmark clears out the underbrush. It carries the lame and the halt. It lifts the burdens off the backs of those whom the burdens crush into helpless congestion. This is what I call *soul* planning. By plans like these the little people can call their souls their own.

5

I went for a walk in Dyrehaven, the royal forest that is Copenhagen's public beech forest. On a path across a clearing I met a "Nisse." He was a small gnomelike man with a head too big for him, hydrocephalic I suppose they call it. He smiled at me in a fraternal way and I smiled back. Funny, I said, he's all alone in the park. He fluttered his hand at me and I fluttered mine back, as the Danish babies do when Mother says, *"Vink! Vink!* [Wave! Wave!]"

Then I met another gnome. He wasn't so chummy.

After a while I met a third. He paid absolutely no attention to me.

Now the Nisse is a Danish institution. He is a mischievous fellow who turns milk sour and that sort of thing. The germs of disease might, if you were fanciful, be the work of such mischief-makers. But to meet brown-clad gnomes in a public park, three in succession, made me doubt my eyes. And then I came on a hundred of them. They were playing on the grass, strange old-faced men with heavy heads that overweighted their bodies, but playing like children.

It was an institution at play. This was their outing. Instead of allowing these men to break down the families that could not possibly feed and clothe and nurse and exercise them, in addition to defeating the iron law of wages, the Danes had combed them out and provided such care for them that they could be relinquished by those who felt responsible for them.

In my childhood such men would have been wandering the roads, just as the sane epileptics would have been locked up with lunatics. But here they had been assorted. And another of those obstacles to a home had been removed before the home had been wrecked by it.

6

That same Dyrehaven (Deer Park) is to Copenhagen what Richmond is to London or Phoenix Park to Dublin or the Bois de Boulogne to Paris. It was royal once, now it is everyman's.

But, by reason of that faithful reciprocation between everyman and his government, Dyrehaven is more than a park. It is vast enough to respond to every single mood of the nation's capital. It is a rather rowdy popular amusement park, where the deer come in to beg for what Danes call Vienna pastry. (One Copenhagenized deer, at least.) This park could give a Breughel his models. It has streets with booths on them, and it can be hilarious. Its humor is broad. Leaving this corner of the park, all by itself, one soon finds a café that is devoted to painters, and these painters, many of them elderly men, form a school of their own. They exhibit together. On the walls of the coffeeroom there are speaking portraits of the presidents of this Dyrehaven Academy, and outside there are bicycles with paintboxes attached to them and a tricycle for one painter who cannot walk. All through Dyrehaven, summer and winter, you come on the painter's bicycle. Near it, at his easel, a grave man will be concentrated on his canvas. He may be a flaunting youth with hat cocked on his head, but he is more likely to be a sober, rather elderly man, and his canvas will not be a Vlaminck. It will be a patient representation, with a completely rational tree rising from a floor of bronze leaves, and behind it a blue sky furnished with white clouds, seen through the well-articulated branches of the said tree, which may be a knotty oak or a beech in lofty majesty. The painter is as much at home with his art as in his comfortable, all-weather clothes. He is in a tradition. It owes something to the Dutch, something to Constable and something to Fontainebleau, a reputable and untroubled tradition.

One of these painters was an old friend of my wife's family, Søren Lund by name. In the summer he must have gone into the country because he loved especially to paint mares with their foals, and this he did with tender observation and fidelity. I saw him once or twice. He was a tall, pure-eyed, long-bearded man who kept modest house by himself in an orderly flat high up in a yellow brick building. Every day, in the ordinary way of things, he got on his bicycle and pedaled out to Dyrehaven. He was as pellucid as a monk, which most of the painters in the café do not resemble, and his pictures, though in a Landseer mode to the casual observer, had his own lovely quality in them. He was untroubled by genius, by that excruciation of the soul that gives the world a Van Gogh, by the nostalgia which makes Gauguin pattern horses against a twilight coral beach, by that Parisian eye, cutting like a diamond, which made Degas see horses in action, destroying Meissonier's formula. What catastrophes to the plutocrats are caused by these heretics who make the up-to-date out-of-date! How sad when the estates are liquidated! But Søren Lund was no Bastian le Page. He painted for love; his mares have white stars on their foreheads and they gaze at one with their own imperturbable vision.

But Dyrehaven has an expanse to which the amusement park and the artists' coffeehouse are only the fringe. In five minutes one has forgotten them. There is a golf course, across which the public amble serenely, sometimes innocently picking up a ball as a souvenir and sometimes stopping to see a man putt, as if he really is no less on exhibition in the park than the grounds in it reserved for the military. This is not only a playfield, a series of plantations, a vast source of firewood, the home of thousands of deer, the site of a royal dwelling, but it is also, and before anything else, a true forest and a temple. The profanity of golf has left to itself the high viking grave in the center of the golf course, and this is but one of scores in Dyrehaven, with the blue Sound in sight of these interments. It is only the tiny youngsters from a near-by home who clamber to the top of the burial mound and roll down for the joy of rolling, before they are shepherded to the edge of the wood, where they clamor as endlessly as sparrows. The riding clubs have a wide area in the plain where they are allowed to follow their will, but even these strings of riders make no more impression than the herds of deer when one has really penetrated into Dyrehaven.

The miracle of this park, to which a hundred thousand people may go out on a Sunday, is that one can be entirely alone in it. If one chooses the hour and the day of the week and the season, Dyrehaven can afford that companioned solitude for which the soul perpetually craves, once it has disentangled itself from routine. "Les arbres dont la société est si facile." It is a quotation from a Hindu poet of the ninth century, and Dyrehaven gives this consolatory society. Sometimes one experiences it in the thickness of untouched scrub and mossy glades. Sometimes one follows a riding path up the slopes, to wander under trees that grow sparsely on these higher levels. Sometimes the beech forest, with its austerity and its silence, grasps one in the noble,

Soul Planning 109

admirable dignity of its depths and heights. As the male deer resound through these magnificent cavities of space, their instinct glorified by the beauty that hallows its lair, one is no longer within a few minutes of a great city. These reverberations tremble through the branches, and one halts to hear them, the voice of a million years.

It belongs to the people, this park. There are no motorcars in it, except royal cars and a dozen belonging to the diplomatic corps. You can cycle through it or drive in a barouche, but for the most part you walk, even in midwinter, when the Danes are sometimes able to be officially Scandinavian and skate and ski. The Gulf Stream doesn't often permit this. Under a foot or two of snow Dyrehaven is a new world, with that quality of beauty one cannot express or even grasp. It is, I think, the tenderness of the blue sky above the frozen snow, which unifies space and confers silence on the world, that leaves one at a loss for words. By this time the male deer has become a bourgeois Mormon and is on the dole.

Whatever few signs there are in Dyrehaven are cut into rocks. There are no police. You are requested not to handle the newborn deer, as the females desert the young that have been contaminated. Beyond that, you are left to yourself, and Dyrehaven does not suffer for it. The Danes treasure it.

7

I was walking there one day with two visitors. They were from England, Desmond MacCarthy and George Moore, the philosopher, from Cambridge. Cambridge, for some reason, had a year or two when it labeled as its own Desmond MacCarthy, Roger Fry, Lowes Dickinson, Lytton Strachey, with Clive Bell, E. M. Forster, Maynard Keynes, Leonard Wolff, to appear in the heavens as a Cambridge constellation. Desmond MacCarthy, in spite of his name, is Irish, English, French and German. Eton did not mar him, Cambridge prepared him and Hazlitt has given to England no finer pages of literary elucidation. As an ambulance man in the first World War he may have had his equals, but as a talker he has no equals; and as we strolled through Dyrehaven the birds ogled him from the trees, in envy of his music. George Moore, one of those crystals from the furnace of intellect that England molds, had already been flicked by Denmark to two perfect utterances, each of which had sung to us like a flawless chime—one a passionate revelation of his feelings about political freedom and the other a sudden terse but unconditional appreciation of Carlsberg Pilsner. We were still free in Denmark. The clouds had not yet descended. It is for the pleasure of reminding myself of this that I recall them.

And as we strolled toward Hermitagen a large group strayed past us.

"I wonder who they are," Desmond MacCarthy said.

There was a brass band, beyond doubt, and a number of the men carried lunch packages and Pilsner.

I asked a young man to tell me who they were. They were unemployed taximen, and they had come out to Dyrehaven for a picnic.

So serene a group did not imply a grim unemployment. But, in any event, there is no rule in Copenhagen that a taximan must be scrupulously unshaven. Employed or unemployed, you could be sure of this, the backs of their necks would be clean.

And they too use Dyrehaven, where they cannot ply their trade.

8

It is not by discipline or propaganda that the Danes are induced to respect their public spaces. If one may speculate on it, as a roving observer, it is the long, unbroken habit of community. If the time seems to have come, for example, to set up statues of nude figures, male or female or even hermaphrodite,

Soul Planning

in the most public of all squares or parks, there can be perfect assurance that no one will deface them or be disturbed by them. Just as you can go to the public bathhouse and feel certain of scrupulous cleanliness, just as you can go to a railway station and reclaim the toothbrush you forgot in the sleeper, just as you can ask the rural postman to take back the library book for nothing and order the next one to be delivered through the same agent, all of these facilities and reliabilities a matter of course, so you can count on a definite standard of decency and of thoughtfulness even, so to speak, in the indecent and the thoughtless. If a broken bottle is thrown away in the park, the man who picks it up will say, *"svineri."* And swinishness is deplorable, intolerable. The norm of Danish life is not to jangle, to vituperate or to play dirty tricks on the neighbors. The adolescent years, on this account, are not student years. They are apprentice years. And the plan is to recapture the young man for school when he has passed through the difficulties of puberty. It is by the shrewd and subtle management of these crises in social existence, plus the long habit of community, that Denmark has the amenity that one notices.

Is it easier for a small country to do it? Are the big countries "too big"? I don't know. America seems to be soothingly polite in many communities, and Denmark, on the contrary, fails in certain definite layers of society. But there seems to be no pronounced roughneck or he-man tradition.

A manufacturer who provided facilities for shower baths in his factories told me that there was a marked difference in the degree to which the Copenhagen, as against the provincial, employees made use of these facilities. The most negligent were in a district that had formerly had big estates. Copenhagen was prompt to take advantage of all that was offered.

More and more manufacturers do this sort of thing. And since vacations have been made compulsory, they buy islands or tracts of seashore to which they can send the people who work for them. It is all very sissy.

9

Statistics as a rule are not instructive. But when you see that tuberculosis deaths have been cut from 11 per 10,000 to 5.2 per 10,000, and when you see that syphilis cases have dropped from 11.4 per 10,000 to 2.3 per 10,000, then you may be sure that public solicitude is active.

Think of what it means to have a tubercular case in a small home. Think what it means to have a syphilitic infection neglected. The breakdown is not merely in health, it is in the structure of the family, in the economic fabric that so little can ruin irreparably. One chronic invalid, one helpless passenger, and the rest of the group slaves in vain to compensate. It is a perpetual tax on nerves, on good will and on vitality.

But the Danish community does what it can to avert these small disasters. The Dutch are not more vigilant with their dikes than the Danes with public health. They do not propose to have the handicapped become public charges and public enemies. They remove the handicaps of foundlings, of the deaf and dumb, of the tubercular, of the syphilitic.

Suppose that a girl has a trace of hereditary syphilis. If she is going to have a baby, that unborn baby is already an object of vital concern to Danish society. The prospective mother is given prenatal care at a public hospital as a matter of course, and from the instant the baby is born until it can be given a clean bill of health the best medical science in Denmark is devoted to the infant.

If there is a case of incipient insanity in any rank of society, the greatest care is taken, for the sake of society, to keep the victim from becoming a public danger. Here, too, the best brains in Denmark are made available by the state, and the cost of these services is a secondary consideration. If the citizen can be assessed, well and good. But the main point is to safeguard the community as well as the patient, and psychiatry is in the hands

Soul Planning

of some of the finest if quietest practitioners in that still vex'd sea of science.

From time to time a subject like abortion has to be legislated on in Denmark. It need not be assumed that Denmark takes an advanced position as a matter of course. A country with a quickly falling birth rate, with a growing capital city and with a new urban and industrial population to make laws for has to churn the topic well over before it decides what line to take. There are congresses, majority and minority reports, pamphlets and sermons by the agitated. It is the same with this as, say, with the question of vitamins in margarine. But when you realize the level of journalism, the level of medical science and the level of citizenship, what emerges is no dictate from a set of highly efficient militarists playing jujitsu with Europe. It is an honest outcome of a searching process of evaluation.

"Materialists," a bishop may say. If it is materialism to wipe out syphilis, call it materialism. De Valera in Ireland was not allowed to enforce prophylaxis for the military recruits in Ireland. That was too materialistic. But the Danish method, humbly rational though it is, has pretty good results to show for itself. There are still congested city districts. A clearance has to be made of old buildings in Copenhagen. But the basic problem of slum clearance, the clearance of those broken families who cannot be integrated just by being rehoused, has been attacked by Danish method at its hundred sources. And as a new social infection develops, Denmark pokes into it. In this sense, schooled in dealing with probabilities, it is plainly materialistic.

10

And yet I call it soul planning. Why all this prenatal care for the syphilitic? Why all this fuss about the pleasant imbeciles? The guiding minds, whether governmental or merely public, have no illusions about the handicapped and no desire to strap burdens on the aching back of the taxpayer. But they prefer drainage to yellow jack, and if they have to stick tubes into the slums, if they have to catch all the gross cases in the filter beds, it is not out of sentimentalism. It is out of faith in the common people, no longer housing the demented who may set a house afire or a continent afire, those expensive geniuses who burn down the house in order to roast the pig.

CHAPTER NINE

Have Danes Got Souls?

"THEY have no *souls*."

Another Irishman broke this news about the Danes. I sat next to him at a session of the Dail Eireann in Dublin, wondering who the bright man was, so expressive, with vivid coloring and white hair, till he told me that he was Shaw Desmond.

The word soul is useful, just as the credit system is useful, but one has to be sure it isn't merely a token of exchange. One has to ask about it, very humbly of course, whether it reposes on confidence or whether it reposes on gold, since if one accepts it one must accept it seriously. It is as vague a word as the language has. The senses do not give a clue to what it means. I do not myself know what an apperception is, but I feel that the soul is an apperception. Eluding capture, eluding observation, it still communicates itself, and while we cannot directly grasp it we can say that we appreciate it, that we hold ourselves aware of it, that we are the poorer without it, so poor that we can never be really rich again.

It's a tough word to define, like *love*. Long years ago I began to eulogize Chicago to Ned Burling. He said, "Who is she?" A light so tender could not dwell so fondly on Chicago without making him wonder whether it was not the light that is neither on land nor sea. But that light also does break on the world. The hormones may be necessary to it, just as the thorax was necessary to Caruso. But what came from Caruso, from his entrails if you like, from the whole Italian mass of him, was a sound that at once caressed, enchanted, enhanced and possessed one's being so that one rose with him to an acme of receptiveness from which pain was excluded and one had the experience of joy. What that experience of joy is, who can say? When Caruso sang and reached his height I was enabled to forget his body, to forget his physical presence and to know, by aid of that tact and intimacy and volume and suavity he commanded, something of the marvelous gaiety, the blitheness, the exquisiteness, the liberation that his wise employment of an art had given him. What there is in a voice to soothe and anoint the "soul" I do not know, but in such moments of harmony and glory, whatever evokes them, the existence of a soul is a useful presumption and all the more useful when one ascends to white snows, to a purer radiance. Those who have no ear can scarcely believe you when you talk of music. They honestly have not experienced it, and they rather question your experience. Those who have not gone to Greece, in the same way, are often a little skeptical of the soulful who rave about it. The seraphic female, the chinless aesthete, the Botticelli spinsters, the pansy and the sissy, are all creatures against whom one revolts because the idiom of the soul verges on the ridiculous, quite as much as idioms of the body. Even the aesthetes who write streamline detective stories or the highbrows who go to funerals in sweaters and slacks have not discovered an idiom that is beyond ridicule. They are being soullessly soulful, that's all.

Once you begin seeing the ridiculous, all is ridiculous. "How *absurd!*" people giggle with delight at the candid photograph. They see that to be caught with your mouth open, to be seen smirking, to be trapped scratching yourself, is a caricature of the correct and genteel man and in this way ludicrous. But is not this amusement also ludicrous? Is it not based on an irascibility? When I am told that certain old-fashioned movements of the body are utterly silly I ask myself if the inquirer has ever thought of people standing up or sitting down. Are they not also silly? A dog with his forepaws hanging down is laughable, but we also stand with our forepaws hanging down. And when we sit we are all flattened out at the points of contact, like those china ornaments you pick up that are flat behind, usually with a price mark on the flat part. Think of a banquet, with all the chairs suddenly removed and all the sitters sitting on air, flat underneath and crouching or bolt upright. I find us ridiculous when we eat, when we snore, when we walk, when we orate. But even more ridiculous do I find the efforts of the irascible to say, How amusing, when they study a murder and to look stonily at the non-murderous, saying, We are not amused.

2

Have the Danes a soul? Well, there are neat little Danish grocers, puffy brewerymen, plump red-veined fishwives and sleek cattlemen who are not pictures of spirituality. Whether they are more or less spiritual than an Irish pig jobber, an Irish coal miner, an Irish dock laborer or an Irish publican could be argued from dark till dawn. I have lived in an Irish provincial town where the Celtic twilight was waning, and I often asked myself, Have these people souls? And within an hour a chance word, a lisp of a look, a whiff of ethereal revelation, and I knew that behind an apparent blankness there was as much ardency of spirit as I could fathom in a year. Those little black boxes in the chapels are theaters of it. The Big House is a warehouse of it. Every doctor, every solicitor, every bank man, has glints and glimpses of the drama, and even the publican, a hollow-cheeked, book-reading, crack-laughed individual, could mint treasures of it in an evening's walk. Dostoievsky, that soul broker, could have flourished on the annals of that single town, and yet the citizens sit yawning, the cats sit yawning, under trees that are tangled with the moon. In the mists from the river many a soul has shivered in ecstasy, but it has gone as unperceived as the globules of crystal on a cabbage leaf or the rivulets of secret tears. There are Dead Souls in this town, with their eyes like two candles by the coffin, but it is living souls that see them. Only living souls do see them, and it is the eternal duel, between these living corpses and these gravediggers without spades.

Yes, Shaw Desmond may say to me, this is Holy Ireland, but answer me for Denmark.

Allow me to laugh.

Just because people are blond, they are not cheerful. Just because they are orderly, they are not pigeonholed inside. Just because they are clean and punctual and discreet and polite, sitting in rows at a concert as packed as books on a shelf, it does not follow that inside they are like tins of condensed milk in a carton. I look round me at a Danish concert, and I know that disease, penury, ignobility, ambition, lechery, insanity, have churned and inflamed and incited a considerable number of the dreamers in the hall. I also know that out of these fantasies have been composed the lives that thirst for the incommensurable in its less destructive form. They do not wear their souls upon their sleeves for Shaws to peck at. Denmark is ironic. But we must allow them souls.

In early years I reviewed a book by Arnold Bennett, *The Old Wives' Tale*. One of the young Irish writers, who was eight years old when it was published, has assured me that it is quite second rate. So be it. Bennett wrote to me about my review, and later we were to meet. I liked him. He was an Englishman in his phlegm, a little on his guard, sometimes curt, not too easy to be natural with, but with some curious richness of nature, a flash of jewellike candor at times, a magnanimity and a warmth. We were in Copenhagen not long after seeing him, and then he was dead, just like that, years before he should have died.

He was enough older than myself for me to feel a certain piety about him. We walked along the Canal in Copenhagen, grieved at this news as one grieves at a tree cut down or any brave living thing smitten. I had read him thoroughly and fallen foul of him too, but his death was a light gone out in the avenue, and we knew it.

We were walking by Christiansborg Slot, and we saw people mounting the steps of the church, going in under the pillared portico. Signe said, "It is the Palestrina Choir." Often Bennett had written about quartets in the Five Towns, with that sage air he had, as if he had Bach in him. We went up the steps. There was no need for a ticket, and we went in.

We could not see the choir, which sang from a balcony out of sight. The voices were grave, pure and disciplined. It was an evening when we heard, or at least remembered, only the singing, and that evening it was limpid song, carried from the sobriety of the bass to that spire of adoration which only the adolescent attain to. Out of its passion we drew assuagement and were freed by it. It was a consolation. But on many evenings afterward, going back to the same choir, at least as poignant as the singing has been the audience. They come, as the choir does, because they wish to. They are of all ages, of all stages of fortune. In their faces there is a strange light, not always, but often. The Italians in Florence saw this same light and painted it, up to Savonarola's time. Denmark is not Catholic. The choir that sings Palestrina also sings Lutheran music. But here, caught in this net, is the same gleam as dwelt in Florence.

3

But the soul that was alight in Florence did not satisfy Savonarola. A new spirit had been breathed into Europe. The faith that had possessed it, that had sufficed it, was no longer enough to tranquilize the restless and inquiring man whom new discoveries had disturbed. Authority was shaken, and scoundrels emerged on every side to assert and seize authority, so that in the midst of dazzling revelation there was perfidy and baseness. The priest in Savonarola was outraged. He was a perfectionist, one of the old order, who saw in the new age a tragic departure from spirituality, and the soul to him was the classic theological soul, "the immaterial part of man regarded as immortal or as subject to salvation and damnation."

The soul, as the theologians conceive it, apart from the soul that lights up in a particular way, is possibly what Shaw Desmond was thinking of. And this soul, certainly, is by no means to the fore in Denmark.

In Ireland, on a Sunday morning, boots are blacked and white shirts are pulled over heads and hair is brushed and the best leg is put forward because on Sunday morning you go to Mass, just as sure as the sun is up for breakfast time. The entire population, whether it is Black Protestant, or Catholic, makes its way to church and chapel. That's that. Only paralysis or the throes of childbirth can excuse you from joining the throng. It needs no Gallup poll to tell how many go to Mass in Ireland. They all go, one-legged and two-legged, and the exceptions are lepers.

On a Sunday morning in Copenhagen, I was soon to remark, there is also an extraordinary activity. Households and apartment-holds throb with preparation. What is afoot? Are they off to church? No, they are off to the woods, to a *skov-tur*. Thousands go by bicycle. Nearly a hundred thousand will go by train. They take food with them and perhaps bathing things, and they make a long day of it. They go by a sort of capillary action, repulsed by the city, attracted by the country, and they obey the sun like true worshipers. As Copenhagen grows bigger the *skov-tur* grows more urban. The youth, that is to say, go to huts and cottages for the week end, and they go in bands and batches. But this is not churchgoing. It is the most secular Sunday conceivable.

Children are still baptized. A very few of them are "confirmed" at the City Hall. Quite a good number are confirmed in church. It is rather a social event, and confirmation gifts, while not as imposing as wedding presents, are a type of honest graft that few young Danes despise. The puberty rites in Denmark really mean that you acquire your first serious watch and your first fountain pen. A church wedding is not so common as a confirmation, but it is one of the supreme events of a young lifetime. And, at the bitter end, the church is again invoked. It remains the high institution for births, deaths and marriages.

But if English friends visit Copenhagen and ask you to take them to buildings where they can, so to speak, bate their breath officially, they are pretty sure to be disappointed. They complain to me sharply. They say the churches are too bright, too lacking in mystery, in the religious sense, and too, too ghastly. They are as unhappy, I suppose, as a salt-water fish in fresh water. Their gills are different. They put their objections, however, in terms of light. They feel overexposed. They shrink from the publicity.

Into these emotions I have no way of entering. There is one church in Copenhagen that has become a public library, and this never fails to thrill me. The silence, at any rate, is religious and the lighting rather bad. But Danes appear to have a different sense of mystery and, for that matter, a different sense of sin from their English cousins.

Those who have studied Søren Kierkegaard can no doubt elucidate the Danish soul, in so far as one of its most piercing critics has penetrated it. I have not yet read him, it shames me to say. But supposing him to have combated the official Church, the institutionalized Christ, while himself being a convinced, truthtelling spiritual man, there does appear to the outsider to be a degree of religion-in-solution in Danish life that perhaps is traceable to powerful dissolvents of an intellectual type special to the country, removing the accretions without destroying the fabric. How else, I wonder, is there so little pestiferous moralizing? And how else, on the other hand, is there an escape from this kind of pernicious platitude without a complete loss of direction, a moral hodgepodge? There is a felicity about Danish latitude to which one is tempted to apply the word civilized.

In London I have sometimes extended my long nose and sniffed a latitude that was worse than platitude because it seemed to be a conspiracy to wink and hoodwink. It is what is brutally known as corruption. No one casts the first stone because all the stones are rubber and they bound back. Such a society depends on rejecting any member who gets a white ball. It insists on mystery, because in the dark all cats can be as black as they wish to be.

This latitude is the sure proof that moral stricture is exaggerated to such a point in the surrounding community that, to even up, you have to carry a hip flask and to bootleg. The hijacker comes later, and then the aggrieved middle class buys the *Tatler* and the *Bystander,* to gloat on the smart set with thrills of outrage. Prohibition in America was the most legible and fantastic of all experiments in repression, and by writing itself out from under this experiment the Catholic Church in America gave an instance of what a wholesome moral latitude can be.

But Denmark goes the Catholic Church one better, and all along the line. It has a wholesome moral latitude that would leave Manchester gasping and would leave the Catholic Church frowning. It is a crimeless country, to put it broadly, that does not believe in, or practice, or even recommend repression. When you turn Denmark wrong side up you find it is the same on both sides. Those moral slums that fringe the Puritan City of God—they do not offend you in Denmark because they do not exist. John Calvin has, of course, had his Danish counterparts. There are strict sects in Denmark, strong Prohibitionists of every kind in Denmark, upright men who propose severity and asceticism. But the peculiar twang you get from the tense human will, the twang called fanatic, is repugnant to the Dane as such. He says, "Yo, yah," and lifts his eyebrows. Those mountains and those valleys and those swamps, all the geography of John Calvin and John Bunyan, have to be sought elsewhere in general. And if to have a soul you must be ironshod and on your way to the Delectable Mountain, the number of souls in Denmark is limited.

So near to Germany and yet so little Germanic! The Danish spiritual adventure deserves a deeper study and a greater knowledge of literature and history than I can ever command. But whether I am judging it too superficially or not, too much in the wake of Georg Brandes and his rationality or not, I must declare that only once in all my personal dealings with Danes have I run into what I call repressiveness.

The German woman hasn't come out of the kitchen, we are told. Well, what has she done in the kitchen? What can she ever do in the kitchen, until she comes out of it? The Danish woman is good in the kitchen precisely because she is not condemned to it. And the status of woman in the North, as against the status of woman in the military countries, is part of a liberation that runs through the whole of social behavior. This liberation, in turn, deprives curiosity of its meat. Where the apples grow by the road there is no adventure in stealing them. What would be shocking and titillating in England and Ireland, in human behavior, is mentioned in Denmark as you'd mention tonsils or shingles. Some people have their tonsils out, some don't. The Danes do not divide into passionate schools about it. But they are sorry for a bad case of tonsillitis.

They do not, in short, regard salvation as the probable outcome of manners and morals that happen, at the time, to suit the ruling class in a community. They do not hand their political enemies a ticket if the enemies happen to sleep with A rather than B, or drink A rather than B, or eat A rather than B. What human beings do, in these departments, concern them very much, but in the region of personal preference and sanction. So long as conduct is not intrusively bad, the Dane is not fussy. His community is so real that if conduct is definitely bad it is bound to be intrusive. Then it breaks a law and he deals with it. For this reason his lawmaking is extremely serious. He is a citizen. And if you do not offend him as a citizen he drives you in daisy chains.

But mystery, chiaroscuro, Dante, T. S. Eliot? The Soul? You must search for that with other Hells and Heavens in mind. In Denmark, with the material in hand, a new conception of Hell and Heaven may arise, so tragic that it becomes omnipresent. But I do not think that anything can destroy the achieved liberation.

CHAPTER TEN

Danish Modesty

AS I THINK over the Danes, the fact that they are unassuming is perhaps their greatest charm for me. The world at present is noisy with the assuming. But to speak of modesty is dangerous. Just as the world is fooled by self-assertion, it is fooled by false modesty, and that is the last thing of which the Danes can be accused.

The old story of Balzac and the lunatic has often consoled me in the presence of a prig.

"You have never met Balzac," said one well-known Frenchman to another. "You are to meet him tonight at dinner, but forgive me, I must have my uncle there, and it is pretty unfortunate, he's quite mad. He thinks he is God."

After the dinner as the guest was leaving he thanked his host profusely. "But Balzac hadn't much chance to speak, had he? Your uncle had a bad attack of being the Deity."

"That wasn't my uncle who shouted us all down," said the host. "That was dear Balzac. The man who never opened his mouth, he's the man who thinks himself God."

If a man is strong, well and good. But if he is strong and silent, watch him to see if his tail wags. If it doesn't wag, he probably thinks he is God.

2

The Danes are not quiet out of a sense of disproportion. Nor are they modest because they have been taught from childhood to use the soft pedal. They are modest, as a rule, because they have slowly and painfully learned to see themselves in proportion to other people—sometimes people better endowed and, in certain respects, more accomplished. The Danes travel. They study foreign languages and foreign literatures. They break down their insularity. And in consequence they do not tend to overrate themselves. They are so alive to social achievement, especially among others, that they have become relatively unassuming. And in the bosom of the family they often shake their heads and are severely self-critical.

"We are butter fat," you hear them say, "we eat too much. We have no tragedy, no passions, no sublimity."

When I first heard these words from a Dane I was amused. In a Europe where poverty had bred unlimited tragedy and intolerable passion it was a relief to find some country that was butter fat. But these Danes were right. They knew that the unsocial man, the daemon, demands to be released. A Scandinavian like Strindberg, a Russian like Dostoievsky, a Frenchman like Baudelaire, an Irishman like James Joyce, a German like Nietzsche, an American like Edgar Allan Poe, had something to say that Denmark did not obviously heed. It was not a question of the utterly puerile censorships of a genteel era. Danish liberation in this respect was to be counted on. But it was a question of unleashing the ego for wilder flights than the bourgeois feel they can afford, creative flights that reveal the landscape that has never yet been perceived, just as man flying in the heavens sees a beauty below that had never been perceived by mortal eye, though it had been there since the dawn of creation. This urgency, so evident in French painting, so evident in German music, in English poetry, is alone enough to keep the Danes from being complacent. From the first contact with them I felt none of that dreadful stubbornness of the ego which sometimes shoves one back from the barbarian—such a barbarian as threatens us in the power-loving, the bumptious, the aggressive.

3

Matthew Arnold used to call the English aristocrats barbarians. Why is it that they sometimes show bumptiousness?

These aristocrats owe it, I imagine, to those sterling members of the English lower middle class who, as H. W. Nevinson has so acutely pointed out, are the truest conservatives in the world. It is the lower middle class, on the whole, that gives English aristocracy its *Family Herald* illusions. It is the nanny who does it. And nanny didn't go to Eton.

The aristocratic baby is nanny-processed. Nanny does everything for the baby except actually give it birth. She naturally appropriates it. The shyness and estrangement under the clear, unembarrassed tones of the charming young have been induced by nanny. It is her fierce sense of propriety, her etiquette, her ideals, her sex fantasia, her religious fantasia, that mold the little blob of ancient race, and whether the child ends as a tongue-tied nonentity or as just a piece of blotting paper may be determined by nanny, with the groom, the governess, the chauffeur and the tutor completing the interior to which rank will give the façade and the appearance.

Go into Central Park any bright afternoon and see the nannies processing the babies of the rich. It is instructive. See the nannies in Kensington who hold aloof according to the rank in the perambulator.

There are, of course, good nannies as there are good parents. There are aristocrats who deserve the name. But much that is barbarous in the group that Matthew Arnold called the barbarians comes from the traditionalists who bring them up. It is not easy to sort out the illusions that are native to the nannies and communicated to nobility from the cradle, but some social student ought to tackle this. A ducal nursery should be the experiment station.

Among the best efforts of the Chinese, one is told, is the art of self-depreciation. The English too are inclined to say, "I fear I'm rather stupid," or "I don't play a good game, I'm afraid," when they're not at all stupid and when their game is not only superb but the thing they are most proud of. This mock modesty is inculcated by the nanny. Take it in regard to heroism. A hero who risks his life to save another must mumble that it's nothing, in the *Family Herald,* as if he did that sort of thing every morning before breakfast and as if any fine achievement must be unmentionable.

This is a pose. To be kissed on both cheeks for your heroism would be preferable, or even on the tip of your nose. If I were ever to do a heroic deed I should tell about it, modestly but repeatedly and in detail. Once, in fact, I did stop a runaway, and I am willing to tell about it. This poor horse was something of an introvert. It had started to run away in Lincoln Park in Chicago. It was then in perfect good faith. By the time I met it the adventure had been going on so long that it had time to see the error of its ways, but the driver was so scared he could not pull up the horse, and the horse could not stop running away without losing face. As I walked up Michigan Avenue I saw the predicament. The horse's expression was utterly tragic, we exchanged a glance of comprehension, I ran out, it nearly fell into my arms, the driver staggered from his seat—— But I fear you are bored, I was about to tell the story. Had I deeds of heroism to relate to my grandchildren, so that they could hug my knees and say, "Tell us again," I'd be the happiest of grandfathers.

What charms me about the Danes is that while they have no nannies, in the *Family Herald* sense, and while they have no mock modesty, they are a genuinely modest people.

Danish Modesty

Every year in every quarter of Denmark, as the Carnegie medal awards make clear, there are acts of courage that amaze and delight one, but best of all is the simplicity with which a man can take it.

What is one to do when a maniac stands out on a window ledge and says, "I am going to jump"? In a Jutland town such a maniac held a crowd in horrible suspense before he leaped. He did in the end leap from the fourth-story window, but as he neared the ground a workingman ran in to try to break his fall. Though he was himself badly injured, the worker managed to do it. He was in hospital for weeks. When he was asked "Why?" he answered, "Could I live with myself afterwards if I had stood by and watched another human being do that to himself?"

An aristocrat like Karen Blixen, who wrote *Out of Africa*, answers in precisely the same spirit. When one asks her how she came to rush at a lion, armed with nothing but a stick, and beat the lion off, she responds with perfect directness, "But what was I to do? He had leaped on the back of one of my poor cattle."

Another Dane, telling in my presence of stopping two big horses that ran away with a heavy truck behind them, amazed me by saying that all he did was to vault on the back of one of the horses and in this way bring them to a standstill when he had dragged up the reins.

"But you vaulted. How could you vault up like that?" I asked him.

"Oh, that wasn't hard," he said seriously. "In those days I was just like a little monkey."

The game of self-depreciation doesn't come in. They are not like those air pilots in films who unhesitatingly take up defective machines without a grimace. They don't say, "I'd rather not speak of it. It was nothing." If you say something is nothing, you make too much of it, the "pride that apes humility."

4

A taste for modesty, however, is an acquired taste. Just as a baby in the cradle reaches for the gaudiest object first, so human beings choose the blatant and follow the blatant, unless they have been civilized. Look at the uniforms of those prodigious twins, Göring and Mussolini.

My first impression of a demagogue was at an early age. This man called himself Sequah. He sold patent medicines, cured "aches and pains of any sort whatsoever," extracted teeth, made the lame walk and, by means of a decoction called the Prairie Flower, turned the rheumatic into athletes, made the dumb speak, etc.

He arrived in town with a coach and four. He had outriders. He had a band that played music, soft while he discoursed and loud while he extracted teeth. The band drew the crowd and Sequah drew the teeth. Instead of filling them he pulled them, and he threw the gold to the crowd in the form of golden sovereigns. He was the only dentist I ever saw who wore a scarlet coat trimmed with gold braid. He was a gorgeous dentist and a superb spellbinder. All the ordinary doctors were deserted by their chronic cases for this great promiser. He knew the secret of perfect health. The fountain of youth was in his half-crown bottles. The word went over the county, and the lame, the blind, the halt, were brought to him by the hundred. He whooped it up better than any Mission. Even after he left town men and women who had limped for years walked without their crutches. They swore by Sequah. The town was dull without him. In a month or two the crutches began to reappear. The orders for Prairie Flower diminished. A few fly-specked bottles remained on the chemists' shelves as the sole monument to Sequah, the Medicine Man, the magnetizer, the hypnotizer, the Billy Sunday of rheumatism.

We had all been dazzled by Sequah. The dry and critical

called him Se-quack. We resented it. It was the Promised Land he invited us to. Hundreds swore that they had benefited by him. Hundreds did benefit by him. And those who had a low opinion of the populace could only retort, "Wait and see."

Even in the beginnings of the Grundtvig movement in Denmark there were critics who saw in it a danger of complacency. They decried the enthusiasm in it. They said that it appealed to the two besetting sins of the Danes, laziness and vanity. They believed education ought to be professional. They feared the smattering of it. They argued for the plain, hard way.

But the plain, hard way is a matter of acquired taste. John Wesley had to stir up the English common people in a crude way. The Salvation Army, with its bands and its uniforms and its promises, had to learn a lesson from Sequah. A preference for the showy way, the quick way, is the natural preference of the multitude. It was only in due course that the Danish multitude acquired another taste.

One of my earliest experiences of untutored taste occurred at a lecture on beauty, in my native city of Kilkenny. A bearded gentleman, T. W. Rolleston, well known among the aesthetic in years gone by, thought it would be an excellent thing to enlighten Kilkenny on beauty in furniture. He had lantern slides, and among other objects that he displayed to us was a picture of an ordinary commercial grand piano of sleekly polished mahogany, evidently expensive, and a picture of a grand piano in a light-colored wood, on the simplest lines, plain and unvarnished. At the sight of the plain piano everybody laughed. They all heartily applauded the polished mahogany. When the applause died down Mr Rolleston tried to explain to them how wrong they were not to prefer unpolished mahogany. He made no impression on Kilkenny.

Was Rolleston right? Was Kilkenny to blame? Even now it seems to me natural that we should have applauded the glistening object rather than the plain one. Something in us wanted Sequah to perform miracles. We react to stimuli such as his.

As an English hack writer once said, "There's magic in—The music of—The band." It takes many years not to be rather numb when you come from the big noises to relative silence, when you come from the bright lights and look at the plain, unvarnished Danes.

5

Even the quantitative, as I have suggested before, puts the Dane at a disadvantage. As a small area and a small population, Denmark has to admit that sort of insignificance. As a consumer of steel rails, try as it may, it is unimportant. As a market for hurricane insurance it is nil. Were every Dane a centipede it would be a good country in which to sell cotton goods or boots, but in realms like these, where the quantitative test is the real test, the frog cannot blow itself up to be a bull. All the money spent on education in a year before it was invaded could not have given Denmark more than a hundred big bombing planes, putting a bombing plane at a million kroner. As a military power Denmark is nothing in and by itself, and when an intelligent Dane adverts to this he cannot help being subdued. The immense quantitative superiorities that are asserted in totals rather than averages reach huge numbers of billions that leave a Dane mute and stupefied. He thinks in small totals. His unit is the krone, not the dollar or the pound. In this respect he is a little fellow.

But the concept of a small Dane, as distinct from a small Denmark, is an absurdity. Danes are not small just because they belong to a small country. It is one of those habits of comparison that the modern world falls into, this comparison of political and economic units transferred to the individual and spiritual unit. A prize gooseberry, even, might grow on a small gooseberry bush.

But the outsider like myself must not be stopped by the fact that the mahogany is not lustrously polished. Remembering that the Dane himself is modest, let an outsider ignore the com-

Danish Modesty

parison of grandiose with little and measure excellence with excellence.

Denmark has no illiteracy.

Denmark has eradicated syphilis.

Denmark seeks no profit out of Greenland.

Denmark publishes fifteen times as many books, proportionately, as the U.S.A.

Denmark builds railways in Persia.

Denmark rebuilds Waterloo Bridge across the Thames.

Denmark is high among the shipowning nations.

Denmark has won more Nobel prizes in science, proportionately, than any other nation.

Denmark has Tivoli.

Denmark has a great brewery managed by five professors, and all this brewery's surplus goes to the arts and sciences.

Denmark has almost no murders and no capital punishment.

Denmark has urbanized its farmers.

Denmark has ruralized its city dwellers by developing "colony gardens."

Denmark exports high-grade goods with clocklike regularity.

Denmark has famous doctors.

Denmark builds fine ships and has built half the Diesel-engine ships in the world.

Denmark exports cement machinery to the U.S.A.

Denmark has a high standard of seed control.

Denmark controls the breeds of stock on the farms.

Denmark has extraordinarily cheap electricity.

Denmark has electricity on the farms.

Denmark exports serum from its fine Serum Institute.

Denmark has clean cities, including the capital.

Denmark has cheap and excellent telephone service.

Denmark has efficient public-owned utilities.

Denmark has excellent fresh-fish markets.

Denmark has a fine system of public libraries.

Denmark has a most competent postal service.

Denmark paid good interest on current deposits and a better interest on frozen deposits.

Denmark spreads income-tax payments over the year.

Denmark endows its Royal Theater munificently.

Denmark has excellent ballet.

Denmark preserves its "beauty spots."

Denmark makes butter into a lyric.

Denmark specializes in strawberries.

Denmark cares for its old.

6

These are small excellences that occur to me casually. Most Danes would not make much of them. There are too many great excellences in the big world.

But Danish modesty, genuine as it is, should not mislead anyone into supposing that the meek—and they are really meek—can be readily imposed on.

It was my luck on one occasion to show Copenhagen to a genial, prosperous visitor.

Copenhagen had charm for him. He had traveled a great deal and he could not be vastly excited about it, and at times he found it hard to pump up the exclamations that were expected from him. I was on his side. Even though I kept saying, "Don't you think it's good?" and "Isn't it well done?" it was an extortion I was ashamed of, just as I am ashamed to stand over one of my readers. What can the poor victim do? He has to say, "Why, you leave me speechless." He has to give a gasp and nod his head whether he approves or is bored. To extort praise, either for your work or your child or your preferences, is to go the wrong way about it.

But our visitor could not get away from the feeling that a lot of the stuff he was seeing was small-town stuff. While he smiled and was genial, in his big and buoyant way, he wasn't bowled over. In America, he told me, a police sergeant's stand-

Danish Modesty

ard of living would be higher than that of many of the people that Denmark thinks important, and a good number of these people get along without comforts and conveniences that the police sergeant would hold essential.

Could I deny this? No. The almost entire absence of police, perhaps, could be argued as a comfort of another sort. But the sternness of life even in a good trade-union model apartment, or the starkness in certain vaunted boats and trains, had to be admitted by anyone who knew the comparisons he was inevitably making. We had, after all, been to a couple of golf clubs in Florida that were so charming, so surpassing, that I licked my chops in retrospect. Between Dyrehaven and the Seminole, for example, the contrast could not be made.

"But," I said to him, "you can be massaged, and massaged by just as good a Scandinavian as you'll have in New York, and you'll have the whole works for a dollar."

He tried it. The masseur, learning who this magnificent colossus was, pummeled him till he was so sore he could hardly walk. But it was worth it. He went back and had another dollar's worth. In this I was vindicated.

Then he took me to dinner. We had one of those dreadful headwaiters who is to be found in an international restaurant. He seemed to look on my host as a man who had to be steered to one expensive dish after another. It was irritating and absurd. My friend tolerated it. But at the end of the evening, looking over the items into which he had been steered, he found a dubious one. He pointed it out. The headwaiter became dogmatic.

"Very well," said the visitor, "you won't straighten it out. I won't pay you. There's my name and address. So what!"

Considering the provocation, I understood it. I should myself liked to have seen the headwaiter boiled into mock turtle over a slow fire. But, said I to myself, this is little Denmark. I very much doubt if you can get away with this. We'll see.

Still, it was a demonstration. We were meeting fraud with

force. It was what they call a "gesture." A large tip showed indifference to mere money.

The management could not know how irritating their man had been. They could only check up the bill and the kitchen dockets. All seemed to be in order. They were sorry, but they presented the bill.

My friend said, "No!"

Then, at his hotel, appeared a dignitary known as the King's Proctor. Whether he appeared in scarlet and knee breeches I know not, but he appeared and impounded our visitor's baggage. No pay, no baggage.

We felt badly. The weather had been so well behaved, the city had been so bright, the sea had been so warm, the general impression had been so favorable. And into this idyl walks the King's Proctor and seals up the baggage.

And only the day before, when my friend wanted a small repair done to his coat, the big shop had refused to take any pay. "We never charge for a thing like that."

"But I am not a customer," he said.

"Well, that may come," the salesman smiled. There was no charge. And into this Paradise came the beadle with a mace over his shoulder. Our friend had either to leave in his dudgeon with one shirt or to give up his dudgeon and recover his shirts.

He paid. But I don't think he loved the meek Danes.

CHAPTER ELEVEN

Danish Compassion

FROM MUCH that I have said, you may have gathered that the Danes are compassionate. I should like to expand this.

Compassion, as I seem to find it in the Danes, is not in general a heroic virtue. The hero is a lad who sees his duty and does it. What it costs him to do it he does not count; what it costs others he does not always count either. From the hero to the man of iron is a short step. This man cares less than the hero what happens to the other fellow. He wants his own way, and to achieve it he is ruthless. The line he takes is the direct line. Those who stand in his way he bends or breaks, and if they do not yield to him readily he is incensed. From this to the overweening self-assertion of the tyrant is no long step. The tyrant is soon able to pervert his account of those who oppose him or withstand him. In the full flower of his strength he is not only self-minded, he is overbearing, vengeful and cruel.

An interesting problem arises when the strong man finds it suits him to assert moral responsibility. His account of those who oppose him is then opened to debate, and if they have loud voices and good lung power they are so vigorous in being heard from that the natural ruthlessness of the strong man is curbed and all sorts of people—lawyers, reformers, editorial writers, the Society for Prevention of Cruelty to Animals, the Society for Prevention of Cruelty to Children—come nobly into action, producing gout in the strong man, sending him to Bad Nauheim or Vichy.

The meat-eating strong men who at the same time pretend to moral responsibility have a tough struggle. They incline to be choleric and irritable. This has led to that new phenomenon, the vegetarian tyrant, no less willful and cruel than his full-blooded counterpart but too shrewd to be gouty. To look for conscience or compassion in these green-hearted men is highly erroneous. They are so consumed by ambition, so utterly self-centered, so intent on having their own way, that no other lust has the slightest chance of swaying them unless they become pathological sadists, not only willing to inflict cruelty but convincing themselves that the sufferings they cause are a magnification of their importance, a sign that their existence is justified and a final proof that values have been successfully transvalued, since nothing can stop them.

As in the case of certain of the Roman emperors, sadism undermines these green ones, and they blither into insanity, whereupon their guards pluck up the nerve to murder them. The transition from the throne to the dump heap makes even Gibbon unreadable. These horrors, with which the emperors bloated themselves, could never sate them, but the ordinary reader has not the stomach for them. He recognizes that to blunt his natural horror, to open his mind and accustom his nerves to cruelty, is the end of fraternity and peace. Even to witness bloodshed as a sport, or to kill cornered animals, has elements in it that the good man, the sissy, revolts against.

There are jobs, however, that the average man must not wince at. He must kill animals in order to eat them. He must put criminals in prison. He must kill his enemies. No matter how

Danish Compassion

compassionate he is he has to face the facts that are irreconcilable with his own survival or else risk extinction.

2

One of the practical tests of the Danish social attitude is provided by murder cases. During the years we lived in Denmark I paid some attention to every murder that was committed and followed them in the newspapers. In recalling these murders, however, I have only memory to rely on, and I trust to be forgiven if I am wrong in some details. Unlike the brilliant Miss Janet Flanner, whose accounts of French murders are titbits of insatiable curiosity, I have never found a murder "humorous." I have never played football with a decapitated head. The temptation to do this, indeed, does not exist in Denmark, where murders are few and decapitation abandoned.

The object of the Danish state is to prevent murders, and it has gone about murder prevention much as Massachusetts goes about mosquito prevention. It has studied every social situation likely to produce murderers. It has attacked these nesting places in time to kill the eggs. The result is a society in which the average of murders is extraordinarily low. While adolescents have plenty of stimulating films to look at and plenty of gory books to read, they must go without horror in the daily paper. The supply is limited, and the papers do not specialize in making the murderer interesting.

There is one community in the United States, the tiny community of Martha's Vineyard, where murder is almost unheard of. There have been six murders in about three hundred years. Small as this number is and select as this delightful community is, the people in it being a large family and as gentle and friendly a group as you can find in the entire country, the Danish percentages for this particular crime are correspondingly low.

Those found guilty of murder in the years 1930–38 can be set down as follows:

	Men	Women	Total
1930	5	1	6
1931	12	1	13
1932	7	2	9
1933	9	4	13
1934	8	2	10
1935	7	2	9
1936	8	1	9
1937	8	1	9
1938	6	1	7

The total population of Denmark, it should be noted, was 3,700,000 in the middle of this period.

3

Copenhagen is a city of a million inhabitants. Though there are no slums on the outskirts of the city, there are still a few streets in the center of the old town that are occupied by more or less wretched people. Under the sagging tiles of old tenements, doomed to be torn down, there are city folk of the kind that are to be found anywhere, odd characters and twisted characters, sneak thieves, pimps, prostitutes, casuals of one sort and another, a group so small that its members are pretty well known to the police but seldom in real trouble and kept in order by, at worst, occasional short detentions.

At the top of one of these tenements there lived an old flower woman. She was one of those crones who buy up the faded flowers at the finish of the market, and her business was to make them into wreaths that she sold very cheap. She lived alone, supposed to be a miser but at the same time reputed to have a soft spot in her heart for stray animals and occasionally renting her extra room to a stray boarder.

At this particular period she had allowed a young couple to live with her. The man was a weak young fellow who had been in trouble for stealing a bicycle. He was ostensibly a messenger, but in reality he lived off the earnings of his roommate, a girl who hung about the cafés. He was neat and presentable. So was the girl. Cash was short, however, and the old flower woman got so tired of their promises to pay that at last she closed the door on them but retained the cheap suitcase that held the girl's belongings until such time as their debt for the room was canceled.

The evicted couple were angry at the trick the old girl had played on them. At first they went down to the street, on being shut out, then went back again, the young man furious, the girl hanging back. The people in the flat below heard high voices up above, the young man's voice raised above the old woman's. After a while there was a thud, the chandelier in the flat below shook with its violence, but nothing was made of it until the police came. It was the young man himself who had summoned them, saying he could not get in. His story was soon pieced together. He and the girl were put under arrest, and he was promptly charged with murder. The case against him was circumstantial, but as the old woman's body was scarcely cold by the time the police crossed on a plank into her window, finding her prone on her bed under a piece of carpeting, evidently choked to death, the accusation was a highly natural one, and his protests were almost as idle as they were feeble.

There was no third degree, however. The police knew the youth. They were convinced he was guilty. But in spite of his bad reputation, his presence on the scene and the incriminating row, no indignation was whipped up against the accused. The girl did not stand up for him, and he was held for trial.

While he was awaiting trial an ex-waiter came to the police. He told a muddled story, the gist of it being that he had spent the night with a sailor whom I'll call Nils, in the course of which the sailor had said, "I throttled that old witch last night," and then mumbled he had thrown an empty purse down a closet.

The sailor's last name was unknown to the ex-waiter, but when the police showed him an album of convicted criminals he suddenly halted them. "That's him. That's Nils." And the police knew the man. That evening they traced him to a shack and the next morning arrested him.

The story they dug out of him was this: he and another derelict were sitting in a café, thirsty and penniless. Where to get the price of a few drinks? They had once boarded with the old flower woman, and Nils said to his mate, "We'll go up there. We'll pretend we want to rent the room. And while you are arguing with her about the price I'll slip in and steal her savings."

They acted on this. They were already inside when the indignant couple came up the stairs. During that altercation they hid. The companion managed to slip out after the evicted boarders. Nils hid in a closet. When all was still he crept out. The old crone, half blind, thinking he was the youth who had come to get the suitcase, rushed at him tooth and claw. Nils clutched her by the throat, and she was a dead woman before he relaxed his terrorized grip. She thudded to the floor. He lifted her up, covered her and waited till he felt a lull, then stole out and down.

The purse he had picked up was cast into an earth closet. The police traced the contents of this closet to the land where it was periodically emptied. They went out there and found the purse. The story tallied, and Nils supplied every missing link. By that time the pimp was completely exonerated, except that there was a suspended sentence against him.

What struck me about this murder was the openness of the police, even after they had built up a strong circumstantial case, to follow up every clue, whether brought to them by suspect characters or not. The ex-waiter was not a stool pigeon. He was one of those socialized Danes who, when they know of a mur-

Danish Compassion

derer, feel bound to inform the police. It is one of the curious facts about Denmark that the law is a product of the community, that the citizens abide by it, that they do not hold with the lawbreaker and that the lawbreaker himself does not declare a vendetta against his accusers. A further curious fact is that a crime once atoned for is off the record, and to bring it up against a man whose honor has been restored is libelous and severely punished. Hence criminals are deprived of civic rights for a term of years, and they have no "honor" until these rights are resumed legally.

4

A respectable elderly woman who lived alone near the railway tracks in a small provincial town was found murdered in her home. The motive was evidently theft, as her watch was gone and some other belongings. The first theory was that a tramp had killed her and made off by the tracks. The whole town was greatly upset. Copenhagen detectives arrived on the scene, a whole murder squad. All Denmark was distressed at the brutality.

The watch was traced to a Copenhagen pawnshop in short order. Meanwhile, however, a local teacher had told the police that she very greatly feared it was a pupil of her own, a problem boy, who had done it. He was now a barber's assistant. On inquiry, the police found he was one of those bright and talkative young barbers who deplore crime as they shave. Everyone in town who had a scrap of evidence went to the police with it. Soon the young apprentice was arrested. He had killed the elderly woman, an old friend of his. And as he was about to strike the fatal blow with a hammer she had looked at him with horrified astonishment. "*Men dog,* Hans!" It was an exclamation of pure incredulity. "Whatever is this, Hans!" She might have uttered it if a cat had upset an ink bottle.

In this case there was no one who had reason to suspect the

murderer who did not come forward. The man who bought the watch was of great help to the police. So were several persons who had concluded on their own account that the youth was guilty. He was put under psychic observation after arrest, but the best state psychologist could not find he was abnormal. He was found guilty, but I believe he was given an indeterminate sentence.

5

A small girl whose parents were working people in the provinces was sent for vacation to Copenhagen to her grandmother, I think it was. This grandmother lived in a poor quarter near the central railway station. One afternoon the child's mother was to come in to Copenhagen to see her seven-year-old daughter, but the daughter had not come home from the playground when she arrived. After waiting a while the alarmed mother went to the police. There was no trace of the child from the time she left the playground. She had disappeared in broad daylight. Her companions could give no clear account of her leaving them. She was a perfectly cheerful, simple little girl of the ordinary trusting Danish kind, and she was no more noticeable as she skipped around than a city sparrow. The more the other children tried to account for her, the more brittle their evidence seemed. She was gone. That was the ominous fact. The police did not disguise that they regarded it as ominous, and they even asked the public by radio to give them what help they could to clear up this mystery.

Some of my friends thought this was crude and alarmist. All sorts of idiots, certainly, rushed to the police with stories of little unsuspecting girls seen walking hand in hand with plausible elderly gentlemen. There was a sudden burst of solicitude for unattended children. It was as much as one's life was worth to glance at anyone under eighteen. Copenhagen clucked and ruffled.

Danish Compassion

But what were the police to do? A child was gone as if swallowed up. It was sinister.

And it was sinister. A worker phoned the police that a neighbor of his, home from his work as a stoker on board ship, was acting furtively about his little flat. He would allow no one to go into it. It was in the quarter where the girl had vanished. The police acted on this tip, as on so many others. They made a search in the suspect's flat, found the little girl's body hidden away in papers, discovered that he had brought her to his room by offering her candy and then, according to his story, choked her to keep from telling that he had done this.

A small, insignificant man, under the average in intelligence, he was protected by the police from a hostile crowd. A small band of high-collared Danes whose chins seemed to me to point too straight to heaven immediately demanded the restoration of the death penalty. The man was put on trial long enough after his arrest to ensure a cool verdict. He was sentenced to fifteen years or something like that. The trial was given no prominence in the papers.

This murder might have been detected by the police without the aid of the public, but I greatly doubt it. It was through information from a man whose name and address were at once published that the guilty man was found. The citizen's loyalty was not to his neighbor in the tenement house. It was to the community. As an Irishman, to whom the idea of an "informer" is detestable, I do not instantly leap to applaud this co-operation with the police. I never liked teacher's pet at school, and I never liked any boy who gave the show away. The Danish practice, on the other hand, is free from all the complexes that a suppressed nation is bound to accumulate. Gurli's murderer is not being hounded down by a remorseless gang of gendarmes whom the public hates. He is being tracked with somber fidelity by policemen who deplore the job, and the citizens go to help them as they would if there were a fire or a catastrophe.

The informer is not vindictive. He is dutiful. And especially, having the victim in mind, he is compassionate.

6

There are unrepentant murderers even in Denmark. There was a seagoing Dane whose violence estranged his wife. She fell in love with an older man who straightforwardly went to the husband, told him he was in love with the woman and proposed to marry her if the husband would release her. The husband at first agreed, but in order to clear up the details he asked the lover to come to see him. The lover had no objection. He went to the husband's flat. A friend in a car waited in the street. In a short time the seaman came down. "I have killed him," he said. He had waited until the lover stepped into his room and then clubbed him to death from behind.

This horrible crime he defended on the score that his wife's first duty was to their child. She had no right to leave him, he said, and he boasted in court that he was proud of what he had done. He was given a ten- or twelve-year sentence. He appealed against this. The higher court gave him fifteen years. His sense of his moral prowess had come to be tiresome.

Why ten years, at first? A friend in the Department of Justice explained this. Experience in Denmark has shown that a man who comes out of jail within a decade can knit himself into social life again. He has not become estranged from it. He still has living connections with it. But if he is in prison for much longer he changes insensibly. He loses touch with the outside and he loses adaptability. His real home is inside the prison walls, and society has to carry this dead weight in one way or another so long as he goes on living. For this reason, if his behavior warrants it, the Department of Justice does its best to send him back before the common touch is gone. Its object is to integrate him as a member of the community.

7

This seafaring man who murdered his rival was far from a typical Dane. In cases of jealousy like this, suicide is much more probable than murder. But in any event his truculence was unusual. He had no twinge of remorse, and the court could not squeeze it out of him.

No one who knows the seafaring Dane would deny that the following story is truer to type.

We were walking along the water front in Marseille, perhaps fifteen years ago, and we stopped to look at a vessel that was flying the Danish flag. As we stood there a Danish seaman was coming ashore, dressed in his neat blue suit, and soon we were going up to Notre Dame de la Garde in his amiable company. We chatted along for some time, till finally we sat down in a café and finished hearing his simple narrative of the women he cared about.

Marseille was just the town to hear this in. Not since I first went to Chicago in 1904 had I been in a place with such romping, variegated life. It was ugly, but with a brazen, breezy hilarity. The traffic was singularly confused and impatient, yet with yelps of surplus vitality. Such disorder was in some way exhilarating. It was, I suppose, the tempo of the Midi, but with a dozen nationalities pouring up and down, transient, curious and carefree. Our open café, plunged back into shadow yet filled with figures, was a buzz of talk, with lively waiters in white aprons bearing their trays aloft, amid heads that tilted and turned, flicked by expectancy. Every salient man that came in was watched without shame, and every flagrant female was ardently, openly stared at. It was a show, a human circus, to the roar and honk of traffic, the cries of newsboys, the yells of porters and truck drivers. And in the midst of this, seated between us, the quiet-voiced Dane unfolded his story.

He too had gone to sea, leaving a wife behind him. It was a

long absence. He returned after several years to discover a child in the home, the son by another man. She said the other man would marry her. To this the seaman agreed and took ship again for as long a voyage as possible.

The next time he returned to Copenhagen he had no home, but as he sat in Nyhavn he saw his wife. She had been deserted by the man she had been living with. After her divorce he had not married her, she was picking up her living in the drinking places that line the quay in Nyhavn.

Rather than come back to a port where he was bound to see her he had shipped on another long voyage, this time on a freighter going out of Liverpool. And in Liverpool he had fallen in love again, with an Irish girl.

"And you are going to marry her?"

"No," he said. "I want to marry her, she is the girl for me, but while her mother is content we should live together there's not a chance of her agreeing to our marriage. She says it wouldn't be right in the sight of God for her daughter to marry a divorced man."

"You have nothing for which to blame yourself," said my wife toward the end.

"Yes, I have," he said. "That child in Copenhagen has no father now. I ought to have given that child a home." His mild, blunt face had the most stubborn expression as he said it, and he was really blaming himself. He was still a member of a responsible community. To put up with his wife for the sake of the other man's child did not seem fantastic to him. The child, as he said, hadn't wronged anyone. He was willing to father it.

As between the tough seaman who killed his rival and the tender seaman I describe there are probably a hundred varieties. But the arrow swings more to the tender than the tough. And then, one must remember, there are those long absences. The murderer was not a man who went away for long enough voyages to learn to be lenient. He was a coastwise seaman.

But remorse is not confined to the culprits. One of the Copenhagen magistrates spent an evening every week in the offices of a legal aid society. And the very couple whom I spoke of in the first case, the pimp and his lady friend, turned up at her office (the magistrate was feminine) to ask what could be done to make the old flower woman give up the suitcase she had impounded.

"How much do you owe this landlady?" the magistrate asked.

"Fifteen kroner," said the youth.

Fifteen kroner. The magistrate started to dig out fifteen kroner of her own money, but it was near the end of the month, she was running short, she hesitated. She sent them off without the money but with a clear statement of their rights in the matter.

And next morning, to her horror, the couple was brought before her in the preliminary stages of the murder charge. Her remorse did not vanish until she saw the youth cleared of it.

8

When the law is so sensitive and solicitous, and when the citizens are in truth at one with the law, I cannot imagine how the situation can be improved by the introduction of a military dictatorship, issuing innumerable decrees, employing spies and special police and creating an instant division between authority and the consent it is entitled to. It does not take long to bring law into disrepute when the source of the law is disreputable.

The outcome will not be submission, I venture to believe. But can it be revolt? It must of necessity be a most tense and watchful situation, in which good will will have to be suspended. Only by shameful and unmentionable methods can the authorities then produce their informers. No great people, in the long run, can sustain such abominable intrusion.

CHAPTER TWELVE

Danish Curiosity

HAVING DWELT among murderers for a few pages, we may perhaps flit to England and bathe in the home of virtue.

I think of Oxford not as a city of spires, or bells, or poets, or lost boat races. I think of it as a city of women students. The men are well in their way, but some succumbing to pose, others recovering from it, the ratio of pose per man student being high. Even such saints as Newman, transported beings as they were, did contrive to differentiate themselves so excessively that their very presence must have thrown everything out of scale. Perhaps in a community so special as Oxford the Newmans were at home, as rococo is at home in its time and place, but when the young, so imitative, copy the mannerisms of saints, when they have the effect of insisting on themselves by one trick and another, I find myself unconvinced. The game is too easy.

Yet on my first visit to Oxford I had a sense of relief after London, as if a physical fog had vanished. For some time I could not find a reason for this, and then it came to me clearly: the girls' faces were luminously intelligent. When one looked at them—and life largely consists of interchanging glances—one saw that they were not lumps of pretty but insolent flesh. They were often not particularly pretty. But they were more than alive, they were illuminated. Quite unknown to themselves, a preoccupation had taken possession of them, and merely to observe them in passing was to have a part in it, like receiving a little shot of electricity.

In the lobbies of the League of Nations Building in Geneva I remember a different throb in the air. The young women of the Secretariat vibrated with a liveliness that was not all intelligence. They were tingling with the variety of male attention that this peculiar international grouping was rife with. They gave off sparks, you might say, as they brushed from department to department. It was a fascinating place, combining the manners of young diplomats with the provocation of a feminine elite—an elite of self-supporting, detached, competent and on the whole striking young women. They had better coiffures, better shoes, than the girls in Oxford. They were also less remote. Even their distinction of manner—and they had come from all over the world—did not cancel an awareness of the male which made their internationalism more piquant.

In Copenhagen, it seems to me, the casual contact is with girls who have something of the Oxford mind in them, something of the Geneva Secretariat in them and yet another, a more disarming quality. They are more passive than the Geneva career women. They are less coquettish. And the child in them is more evident. Where intelligence has fully flowered they are exquisitely radiant. Where it is still veiled they are in a mild quiescence. They are not even particularly smart, to note their appearance, but they are smarter than the Oxford ones.

They are at their best in October. They are still burned by the sun. Their hair is astonishingly light against their tanned skin. And their eyes, sea blue, cornflower blue, pale aquamarine, have in them the luster of renewed intimacies, of Copenhagen revivified. The city itself, blooming quietly at twilight, is a good background for them. They move through it with a glint of rapidity, unforgettable.

2

One of the best elements in Danish intelligence is its flexibility. The Danes are unusually open-minded. Loyal as they are to their own country, and their patriotism is immeasurable, they hang in Europe like one of those open crates that you see in their canals, enclosed and yet plunged in the stream, washed but not washed away.

So small a country as Denmark would go stale if its people did not get out. But to escape from it to larger and more varied countries is a rule of its being. Over to Sweden or Norway, down to Germany, to Italy, out to Asia—the Danes keep on the move, and this is no longer the exclusive privilege of the well off. The workers of Denmark, no less than the salaried people and the employers, crave the stimulus and joy of travel. It is this mobility that makes them seem so frivolous when contrasted with the more immobile Norwegians or the more stately Swedes.

We decided ourselves, in the early months of 1939, to escape to Norway. We took the *Kronprins Olav* to Oslo. It is no great adventure into the wild unknown. You leave Copenhagen in the afternoon and arrive at Oslo in the morning. What you have to overcome is not hazard but inertia.

The sun shone as we embarked, and the dock was highly animated. From every taxi there projected bunches of skis. The girls in ski costume were a little self-conscious, but no steamer could have been better for vivid colors and definite forms than this modern *Kronprins Olav*. So long as the Victorian tradition was dominant, most steamers had to be as lugubrious as funeral parlors. Who designed the carpets and the woodwork? Out of what bearded contractor were these inspirations pumped? Only in America, where the gay river boats managed to resemble summer hotels, did one get completely away from the feeling that one ought to sit down and eat mutton. But with the coming of automobiles and of the more scientific dental clinics the designers of the passenger vessels, which are no longer "steam" ships but often oil ships, have cleared away innumerable knickknacks and confused cupids and pillars and scrolls, have smoothed the details into flatness, swept the lines into clarity and spread colors that have no sense of sin. It is mechanized, if you like, and very close behind it are the plate-glass factory, the steel mills and the linoleum works. All the feeling of the hand worker is gone; it is the blueprint and the factory worker that produced this. I sometimes think my hair ought to be more mechanized when I sit down in so barbered a décor, and I understand why young women feel that their features should be masks and their hair in cement. But when Danes poured into these lounges and restaurants the liveliness of vacationing was heightened by such clean and simple decoration.

I was on deck before sunrise, out of restlessness. We had by that time anchored in the harbor of Oslo. It was a magnificent but somber scene. The sun already tinged the sky with streaks of sullen red, and against this sky there was a pointed black hill with an eye of light moving across it, which must have been a tramcar bringing people down to work. The water of the harbor was black with bars of light in it, and there were melancholy heights of land about it, shapes that were massive, brooding and bold. I felt myself alone among these vast presences in the chill damp of the harbor, and they had majesty for me. It could not have occurred to me that within a short time this majesty was to be affronted by an underhand invasion. One or two servants within the victim's house would aid it. An indelible chapter, so long as these mountains brood on Oslo, the violated capital. The honor of a great state permitted it, the honor of an army and a navy. A noble chapter in the history of the Germans!

3

We went to a little hotel north of Lillehammer. It took no more prowess on our part than to buy tickets and to board a train. To reach the hotel in the end we had to motor for an hour or so. Most of the time it was on a single line that went up, and pretty smartly too, with steep snowbanks and forest on either side. Once in a while we had to wait so that woodsmen who had been cutting logs could bring them down. They gave us a keen glance out of their shaggy, long-jawed faces. A Norwegian on skis shot down the road without a quaver. We breathed clean air into our mouths, our lungs, our blood.

The hotel itself was perched on high land where the pine trees thin out and cease. It stood out uncompromising in the field of snow, a typical modern block of cement with eyelets in it. But we had chosen it because it had soundproof rooms, hot water and all the rest. It was indeed a model hotel, with a young proprietor who fathered and mothered us.

A hundred yards or more from the hotel, with its bathrooms, its electric lights and its central heat, there was a little wooden pen or paddock in the snow. It was an enclosure for reindeers. And the first time we were making its acquaintance a sleigh darted out from behind it to climb the hill, drawn by a reindeer that tossed its head and dashed off with a saucy recklessness. The man behind the reindeer was a bundle of robes. It was the North come true, a Raphael Tuck Christmas card.

But it was not the marvel of the reindeer, the excitement of learning to ski, the extraordinary delight of pine trails in the winter sun or the sublimity of the snowfields that leads me to talk of Norway. It is the light it gave me of the Danes as migrants.

At a table near us there was a young couple whom I had noticed on the *Kronprins Olav*. She was more than good-looking. She had a grave and limpid expression that was pleasantly dis-

Danish Curiosity 155

owned by an arch little hat. He was a blond Dane, rippled by a breeze of something natively free and audacious. It hardly needed a detective to tell that they were on their honeymoon, and by chance we had happened to learn that while the youth's father had spent years in Australia the girl's father had spent years in Chile. The youth was of a Danish noble family. A soldier by training, he was a seed salesman by trade, but he talked eagerly of seeing the world. She had already seen a good deal of it. She had gone to school in Florence, I think, and had lived in the South Sea Islands. She was completely at home speaking English and at times made observations of such insight that, had it not been for occasional glimpses of the child in her, I should have suspected her of uncanny wisdom. Her father seemed to have been born with a migratory impulse like a fish or a bird, and her delight in him was like that usually inspired by natural phenomena such as geysers or volcanoes. I was disturbed by her desire to ski as much as her husband, who bounded down the hills with a wild gleam in his eyes. I expected to see her laid out in the lobby of the hotel, a Venus de Milo in a coffin, minus a few limbs and a nose. But beyond a few bruises and gashes she was not marred, and their future will undoubtedly include Africa.

At another table were some old friends of ours. We had first met them in 1922, when they were home from China. Their daughter was about to sail to Canton after months in Germany and France. They themselves had lived for a decade in China, and the husband knew India and Siam. He was the director of a great steamship line and born in the same small town as my wife, Nykøbing, Sjaelland.

With them was a bank director. He had, I believe, been left a penniless orphan; but instead of being thrown into the discard, which might have been his fate in a big country, he was so nurtured by the state that his mathematical abilities were cultivated. Later he had become a typographer, then a leading man in the trade-union world and at last a minister in the cabinet.

He had journeyed all over Europe, and not long after seeing him in Norway I saw him in Washington.

At still another table there was a Copenhagen wine dealer. He had a son in Madeira. His business took him to Germany a great deal, especially in the vintage weeks. His daughter had spent months at Oxford and in London. He spoke English and German with great facility.

It is not too much to suppose that nearly every Dane in this small hotel, man or woman, had spent months or years out of Denmark, most of them well versed in several languages and all of them what you might call "carriers," agents in that cross-fertilization of a culture which makes it healthy and strong.

Yes, you may say, but these were cosmopolitan Danes, the kind you might expect to meet at a winter resort. They are the sort of people whom you meet in every country, the sort who break away from the small town or small country, the sort who travel. If you went to San Moritz you'd find Danes there. If you went to Monte Carlo you'd run into a Dane. You come across them in Florida, in Burma, in Calcutta.

> *And there was Hans, the blue-eyed Dane,*
> *Bull-throated, bare of arm,*
> *Who carried on his hairy chest*
> *The maid Ultruda's charm.*

All over the globe, shaken out of the natal pepper pot, you find these specks of Denmark. That proves nothing.

4

I don't know. I have no statistics on my person about the number of Danes who go abroad in normal times. It is only my guess that they are a much-traveled people, and certainly those who stay at home are avid to hear and read and know about the world. Aage Krarup-Nielsen, who first came to us in New York when he had written a book about whaling in the Antarctic, has

Danish Curiosity

spent the whole of his subsequent life traveling all over the world, returning home with books about it and lectures and films. His success has been extraordinary. And it is rural and provincial Denmark that cannot have too much of this assiduous and intrepid observer, Aage Krarup-Nielsen.

Few books sell so well in Denmark as books of adventurous travel. The enormous vogue of Kipling depended, to some extent, on this appetite for a wildness out and beyond, an *outremer,* a ravishing strangeness. To hang a cage with a parakeet in a tree above the sleeping princess and then watch in hiding until her Danish eyes beheld that flame of color is a form of courtship that a Dane from overseas would know to be irresistible. The magic flute for a Dane tells of far lands and glancing leaves and birds of paradise.

But it is not just bookish curiosity. One evening in Copenhagen we met a very polite and agreeable man at dinner who taught music as a profession. We lost sight of him for a while but ran into him at a concert and were happy to be invited to have tea with him. He lived by himself in an enviable soundproof old-fashioned flat from which all vestiges of dogs and children had apparently been sheared away, leaving it fit for autocrats to live in.

"And where have you been?"

"In Italy," he said, beaming, "and Sicily, and back through Dalmatia and Venice."

We had not left Hellerup.

"Good lord," I said, "you have an easy time. Did you go alone or with friends?"

"I worked hard every minute," he replied. "I took a batch of working people."

"For fun?"

"Yes and no," he said. "I happen to be good at languages, four or five of them, and I was asked to conduct a party of thirty. I hadn't an instant's rest except on one short sea journey, but I enjoyed every second of it." He looked it. "I was courier, doctor, father. I arranged for the hotels, the boats, the trains, the buses. I didn't lose a soul on the whole trip, and I never liked people so much as these. It was glorious."

His prize story was of a dame in the party who saw a bevy of Rubens goddesses for the first time and turned to her companion with her eyes glowing. "Chock-full of vitamins!"

Here was this rather reticent man whom I had supposed to be one of those bachelors who come to dinner at a moment's notice and can be counted on to see a lady home. It had never occurred to me that he could be just as polite, agreeable and helpful with the wives and sisters of trade unionists. Our afternoon was spent in hearing about this thrilling voyage, for which the workers paid a reasonable co-operative price and had a glimpse of Florence, Rome, Naples, Venice and the rest, the Pitti, the Sistine Chapel, the Villa Medici, St Peter's, Tivoli. What most delighted our friend was the stonemason who examined Roman antiquities with the eye of a craftsman. At every turn his own spirit was refreshed by the good sense, the seriousness and especially the novel approach of men and women who were willing to put up with any small inconvenience for the sake of a vision for which their schools had long prepared them. He came back eager to go again and yet again.

When can it be? Many beautiful things have been obliterated. What remains, the common treasure of Europeans, is not on view. The millions of workers who were yet to discover their heritage have been cheated by two sons of workingmen.

5

But whatever the immediate future, Denmark in the long run cannot be landlocked nor sealocked. It never has been. Small as it is, it has sent out streamers across the world and drawn nourishment to itself, spiritual and physical. Those processes by which it digests what it acquires are sufficiently thorough and vigorous to break down and make over its nour-

Danish Curiosity

ishment. It is no land of quick and superficial adaptation. But neither is it stolid or backward. Even in twenty years I have observed many swift revisions of habit, many betterments learned from abroad, many modernizings. It does not require a centralized higher-up to decree these changes. They are spontaneous. What the higher-up has to do in Denmark is guide these spontaneities, to regulate them. The individual thrust of creativeness and inventiveness can be counted on.

6

And it is in this individuality that the argument for a small unit is so strong. Take just one business, the publishing business. Where a country like Ireland has the same language as a world empire there is almost no incentive to local publishing. A few firms have made the effort to build up a local business, but they are in competition with London publishers, and sooner or later their authors desert them for the big firms, the big sales, the big royalties. Even if these big sales and big royalties may never be realized, the Irish authors look to London and to New York. Not one of them of any literary consequence has ever been able to live by sales in Ireland.

Denmark has a dozen good publishing houses. By the very fact that the Danes are forced to cultivate their field intensively, owing to the restricted public that reads Danish, a great deal more has been done with the Danish book consumer than has ever been done with the Irish or Scottish book consumer. The Danish publishers have mastered world methods. They have applied them to the home market. The result is so staggeringly impressive that people do not believe it. When I say that ten thousand of Alexis Carrel's book, *Man the Unknown,* were sold in Denmark in the first week of its publication, *ten thousand* of a highbrow book that probably sold a hundred in Dublin (four hundred being a maximum sale of a serious book in Dublin), then you may estimate what the Danes have done with their public in this one publishing business. As many as 125,000 copies of a masterpiece by a famous Danish writer have been sold in Denmark in the ordinary trade edition. This would correspond to a sale in the U.S.A. of about five million. No such similar sale has ever been achieved in the U.S.A. The Danes knock the Americans all hollow when it comes to book sales. But when you say to a Danish publisher, "America," he says, "Ah, America," as if America were the last word in enterprise, in stupendous sales, in heroic achievement. The Dane is not fooling. He is inherently modest. Every week he reads the *Publisher's Weekly* and the *Herald Tribune* and the New York *Times*. He thinks, "Danish is not a world language. We are a little country. No one ever heard of us."

There is a weekly in Copenhagen that has a modest sale of half a million copies in Norway, Sweden and Denmark. It is a popular weekly, a mild café au lait. This sale would correspond to a sale in America of five million copies. In this field, too, the Danes are not backward. But the funny thing is the part that localization plays in such an achievement. Oklahoma has not a dozen publishing houses. Oklahoma has not a magazine with 250,000 circulation. Sometimes I think that the small country does favor an intensive development beyond all comparison.

7

It would be worse than absurd, it would be alarmingly perverse, to argue that all the advantages lie with the small unit. I have only to think of London, which alone has twice the population of Denmark, to modify any claims I might be about to make for a small nation. All that I have to say in disparagement of the Port of London Authorities, the brigands of Harley Street, the knaves of Fleet Street, the slums of Torrington Square, all that I could deplore and bewail and mew about when I think of the hospitals, the crawling tenements, the fetid bystreets, simply goes into smoke and blows away when London itself,

Danish Curiosity

that myriad London, blooms in my memory like a forest illimitable and prodigious. Nature, profuse beyond our dreams, has for once been rivaled by her most precocious child. This manmade complex, spread over hundreds of miles, has the merit of mere magnitude, it is inexhaustible; but beyond this it has points of unsurpassed excellence, of subtle and incalculable worth, of dignity, of layered antiquity, of constant care and pride, that only the sustained devotion of centuries could have molded and only the magic of genius could have devised. It is possible, if one has the bare means of subsistence and no gnawing anxiety and of course good legs and a good head, to move around London day after day in a state of ethereal intoxication. The people themselves are stimulated by being Londoners, and whether they are river Londoners, city Londoners, West End Londoners, Hampstead Londoners, Pimlico Londoners or whatever, they come into a special focus if one gives them the slightest attention, and the result is an invincible pungency to which every other London has added. I do not know what makes London so racy. I do not think London was intended by anyone. But out of Britain, on this oozy mudbank, in the most squalid of winter climates, the gigantic excrescence has sucked up a million juices and made itself great. All these browns and greens and yellows, all these purples, these earth colors, these wild splashes of crimson and mad emerald, make a conglomerate that has the camel in it, the African desert in it, the icebergs of the Arctic in it and the squeezed wealth of half a world. What small unit could divulge these secrets? Ten minutes on the Strand raps home the Empire. You cannot hide it. You follow it up Whitehall. You catch it hooking up Pall Mall. You lose it in St James Street. London is at once the most secretive, the most eloquent of freemasonries. It has composed itself out of so free an election that it has become mankind's London. It belongs to the world.

And yet, intoxicating as it is, one of the three or four immensities that only a vast unit can produce, I go back to the small unit and its own pitch of development.

To pass from St Paul's to Roskilde Cathedral is not to pass from the sublime to the less sublime. A string quartet is not less sublime than a full orchestra. A gazelle is not less sublime than a mighty elephant. If the lover of greatness begins to elbow a small nation out of his way, I hope to trip him. If he says, How about music, how about symphonies? I scratch my pate and say, Well, Sibelius, who bred Sibelius? The pitch of development of the small nation is all that has to be scrutinized. I am no hot apologist for Croatia.

My case, in any event, is that Denmark is not this cut-off, suspended, exclusive community we hear about. It is a centered experiment, beyond doubt, but it is by no means thin or self-centered. And for that reason the foreigner who lives there does not stifle in a closed room. He is welcomed warmly, on the contrary, in the feeling that he brings fresh air into Denmark. He is welcomed because he is a foreigner, unless he comes himself to stifle Denmark, to choke it, to smother its freedom.

8

When we elected to live in Denmark a great English lady who was for me the jewel in London's ring—eccentric, differentiated, utterly special and completely natural—took a sad interest in the fact that we were cutting ourselves off. Had it been Italy, she said, or France, she could have understood, or had it been Holland; but she was estranged from us in a spiritual way because we had moved into a remote land, a kind of icebox, extremely hygienic, preservative and impeccable, but chilling. She thought of us as hung up in a refrigerator. For her we were outside the zone of full aesthetic sympathy. She bemoaned it. We had chosen to live on rye bread and buttermilk.

Had England better comprehended Denmark, Norway and Sweden, had England spent a modest sum—say a million pounds—on really acquainting itself with the inner character of these democratic peoples and on making a genuine effort to see how English interests in the political sphere were interwoven with Scandinavian interests, I am convinced that no great English lady could have felt estranged from the North for five minutes. She would have felt more completely herself in the North than she often did in Northamptonshire. All that was essentially precious to her would have been more valued in Copenhagen than in the London of 1936. There would have been less luxury of body but more luxury of comprehension. The failure to penetrate the soul of Denmark came from a lack of psychic energy. In this realm, however, I can never accuse the Danes of lacking psychic energy. No greater admirers of England ever existed.

This admiration is largely based on business experience. But it is also part of Denmark's honest awareness. Denmark is too intelligent to be self-centered. It is too small to be complacent.

CHAPTER THIRTEEN

We Leave Ireland

TO WANDER here and there, to sip the delectation of other countries, did not satisfy the social faith or conscience that was becoming positive in me. Every time I returned to Ireland I had brought news of the North. Manniche's international folk high school at Elsinore was of particular interest, and one of my Irish friends agreed to send pupils there. I had carried back volumes of social study from Denmark and Sweden to give to the minister of external affairs in the hope that he'd see in them the ramified possibilities of small nations. I had retrieved from Geneva the arguments for Ireland's joining the League of Nations, scoffed at in the beginning and accepted in the end. I had, in short, been one of those busybodies, those cross-fertilizing creatures, who are damned as "cosmopolitan." "You cosmopolitans!" said a disdainful woman in Wexford, sweeping out of the house. It was a reproach, and it had a measure of justice in it. A nation demanded more constant devotion from its own. It demanded blinkers, even. No nation could develop unless people wore its harness. No duties would be discharged if people were free-footed and migrant.

2

Man has a sixth sense. He begins, I suppose, with the blind impulse to suckle, in which his lips, the most marvelous of his tentacles, learn their earliest habits. He nuzzles and gropes in the delicious pursuit. His filmy eye and his unpracticed ear come slowly under control. But years later, in the fullness of maturity, he develops that final of his extensive organs—the historic sense, without which he remains a social infant—still suckling, nosing and groping.

In the royal library in Copenhagen, poking among the shelves, I had opened volumes that did not concern me. They had to do with Denmark. They were annals of the years gone by, of Danes long dead, the mere record of the fabric. What struck me in these minutiae was not the dimness of the past or its futility. A certain awe invaded me at this scrupulous notation of each career, this delicate yet merciless analysis. Here was the Past, layer on layer of it, respected by a tribe so steeped in memory that life knitted into life, act into act, until the document had Proustian thickness and I was myself a stray leaf on this canal that held old Denmark in solution. There was no insistence on celebrity, no clamor of a creed, no emphasis on class. It was a heavy yet fluid procession of significance, the Denmark not only of its unions, committees, institutions, but of the loose and the eccentric, detail concerted with detail in a steady flow, the very lifeblood of the people. In those thick volumes, dull as a miscellany to look at, the historic eye had captured every single gesture that could have molded Denmark or have marred it within the range of shrewd and liberal judgment. Here the community wrote itself down, absorbed and infinitely zealous.

It would have oppressed me when I was younger, this compact regiment of Denmark. Now it impressed me. It had coherence. And my historic sense was awake to it and gratified. This was not the vain, miserable legend of honors grabbed and wheedled, medals and ribbons, orders and titles. This articulated the lives of Danes, gave their struggles, their toil and their achievement. This covered zone after zone with local intimacy. And what emerged was Denmark, an organism. They had been produced by it. They made it over. Denmark was at once the parent and the offspring.

Could anyone, I was to say to myself, be so lacking in historic sense as to fracture this development? It is a living oneness. Could anyone mutilate it? Then let the historic sense be inexorably aware of it. It is a sin against Europe, a baseness and a profanation.

I have had good English friends who turned with aversion from our few Japanese prints. They loved China. They could not bear the best of Japanese.

Hokusai is my compatriot. But the Japanese do profane the artist in themselves when they injure China. They are not yet civilized. There is in them the monkey that nuzzles, suckles, cackles. But it has not awakened to mature historic sense. It cannot interchange its history with China.

The Swedish child, on the contrary, can be at home with Denmark's history of Sweden. The Danish child can be at home with Sweden's version of Denmark. The interchange of these national histories is an actual possibility. This is a social maturity.

3

Beside that casual discovery in the dullness of print, we went to the open-air Folk Museum, situated at Lyngby. There, in the fields occupied by a museum, we saw actual folk dwellings transplanted to this historic collection not only from the mainland but from the stark and fog-drenched island possessions. In these rooms under the thatched roofs we examined the furniture, the kitchen utensils, the crockery, the set-in beds, which had been typical in Denmark for centuries. There was no great range of fancy in the folk decorations, no great outburst of

We Leave Ireland

creativeness amid the stern circumstances of tending cattle and tilling the soil. But there was a people's life, a perfecting acquisition of grace and refinement, of higher privacy and ampler ease.

Ireland, I thought to myself, could collect such memorials from the Aran Islands, the Blaskets. But only a few fragments. Any history that has been shattered by conquest loses just this steady progression. The story is jagged and broken. It grins at you irregularly. Its fabrics have not been woven. Its laces are an import from France, an offshoot. Its poplins are Huguenot. It has been stunted, warped, denuded. It is a field of docks and thistles.

But in the royal library again, we went with Herr Ellekilde to his card-catalogue room in the folklore section, and there we learned—my wife through Danish and I simply through my eyes—the nearness of those folk who made Denmark what it is. The Danes have left no folklore to chance. Even with the intense interest of such collectors as England has had the folk songs have blown away like wild roses, and the Irish, while England ruled, had only Douglas Hyde and a few other devoted enthusiasts to catch the sun of folk imagination before it sank under the horizon. The Danish folk tales and legends have been the object of research—a policy of systematic, intensive report, with the results sifted, classified and edited by the experts in the royal library.

I learned of this research through my eyes. Herr Ellekilde brought out the photographs of the men and women from whom material had been collected by the teachers and pastors and editors who had interested themselves in this community task. For an hour I went through a most absorbing national portrait gallery. Here was every type of simple man and woman taken in an instinctive pose. It was a population in review. Here was the village wit, the scamp, the raconteur, and here also the deep-minded and deep-souled man of the soil, the earth-stained and sun-seasoned worker, the man of legends and the man of dreams.

It was an earlier day than this present day of co-operative dairies, milk-fat estimates, patent separators, express milk trains, butter boats with refrigerators and turbines. But it was these men and women who had peered their way through the folk tales to the agricultural high schools that have emancipated Denmark. It was they who became Free Christians or "merry" Christians, stepping boldly into control of their economy, still shrewd and keen-eyed country folk.

Exactly such country folk, with tales as rich or richer, had awaited the coming of self-government in Ireland for their treasure, their fairy gold, to be gathered. The nearest school to a folk high school in Ireland was the Gaelic one at Ring, in Waterford. Here was the soil out of which nationality must be cultivated.

"We want no civilization of thatched cottages," said Oliver Gogarty bitterly to me in Dublin.

What did he mean? He meant, of course, that the men from the thatched cottages were antipathetic to cavaliers like himself. He had another vision of Ireland, a blessed damozel leaning from Heaven to smile on the Hell-Fire Club. He had tales of black-browed Iberians who scowled from the thornbushes. He did not spare De Valera. There were two cultures in Ireland, two races, just as there were in Finland. And they were living in resentment and exasperation.

At times the Danes were so quiet and gentle that a horrid suspicion darted into one's mind: perhaps they are soft. All the people who feel the need of tension in order to be happy, who have hatred in them and wish to give it play, who spoil for a fight, who find good will mawkish—these people do in their souls prefer a less ordered world. They even crave it. I sometimes craved it myself.

4

So the time came for returning to Ireland. During twenty years in America I had written, argued, lectured and harangued about Irish freedom. I had published several books about it, and now it was natural to prove my preferences. Ireland was the place to settle down.

My nationalism, however, had not been the nationalism of a political party. It had been an outcrop of nationality, the inner self, which is a self that has to be respected. However professional imperialists might feel, schemers who asked for federation, meaning subordination, technicians and engineers who wished to simplify it all, there was no response in myself to their plan for Ireland as a small wheel knitting into the Empire as a large one. Its nationality was not yet secure. But it was evident that Ireland's new nationalism made a high and dangerous explosive when it was mixed into nationality. Its exponents were not content to resist the enemies of their integrity; they felt that they had to hate them. This complicated the end that nationality has, which is Self and its realization in its own terms. AE, who could not belong to a party or even go into the Senate, wrote a wise book about it called *The National Being*.

The enemy of the National Being may be respected in his own Self, in spite of the conflict. Frank O'Connor realized this most sensitively in *Guests of the Nation*.

But once nationality is the vested interest of a political party, and once this party monopolizes it, you have the postwar nationalism which is Fascism.

"I suppose," said Ferdinand Kuhn to me the other day, "that the first Fascist was Edward Carson."

That was a new idea to me, but could it be denied? Fascism has since spread like a disease, like the disease of passports, but its first eruption was in Ulster.

Kipling was an incipient Fascist. When AE, in a burst of oratory, struck the golden spurs from Kipling's heels for daring to asperse Ireland it was one Ulster knight degrading another. Kipling's aspersions were out of the Ulster fire and brimstone that he had inherited from Papist-hating ancestors. But it was Carson who literally broke with the democratic process, who armed the Ulster Fascists, at the same time alienating the British army from a spineless Liberal government.

The retort to Carson was another breach with the democratic process. A Gaelic fascism was created; a messianic figure appeared in Padraic Pearse, leading to the Easter Rebellion of 1916, when some Irishmen were said to have "gone whoring with Germany." Out of this rebellion came the Irish Free State, with De Valera and his Fascists rebelling against it in 1922 while England gave the Six Counties in the North to the Craigavon Fascists.

While Ireland was never Fascist in the sense that it broke down parliament altogether, using castor oil and torture to dismay and destroy the opposition, it did develop a New Nationalism that had compulsory features in it—compulsory Gaelic, to mention one—and it invented a great number of "vital lies" that were flattering to the national ego rather than the National Being and that imposed mental prohibition.

You could, we soon found, dig out an intellectual speak-easy in Dublin. You could bootleg an opinion. But you found that it was with a Swede or a Frenchman you were talking, or with aliens of one sort and another. The civil servant had to keep his mouth sealed. The journalist had been much intimidated by machine guns. The lawyer had been tarred and tied to the railings. The jurors had been followed from the courtroom and assassinated. Unless you were a nationalist of the right prohibitive stamp you could have no real communication with the new ruling class. And your communication with anyone was sooner or later to be cut off because the Free State had established, as well as military tribunals with enormous powers, an absolutely autocratic book censorship.

5

In the old days there was a famous story, "A Man without a Country." It was as sad as the story of a dog without a tail. But

We Leave Ireland

since that was written millions of men, women and children find themselves without a country. In some cases the countries themselves have broken down and the populations have collapsed, as if a trellis had dragged down the vines. But in other cases, where the trellis has remained, the vine itself has become infected. Never has Europe seen the like before—an exodus of nationals who have become alien in spite of themselves and for the reason that they are members of a community whose culture is no longer acceptable to extreme nationalists.

The Spanish Jews were driven out. The Huguenots were driven out. The émigrés left. Now it is the nationals who are not eaten up with nationalism.

The plague comes from the political state that bases citizenship on fidelity to a nationalist party.

The moment a nationalist party creates its own army that moment democracy dies, unless it is an army to resist—not foment—invasion. It is the army in politics. The Fascist army, the Nazi army, the Soviet army substitutes soldiering for citizenship. When that flourishes the free mind is obviously a disloyal mind. You cannot combine the searching mind with obedience as the Fascist conceives it.

The combination of the untrammeled mind with obedience to the state, through the device of a reputable opposition, is what I take political democracy to mean.

In Ireland, however, the intellectual yeast which is necessary for the rising of an opposition is, by both sides, adroitly prohibited. In a democracy, in a free country, the opposition can verge on being disreputable up to the point of using arms. Democracy, as a system, can digest everything but firearms in the hands of the opponents. But in Ireland both nationalist parties who had been parties to the Civil War strive to conform to the national ideology they have, which is derived from the only essential culture they have, the culture of the Catechism.

The intellectual, therefore, is no longer a national, even in his own country. He is that strange new citizen, a Man with a Country who is an alien.

6

By the time that the number of books censored reached a thousand I began, as a professional writer, to doubt whether we could remain what you'd call untrammeled. It was impossible to stir public opinion on this subject. Shaw, Wells, Huxley, Sinclair Lewis, Anatole France, everyone you can think of was on the list, the First Thousand, together with all the dirty books and all the books on birth control. But no group existed that cared to make the issue a real one.

Then our own two Irish novels, *Eve's Doctor* and *The Green Lion,* were prohibited by the government censors, branded as obscene and indecent. Against this there was no appeal.

I had made up my mind in advance that if this happened I'd leave Ireland. We put our auction in October. I chose October sixth, the anniversary of Parnell's death. And we cleared out, lock, stock and barrel.

As I drove from Holyhead to London I contrasted this departure with the first, when I had left for America as a boy of eighteen. I left then because there was not enough nationalism. I was leaving now because there was too much. It had been pure anguish to leave Ireland at eighteen. I had a feeling for our country—for its helpless and frustrated present, its crucified past, its uncertain future—that had been impressed on me from childhood but to which I had responded eagerly. To go from Ireland was a wrench almost unendurable. The first three years, New York in 1901–04, were so homesick as to be at times agonizing.

But those were clean wounds. The agony of youth sent to the front unwillingly, of young and old whose homes have been wiped out, of millions transplanted, make those wounds no more than scratches. Most of the recent wounds are unhealed

We Leave Ireland

and incapable of being healed until we cure ourselves of poisoned nationalism.

I reached London in the evening, and from there I went to the home of an Irishman, one of the conquerors. My own family, to the best of my belief, had been dispossessed from Wicklow by his family in 1647. He welcomed me like a friend and we talked of Wicklow.

The feeling that most stirred me, as I crossed the North Sea, was the futility of resentment such as we Irish indulge in. If the group with which one identifies oneself is treated unjustly, the thing is to be patient, to be astute, to be audacious, to act. But let that injustice become a mad preoccupation, let it work into one's marrow and poison it, then the good human fraternity that ought to be our goal is lost forever, and we are given up to feud and vendetta. Better vendetta than a "mush of concession," but I am at least as occupied with the injustices I am about to commit as those I must avenge. The early illusion that because the Irish had suffered injustice they could never commit it had to be forsaken.

It was good to be on a well-run ship.

Denmark would be no Mesopotamia, I knew. But it had never been broken in two, as Ireland had. I wanted to see a country with a healthy psyche. That is the only country that has a chance to prove it is unconquerable.

CHAPTER FOURTEEN

The Capital

WHEN I reached Rungsted, on the Sound, my wife took one good look at me. "You are going into a sanitarium," she said. And within an hour I sank into the arms of Skodsborg, one of those nursing places where they restore your balance without destroying your bank balance. It is run by Seventh-Day Adventists, devoted people. They said it had some of the characteristics of Battle Creek, Michigan. Within three weeks I had escaped from the clawings of rheumatism and felt gratitude to the institution that so soothingly and quietly cares for one—gratitude for everything except "corn" coffee.

In Stockholm, a little later, I mentioned to a reporter that we were going to live in Denmark; I gave him my reasons. On returning to Copenhagen we found ourselves assailed by telephone calls, and when we had asked Central to take the "watch" for twenty-four hours, leaving us in peace, I supposed it was over. I went out to do a little shopping, in the humble manner of the literary. I was on my way up the elevator with a loaf of bread, a jug of cream and my eggs and butter when I heard a cheerful voice, "Herr Hackett?" I said, "Coming." I stepped into the arms of *Politiken*. He allowed us to eat that evening, but he was to have the sole interview next day and we shook hands on it. And the next day I gave him my reasons for leaving Ireland.

"In any event," I said toward the end, "I am an old-fashioned feminist. I'd promised my wife that if she lived in Ireland till I was sixty she could then tow me to her own country as a derelict."

"But you are not sixty."

"No, but she lived in my country; turnabout is fair play. This is her country."

"Oh, Herr Hackett!" He looked a little unhappy, not exactly disapproving, but dubious, unconvinced.

"You don't like to make that point?" It seemed to me a real point.

"Well, you see"—he gave a little shrug—"I have been married four times."

It was sex solidarity. One couldn't offer to be towed to a new country every time, could one? He wrote a most sensitive, capable interview, but he left out my promise to my partner.

2

One of the great comforts, the remunerations, of living in Denmark was to go through the morning papers and find articles in them, day after day, that paid respect not to your prejudices but to your intelligence.

There is a school that conceives truth as "the low-down." No truth is a truth for this school unless it is observed through the keyhole.

Well, if the door is closed on truth, you must certainly choose between casting down your eyes and assuming a prayerful attitude or else looking for a crack in the news of it, either through the door joint, the transom or the keyhole.

To have the door wide open is, I take it, the disinterested ideal. Woodrow Wilson's noble formula—open diplomacy, openly arrived at—corresponds to any good historian's aspiration. But if knowledge is power, the withholding of it is even greater power, and diplomatic newspapers are governed by this. A diplomat has to be a negotiator. In trying to bring the other man to his point of view, which is his duty, he feels it proper to keep back any knowedge that might keep his adversary from forming the right judgment—any, for example, that might arouse his cupidity and give him a bargaining point and so on. That is the stern practice in all business negotiation. Women use it in dealing with the cook. Boys use it in swapping knives. Bishops use it in proposing a choice to a parish priest.

The perfect diplomat should, of course, be a perfect gentleman, but to live in a society whose newspapers only tell you the truths appropriate to a perfect gentleman is to live as a dependent. "I did not see fit to tell you." That is what polite society says to a child. The precocious child is a monster, an infliction. I prefer the slightly stupid child who does not bother me. But in the long run you are chained down by those you chain down, and there is an immense relief in being among people who open the door on truth as wide as possible, circulate it freely in the newspapers and breathe it as naturally as air.

Whether it was the immense influence earned and wielded by Georg and Edvard Brandes or not, some emancipating influence in Danish journalism has saved the reader from inanition. In spite of a certain deterioration as circulation grows, there is intellectual stuff in the papers. The foreign correspondence is ample and outspoken. First-rate men in every field write *croniques*. The interviews are spirited. The degree of candor is high. And all the blare, disproportion, scandal and innuendo that give gusto to journalism elsewhere are only to be found in certain afternoon papers that can be read in fifteen minutes. You do not have to take these at breakfast.

My standards are bourgeois. I can, as I write, think of half a dozen Danes who would disagree with me about the candor of the Danish newspapers of 1937–39. We knew that month by month, under direct pressure from the Nazis, under direct pressure from the Foreign Office also, the complete outspokenness of earlier years, the utter irreverence and frankness of cartoons and editorials, had to be toned down to suit a purposeful Germany. But before I get on the high horse about this I remember journalism in Chicago and New York. How about the Catholic Church? Has not Upton Sinclair written a book called *The Goose Step?* The Danish newspapers are run by human beings who, however fearless, must take into account the intransigeance of the people they are dealing with. If H. G. Wells had to modify his version of evolution to meet the prejudices of newspapers in the Bible Belt in America, one can understand that Danish newspapers have had to modify their version of Hitler's aspect to suit the Nazi Belt in Europe. They have had to modify more than that. I know of one untimely manuscript that got "lost" in the editorial offices of a brave Copenhagen newspaper. But as Bob Davis once said to me about a Sinn Fein murder story, "My baby fingers can't stretch that octave." What I admired in Denmark was the number of octaves that journalism stretched, until Germany unstrung the piano. I found myself saying in Denmark, "Here are these ideal newspapers F. P. A. keeps asking for."

What will happen to them?

There exists in Berlin a file of every newspaper in Germany, and the Nazi editors pick out and follow all the "promising" writers throughout Germany. When any one of these provincial writers in due course can be deemed the right sort he is sent for, and he is given privileges of travel and study so that he can be fitted into the Nazi system. It is a system.

How amazingly different from the Northern method by which two such different people as Ibsen and Georg Brandes should have been picked out, subsidized in their years of struggle but enabled to go their own way, liberated and untrammeled! The diligence and foresight exhibited by the central German organization arouses interest, since the encouragement of talent is such a good thing, but the implacable system by which men are fattened into Strasbourg geese! I don't like it even in Jesuits.

It is just because the Danish papers had no diplomatic mind behind them, just because a Catholic bishop may be in the benign limelight one day and Paul Muni the next, that one appreciated disinterestedness in them.

Yes, soon I was sitting down in Copenhagen to look through my morning newspapers.

3

But Copenhagen itself was more legible. There I did not have to know much Danish. I could look. I could especially look at the faces.

We seldom tire of looking at one another's faces. Outside a hotel in Charleston, for example, you'll see a man in a rocker, smoking a cigar and just gaping, ruminating on all the passers-by. What is he seeing? Is it the white theme and its colored variations, in which Charleston is so rich? What on earth is there to see in a casual glance? But he sits there, absorbed, utterly contemplative. What's he doing; is he just "rubberin'"? His own head, on its rubber neck, doesn't move at all. But his eyes keep shifting. That girl with the high cheekbones and the greasy pigtails, in a red polka dot; he watches her with a fascinated intensity. What's she to him? She isn't a beauty. She's a poor, kinky creature with eyes like saucers and a mind like a vacant lot. Doesn't matter. She absorbs him. Her face absorbs him. It is a face. A human face.

In the same way that the man in the rocker sits rubbernecking, most travelers to foreign cities go rubbernecking. You see them whirled around at home now, but before the Germans started out to dominate the world you used to see them everywhere, gazing around, ruminating, rubbing the backs of their poor necks. A man with a megaphone shouted things at them.

They didn't seem to hear him. They were gaping, trying to read the strange face.

You saw them in the Sistine Chapel, the patient man with a new straw hat and the wife from the Culture Club, he waiting obediently until Marie had studied the ceiling in the mirror that the attendant had lent her. The attendant, at any rate, was taking the strain off her neck.

4

Instead of pitying these tourists I envy them. Few of us who have had vacations in Europe can help having seen a capital city or two. But think of the real roving commissioners, the active and adventurous ones, who saw cities east of the Rhine as well as west, who saw cities in Africa, in Asia, and the old cities in the new countries of South America. Almost the most thrilling moment I ever felt when abroad was the moment when an American, what used to be known as a Single Lady, made her entry into the home of friends in Paris with a quick stride, a fast greeting, and then in her deep, slightly hoarse voice said passionately, "My dears, you must all go to Jerusalem!" We were all sitting there, a little fattened, and she was sparse and trim, with a little glint of vision as if she had peered through a crack into the Unknown. "You must all go to Jerusalem!"

It was not for the distraction it would give us, though that would be something. It was for the light and the crosslight it would throw on man himself, his epochs, his torpidity, his love of beauty, his dramatic sense, his cunning and his caprice. For a caput, a head, is no mere agglomeration. It is the expressive terminal of the body. All that a nation has, its inherent qualities and its acquired tricks and fashions, find a way of revealing themselves in the capital. It is the means by which a nation communicates, gives mobility to its ideas, drinks in and glances out. The capital city is the nation's face, so to speak. You can't help sitting in your rocker and gaping at it.

5

If you think of a few of the capitals you have known, you may agree that all of them have certain features in common. Each of them has to have a means by which water-borne traffic may stream in and stream out. This may be unimportant, like the Tiber or the Potomac. It may be the very imperial dominant, like the Thames, or the canals of Amsterdam, or the Seine, or the waters of Stockholm or Copenhagen. Were New York a capital city, you'd see the North River and the East River as utterly and inescapably a main feature. But for true capital cities there must be a center of national authority and one of national worship. There must be a talking shop. There must be ears, an opera house and a national gallery of sorts. There must be teeth in forts and barracks. However you wish to express it, the capital city, in its own style and tradition, signalizes the functions that the nation controls by features so eloquent, so characteristic, that you read the face—whether it be a smooth modern mask like Washington or a furrowed, time-grooved, benevolent old head like London or a stained golden antique front like Rome—for all that has gone before, for all that now moves it and remolds it, for the strength, the resource, the depravity underneath, the corrosion in the nation's being or its insensitivity, its brutality, its emptiness, its commonplace. Cities are souls. Collective though they be, they gaze at you pleasantly or ironically, proudly or brokenly. They are man's consciousness of himself given a singularly plastic and incontestable expression.

But at a certain high moment, of course—as in Washington at present—the style is elected. You look at Dublin, at its old parliament and its old Four Courts, and you say, "Georgian." You look at Paris, where Gothic and Renaissance have left a richness that robes the city, no matter what bare gleaming shoulder a modern mood demands. You look at Berlin, and you say "barrack." It is housing made formidable. How magnificently rationalized, how powerfully ordered, how ponderous. This is a serious yet a hearty national being. The features of Hindenburg, the features of Bismarck, are legible in the straight broad avenues and the erect, bristling buildings of Berlin. It is not a city that has indulgent reverie in it. It says, like Chicago, "I will!"

6

The marvelous thing about Copenhagen to me is the sparkling lightness of its expression. Oh, not if you pursue it to the rather new, rather dreary quarters that were built in a period of uninspired expansion, a period of eager building contractors who had more bricks than ideas. What one resents about the profit motive, as such, is the single-mindedness of it. There was a period in Moscow when the nudists used to hop onto streetcars, we are told, in such a state of single-mindedness that they hung from their straps like quarters of beef in the stalls, and if you pushed through the car you had to shoulder the pink-and-white carcasses out of your way, the lean and the lard at the ordinary blood temperature. I do not think these nudists had taken all the awkwardness of proximity into account, and no more do I think that the Copenhagen building contractors realized how their yellow brick buildings would poke one in the eye and shove one in the ribs and so grimly or so dully manifest themselves. A barrack is an honest, single-minded, profit-making enterprise. But it is also an obtrusion. The immense tracts of modern expansion that were a consequence of rapid transit, too rapid to be socialized, are in contrast with the inner city which dated from an autocratic period that, in its own way, was thinking of society and, narrow as its society was, infinitely more public-minded, more decorous and gracious than much that has intervened. In the new century, however, the lapse from grace has been detected. A government securely popular has itself resumed the vigilant control of houses, streets and parks, of open spaces and of monuments. The master builder has another patron.

The keynote for Copenhagen was struck in the time of Christian IV. His was the high moment. And where the visitor to Washington, for example, is dazzled by white marble—as if bathrooms and dental clinics had said, No, we are capable of greater nobility than this; let us house Justice, and works of art, and Treasury and pharmacy and Jefferson and Lincoln—in the same awareness of an impulse that came from a rich source the visitor to Copenhagen is dazzled by copper green and gold, by roofs that are thatched with verdigris and spires and towers that dance golden in the sunlight. This is not the blameless white of a capital so far south as to be sun-smitten, demanding the flat roof, the tall front, the cool recess that copings give and colonnades and smooth surfaces. Copenhagen has had no need to blanch itself when the snow is so obliging. But it had every impulse, under this Dutch Renaissance influence, to let fantasy leave the private castles where it had played with green roof and red wall, with corbel and with turret, to employ this festive caprice with city church and stock exchange, with buildings on the canals, with long-roofed breweries, with red-browed tenements, with fountains, cloisters, gardens.

In due course several gems of castles fell into the burghers' laps. Rosenborg Slot, in the heart of Copenhagen, set in its own avenued grounds and flowered walks, was bestowed on a grateful commune, whatever the terms; and Frederiksberg, a few miles away, another royal park and castle, followed Rosenborg's example, as St James's Park and Hyde Park in London. Here the opulence that a king had employed for beauty returned to the people enhanced by age. The king had been society's park keeper.

But when its own turn came the commune took the hint from Christian IV. And not only was the town hall conceived in the familiar style, so was the central railway station, so were hotels and insurance buildings near by, so were smaller if not humbler buildings.

Because Denmark has so little building stone the use of brick has favored this particular prevalent style, and the Danes have it in them to strive for a conformity and a coherence. Even in the bad period this was evident; no one was so unfeeling as to put up an egregiously good building.

But another style insinuated itself into another quarter, and outside the zone of Dutch Renaissance with its incomparable zest, made light and gay in Copenhagen, there developed a style of city palace with more reserve and calm. Amalienborg Plads, where the king resides, is the lozenge-shaped space along which four palaces stand, to form a diamond. They are in such delicate and admirable proportion to the space that, though it is not enclosed, tranquillity dwells in it. It is block-paved, and in the center there is an equestrian statue to a king who has had the fortune to be a sculptor's model and so to be remembered. That is not the statue of a horse or of a king. Seen from any approach, either under the arched portals to the south, or from the Sound, or from the park, or from the House of God, it is a resolving of two animal shapes, the man's and the horse's, into a flowing unity that still stands quiveringly in poise, the conquest of movement that is not immobility. The torture of a lovely movement in the dance is that it dissolves like fireworks. Here is a lovely movement that can never vanish, unless some desecration touch it. It is not an arrested motion, it is a motion sustained and held, just as Keats observed it. It was a Frenchman who accomplished it, but the Danes have placed it with pious hands where it is framed by palaces. It commemorates the king who signed his name to the charter of the East Asiatic Company.

The sparkle in Copenhagen passes, in this Plads, to a finer, thinner gleam. But you walk through it, up to Langelinie, and once again the open Sound dances before your eyes, the shipping spanks along, the women drag their dogs from other dogs, you see people drinking coffee from Copenhagen porcelain, you see yachts in the little harbor, you see abandoned forts that have become rendezvous for trippers, and you say, "What's the holiday?" It isn't a holiday. It's Copenhagen.

7

Now, to be pleasant is not enough. We must have *The Tragic Sense of Life*. (Or have you enough of it, Unamuno? Are you satisfied? You might, by now, be satisfied.) To be pleasant, as a final aim and an inexorable condition, is far from enough. Danes, as a rule, are up too early and at work too early to have many overwhelming illusions about the pleasant. Sometimes a hand strays to the checkbook once too often, sometimes the world is lost for madness—the fair head is as wild a storm center as the blackest—but in general the country is a working country. What is so remarkable, in this so fixed condition of the country as a whole, is Copenhagen's constant pleasantness. It has not, indeed, that *coquetterie* of Paris, as if to invite one to a rendezvous, whatever spleen might follow. That *expertise* in all the sensations, sacred and profane, that enchantment of Paris twilight, violet twilight, never seemed to me to suggest themselves in any other city, whatever Vienna said to those who were fortunate enough to know Vienna. A city that can make a brioche a seduction, that can give to the selling of roast chestnuts the aroma of an adventure, that can suggest illicitness in the very position of the Madeleine, as if a church wore a veil and high heels, that city cannot be surpassed in the extraordinary power of insinuation that, so often in Paris, simply meant that the wine was as it should be. In no other country than France has alcohol achieved the infinite gradations, the resonances, the transitions of a violin. Beer is a percussion instrument. Cocktails are brass. Whether Paris seen by a water drinker would have quite the number of insinuations, seductions and allurements as for a winebibber, I don't know. But Copenhagen has a national presence so uncomplicated by artifice, so clear, natural and effervescent, that even the man who dwells in it is renewed in his sense of it day by day.

For the Parisian, no doubt, the Chambre and the Senate are just as much in evidence as Westminster or Copenhagen's Christianborg. Notre Dame is as emphatic as St Paul's and as the Raadhus in Copenhagen. (I reckon the Raadhus as rather more the dynamic center of faith than any of the churches.) And Buckingham Palace asserts itself in London as much as Amalienborg Plads in Copenhagen. But in the general froufrou of Paris, now contributed by the taxi rather than the skirt, in the ebullience of the crowds who shop and entertain themselves and display themselves, the actual dominance of the city's features is quite lost in the vivacity, the romp and rip of its expression. Its Bourse, its town halls, its railway stations, its Palais de Justice and the rest are all thrown into the medley of a capital that also has theaters, boulevards, hotels, restaurants, kiosks, Lalique and Cartier. The swift smile and the quick grimace of Paris are probably measurably shorter than any smile and any grimace in the North. Its taxi darts and sprints. In Copenhagen, where the civic sense is so domesticated, the parliament, though for less than four million people, spreads itself out on every side with a munificence that every Dane appreciates. It places him, as well as itself. The same can be said of the central railway station. The taxis line up there but in the calm amplitude of the omnibus. The driver gets down, opens your door, bows. This is no breakneck race. And the same is true of the Raadhus. The parvis in front of it is so large that children cannot be kept from roller skating in it. You have equal elbowroom in the space before the Opera. And as for Tivoli, in the heart of the city, the place where Coney Island fell in love with the Opéra Comique, had twelve restaurants and lived happily ever after—you can go in there and get lost.

But while Copenhagen is in itself so pleasant, while all the buildings new and old that house its works of art have the graciousness of a civilization long sustained, and while the parks that are municipal from the start as well as those originally royal are nothing if not amiable—even the botanic one that names every sprig and shrub—and while the ramparts have become promenades that are a symbol and a means of appeasement, there is a stark reminder, right in the Royal Theater itself, that Copenhagen is no sybarite. It is the legend over the stage, "Not Only for Pleasure." This theater, at least, is free from the slavish doctrine that art is only for entertainment.

Then you may remember the motto in front of the somber old courthouse. In Washington on the Supreme Court you read "Equal Justice," a pledge that for rich and poor, a fact not self-evident even in a democracy, justice is even-handed. On government buildings in Paris you read the clarion words, "Liberty, Equality, Fraternity." But in Copenhagen it is a quiet script from the thirteenth century. "A land must be built on law." For seven hundred years or so that has been the fixed, the abiding principle. This pleasant city goes its way without the brandishing of arms, without the mailed fist. If you hear a siren it is not the police. It is Falk, ba-boo, ba-boo, who demands the right of way. Falk is the rescuer, the private company for dealing with emergencies, who sells fire protection, who sends out ambulances, who fishes cars out of the river, sends nurses to you, takes the monkey back to the zoo and finds the baby you lost there.

"A land must be built on law." You do not see this in a vast police force. You see it in the faces of the old, in the faces of the children.

A small child stops you. "Would you be so good as to take me across the street?" and holds out his hand. You look into his solemn eyes, grasp his hand and lead him over. His mother had made him promise to do that, to ask an older person.

Strange, that "Falk" or a stranger on the street can thus be counted on. The land is built on law, is self-policed.

8

No city is ever finished. A man invents the neon light. The word "neon" makes no bones about it; it means new. And every city has to say yes or no to neon light. At first Copenhagen shuddered. It had been otherwise designed. Its masses, curves, perspectives were at their best in lights that intimated. But neon could no more be ruled out of Copenhagen than the motorcars. And now it has a street so lighted from its windows that the street is an interior. Or was, until a blackout ended window lights and neon.

Just as neon had to be accepted, so had the white buildings with colored awnings, the "functional." So had the flat-faced factories. But since the rules for height are rigidly obeyed, the buildings on new lines do not achieve conspicuousness. What other city has remained so calm while growing to a million?

9

If I were asked to declare in a single phrase the charm that inheres in Copenhagen I'd say, It was built to the human scale, it still is handmade.

The gigantesque, whether in height or in extent, has a power to impress the biggest of us. The eye cannot span the height of Rockefeller Center. The eye cannot take in London at night, not even from the air, when that field of jewels, green, red and white, spreads illimitably in splendor underneath. The human senses are stunned into submission when man parades his power over machines, too loud for his ear, too fast for his vision, too monstrously efficient and exhausting. The whole man is then the slave of detail. He takes his elevator to the thirty-fifth, steps out on a signal, click, is gone. Were he electrocuted, it would not be a tragedy. It would be a detail. Once let the whirl accelerate to its maximum speed, too many people come into play, too many papers ask to be read, too many dishes crowd into the menu, too many claims queue up for attention. Relationships are no longer human. The five senses are too inelastic. Not all the harmless pills that help you to sleep, not all the whisky that helps you to have ease of soul, not all the massage, injection, special diet, can enable you to keep that pace of the machine and still be what you call a human being. A war of incredible horror, of incalculable consequence, has to be so served to mechanized humanity that not a drop of blood oozes out of the package. The machine has overproduced it. Any attempt to realize it would fill lunatic asylums.

This breach with man's five senses is unavoidable anywhere. So much comes in that children literally stagger. My niece in Copenhagen had so many schoolbooks to carry that she was threatened with curvature of the spine. The courses are so arduous that teachers fear for the pupils. But if the brain is taxed to this extent, at least there is no frantic pace by day and night. There are no fifty theaters to take in. There are no clanging distractions, no five-minute reports, no demands for pep, no incessant crash of competition.

The modesty and the compassion in Danish character are to be found in the very features of Copenhagen. The city corresponds! It is, in this respect, the capital of Denmark.

Since the city has grown so vast the bus has begun to quicken the city transit, and this must go on. People cannot spend too many hours in streetcars. The businessman drives ten miles an hour faster than the old-fashioned driver. He has to save time. He has to get home for golf. He is quite "modern." Bit by bit, a new type of girl has come into being. In 1920 the girls were straight-haired, long-coated, fond of fawn and sand color, well-nourished, rather serious. The girls in 1939 had every style of hair, wore every imaginable color, were slim, alert, coquettish. But for all the evident or conspicuous changes, this capital of the Danes is still true to the human scale, still aware of man's dignity and man's identity.

The Capital

As the brewery men come out of Tuborg there is a vendor with a handcart to sell flowers to them.

As a drunken, hatless sailor comes up to the policeman at Nyhavn the policeman finds where he wants to go, takes him by the elbow, steers him, directs him.

As a tipsy worker falls from his bike a taximan stops, lifts him into the taxi, ties the bike to the running board. "Where do you live, comrade?"

Fifty thousand of them go to Frihavn to meet the five hundred Dano-Americans coming home. No one organizes it. It is a sunny Sunday afternoon. These are also "comrades."

People tell you of the Copenhagen "grin." This is the glib irony that calls itself sophistication. But while it exists, just as corner boys exist, the city's note is far from crass. Its note is pleasantness.

The sea air blows across Kongens Nytorv. A ship from Greenland is about to dock. You pause for a moment in front of a café on the sidewalk. There are benches over the way. You hesitate. A motorist nods to you. You make your way across. Trees and flowers are centered around the Horse, a statue that has suffered a prolapsus, a statue in the hands of veterinaries. If you look to the left you may have to buy a pear. If you look to the right you may buy tickets for the opera—a dollar each. It is better to go on. You pass a palace that has an art library inside, where you may stop to talk to Aage Marcus, a librarian who knows every English novel, who has a delicate ear for music, who can tell you of Master Eckhart, who is incapable of not doing you a service. No, you leave this temptation and gaze down the row of sailors' dens, from which you hear the sound of a concertina. Five minutes away is the Marble Church, "The Word of the Lord Endures Forever," and around from there the King's Palace. You pass a churchyard and a tree leaf falls. The ships are a few yards away. It is pleasant. Copenhagen is pleasant.

CHAPTER FIFTEEN

We Rent a Flat

PLEASANT as Copenhagen is, it is still on the planet, still under the burden of original sin. What made me "choose" Denmark was the belief that it had gone further, as a community, to give the monkey in man a chance to be human than any other country I had run into. But I did not have the illusion that he had ceased to have monkey in his composition. That is hoping for much. In any event it depends on remaining aloof, whereas by "choosing" Denmark we elected to cease being aloof; we proposed to be residents, to choose a district, to choose a house in it, to choose a servant. In this way we would be more at the mercy of the community than any tourist has an idea of. A tourist may hate his hotel but the facility with which he can move makes up for any misery of the moment. He slides through the community at will. The resident must sit tight. And here the lesson began on the degree to which the monkey is still inescapable even in Denmark.

2

We had dreamed of living on the Sound. "How wonderful," we used to say, "to be in full view of the Sound!" At Hendaye

We Rent a Flat

we had lived on the Bidassoa. In Wexford we could see the Atlantic liners from the end of the garden. At Hvidbjerg we had stayed on the water. (And at Køge.) So it had to be the Sound, as near as possible.

3

The district we chose was Hellerup. Some thirty or forty years before, this had been a district of handsome villas, many of them with parks around them and a line of them built in full view of the Sound. With a shopping street running through the heart of the quarter, a main line of communication with downtown, Hellerup is still a villa quarter. Street after street that runs down to the Sound has kept the peaceful and indeed idyllic air of a garden suburb. The lawns are green. The wooden palings are low, and in spring one sees the flowering trees or the fruit trees, the beds of roses and the houses that are capped with red tiles, their walls white, their windows so filled with blossoms, so freshly curtained and inviting. There is something of the provincial town about Hellerup, yet a town remarkably garnished and almost uniformly trim, at once gay and sedate, the home of an upper bourgeoisie.

We soon began to know this by the dogs. The upper bourgeoisie cannot exist without dogs. They used to be dachshunds in Hellerup. That was in the years when the upper bourgeoisie was under the influence of Queen Victoria, whose etching of a dachshund was once printed in the *Critic* in New York, the head and the brisket in the first installment, the impressive hind quarters in the second. Now, perhaps owing to some other queen or perhaps to the advertisements of Black and White whisky, the prevailing dog is the Aberdeen, one of those rough-haired, animated footstools that look at you with a cocked head, at once quizzical and hostile. These brutes abound in Hellerup. And until the police began to take a serious view of them they made Hellerup more suitable for airplanes than pedestrians.

We did not take a villa. We cast eyes on a very modern building that zigzagged down to the water, its more adventurous apartments actually bulging over the water's edge. It was five stories high, and every flat of the thirty-five had a view of the Sound. It was spotlessly new.

It was the best-placed apartment house conceivable. It was built so that there was no through thoroughfare. It looked out on a row of detached villas in the front, screwing its balconied rooms toward the Sound, and at the back sharing an open space with another, somewhat older apartment building. Ours was "functional." It had, that is to say, adopted certain features from the factories. It had a flat roof for sun bathing. It had great expanses of glass. It was facing south and east with that bold, streamlined, staring look that has something of the emancipated in it and something of the bare hussy.

We furnished it according.

We moved into it with delight. The sun lavished warmth on it. It had a hard, keen definition in it and the repose of its vast space. That means a big room with a corner in which one could dine, a slice of a room cut off the big room and in the back, next to the bathroom, a square cell with north light and a wife in it.

The kitchen was made for a streamlined cook who lived on lettuce. It was neat and metallic.

For this ingenious flat, three rooms in all, they asked about forty-five dollars a month.

4

The people who built it, as time revealed, had not completely eradicated the profit motive out of their system. They were a band of contractors, and for some reason contractors cannot be left wholly to themselves. Each of these contractors had tried to fine down the outlay while remaining picturesquely "functional," so that the resident—who had to deposit three months' rent in advance and sign up for six months, giving six months' notice before quitting—came to realize that there were aspects of the building problem hitherto unsuspected.

Over our heads, for example, there was a young couple that out-Helleruped Hellerup. They had three hunting dogs, enormous beasts that gave their mistress the chance to wear breeches and carry a shotgun. The dogs loved their mistress. Whenever they flopped their eager tails on the floor above us the floor resounded. Our contractors had saved money on sound insulation. As the parties upstairs grew jovial, as the laughter grew bubbling and bibulous, the dogs whacked their tails against the thin partitions that did divide us. At times heels would click-click across the floor, and soon would come a torrential explosion, when the high water pressure rushed to be functional. Nothing was soundproof in the building.

And there were no secrets on the street. The contractors had built garages under the first floor, but they had counted on concertinas rather than motorcars; the long modern cars could not fit into the short modern garages. Hence they had to be parked on the street. Not being a thoroughfare, the dead end was ideal for all-night parking. Some tenants came home at twelve, some at two and some at four. And up from the street rose all the exhausts of hospitality and transportation. We came to know Sandy. We came to know all the men who knew Sandy. Sometimes at two in the morning, my soul in corkscrews, I'd go out on the balcony to say a word or two to Sandy. He did not understand me. He spoke Aberdeen.

In due time the young sportswoman moved, with her gun and the three pointers. Instead arrived a couple with three children. By some odd quirk in the lady she never managed to convey her mind to her children while in the flat. No sooner did the dear ones reach the street than the mother was in full blast from above. She was private in public.

Directly below us we had the luck to have a retired couple, a cashier and his wife. They were dogless and childless. They had given up living in a villa to end their days in the peace and quiet of a flat building. No more coal to provide, no more furnace to worry about, no servant to leave in charge, no snow to sweep—perfect peace, while one smoked a cigar and watched the ships go by.

A hunted look began to mark this poor man's ravaged face. By the time he was getting used to the dogs and the motorcars another family with three children moved in under him. It was another of those families that do not pass their exhaust through a silencer. They displayed their carpets and their confidences on the balcony. It would have been all right in Bagdad but it was fatiguing in Hellerup. The cashier got dyspepsia. His wife took him for long walks, but his hands trembled. His nerves were on edge. His light blue eyes became bloodshot.

Instead, however, of shooting his neighbor this exasperated man took counsel with us and with the other tenants who agreed with him. As soon as the children began to use roller skates he invoked the law against the use of roller skates. When the radio was played in the open window after eleven P.M. he invoked the law against this public nuisance. In short, he became a policeman. It was not long before there were so many encroachments to report, so many inconsiderate or exuberant acts to shut down on, that the first battle was won. The family below him retreated to a building less bristling with neurotics.

As months went on, the retired cashier changed from a hunted man to a hunter. He had decided that most of the tenants were ready to co-operate with him, but there were a few that were not "house cultivated." To bring these into line was an occupation on which he throve. He became the unelected sheriff of the whole building.

There were already a couple of dozen children in it and without a playground. They turned the dead-end street into a playground, yelling with glee as they raced over the wall, along the beach, back by the garages. Small boys and girls from neighboring buildings came to gain strength through joy. There were mishaps, anxious mothers on balconies, cries of anguish, cries of consolation. Not until the sheriff persuaded someone to turn an unused ground-floor flat into a playroom did the insoluble seem soluble.

After a year's work on us the cashier and his wife took a vacation. He then renewed his lease. Within the law he was determined to mass public opinion in the building against the obtrusive and noisy. But as he gained power he became tolerant. He moved from the Left to the Center.

5

He had help from outside. One of the more dashing tenants bought a new car, and his joy was to rip home late at night, clatter to a stop, close the door with a bang and bury his head in the pillow till ten in the morning. At nine one morning, however, the new car became vocal. The horn started to blow without intermission. At first we thought that a prince was born, or a victory won, or a holiday proclaimed. We gazed from every window. A crowd of boys collected, near enough to peer but not near enough to help. With an occasional lapse that meant nothing the horn continued to blast until our friend who owned the car, hearing his child crying, leaped from the voluptuous bed and rushed out in his striped pajamas.

He had that indefinable stylishness one sees in the films. He looked as if he had just graduated from a department store. As he sleeked his hair and sat into the machine we took the show to be over. Not at all. With undiminished zeal the wicked horn kept up its toot. The young man, a little ruffled, began opening everything that would open and shutting everything that would shut. The horn went on.

Down the middle of the road came an elderly man with a red face and tousled hair. Help at last! The boys eyed him and let him pass through.

"What does this mean?" he demanded.

"I don't know," said the silk pajamas.

"If you can't control your car," said the red-faced man, "you are not fit to own one."

"*Men kaere!*" expostulated the fashionable young man. "But dear!" Yes, but "dear" stumped away, beyond all blandishments.

At last a boy helped. The horn ceased to howl. The crowd, casting a last look, dissolved away.

Once the street was clear, except for the Aberdeen, the undiminished horn resumed with vigor. Blah! Public opinion surged in every one of us. A very ruffled youth, still in stylish pajamas, rushed to the offending car. Blah, blah, black sheep!

It was obviously out of order.

Not till a mechanic came with a screw driver did the frightful noise cease. "The damp! Caused by the damp."

The damp permanently affected the young dandy. He and his arrivals and departures became less brilliant.

6

One of the revelations of Danish character came from two women in this flat building. One was the tenant overhead. The other was the laundress who visited us twice a month to do our work in the modern basement.

At work from early morning, she spared herself no physical effort, so that she was in the pride of well-being, her limbs muscular, her body straight, her movements quick. Her face was as clear and candid as her body was athletic. She was professional in her dealings, quite frank about the time she needed for herself and the pay she required, but eager to fall in with our wishes whenever she could do it. Her work was not fine, just good, honest work, careful and thorough. She came and went without a fuss, and just a glimpse of her was as good as wine, she was so lovely and so sympathetic.

We asked her to come to work with us. Her whole idea in being a laundress was to have time free in which she could study, and we promised her free time so that she could go on studying. It tempted her, yet at the same time she was visibly disturbed and almost agonized. She decided against us. "I am clumsy," she said. "I do not believe I could satisfy you." But she stayed on with us, helping us in every other way, one of the comforts of existence.

The woman overhead was also young, of good figure and carriage. It was evident that she too had been a working girl. But where our laundress's features were serene, this woman's were discordant. Her blue eyes had a frosty, hostile stare, her teeth were a little prominent and fanglike and her cheekbones were rudely carved. Whether her early acquaintance with poverty had been peculiarly harsh I did not know, but she had clearly married a man of finer nurture than herself. This had given her a difficulty to adjust for which, not being patient or good-natured, she was inadequate. As a result of this inadequacy life had become for her a battle with superior beings that did not appreciate her. Instead of realizing the basic fact of existence, that the universe is less hostile than indifferent, cruelly indifferent if you like, she saw in it a setting unfavorable and even inimical to herself, and thereupon she went about punishing it for not loving her, in such a way that it could not possibly love her.

Perhaps this discordancy, betrayed in her harsh voice, her bad temper and her spite, may have had an origin purely physical. She may have needed an operation. Or perhaps only by such discordancy does the world know how unhappy some of its poor children are. Like the horn that tooted so raucously, she may have been calling for the screw driver. But on ourselves, who had no wish to injure her, the effect of her incessant protest was disastrous. It was as if a gypsy had moved to the flat building who insisted on burning fires in the middle of the floor. Instead of conforming to the habits of the more effete class into which she had moved, her notion was to punish it for its feebleness. She clattered, banged and crashed in rude resentment. Her husband was on the road as much as possible.

When the Inferiority Complex has fierce energy behind it what is the world to do?

You would believe that neighbors under any circumstances could arrive at a *modus vivendi*. But the essence of an Inferiority Complex is that it cannot find a *modus vivendi*.

After she had shouted from the balcony to the street she stated her objections to us. "They should not expect the rest of the world to be mum all round them. They should go out to work. People should not do their work at home."

We tried conciliatory smiles, absent treatment, dignity and ear muffs. We tried righteous anger.

But in the end she won. We gave up the apartment.

One of our fellow tenants had meanwhile started war with another pest. He did it by inserting an advertisement in *Berlingske Tidende* that ran something like this:

> *Bachelor seeks an apartment that overlooks Hellerup Harbor, in a modern building with every modern refinement but must have neither bedbugs nor dubious ladies.*

The bedbugs were put in to make it vicious. The Dubious Lady was his target. Had she lived her night life with her Dubious Gentlemen, of whom there were many, it would not have disturbed him; but it was her desire to parade herself and her dog, her desire to make the reinforced concrete ring with her merry laughter, that lost her the vote of the Bachelor. Still, she broke no law. It was the Bachelor—who, however, had printed his name and address to relieve his feelings—that was forced to retire from the field of battle.

7

Now there must be blackout in that dead-end street. There can be no uproarious comings and goings because there is no gas. The children are probably subdued, and the cranky German whose villa was on the Sound is no doubt the happiest man in Hellerup. The Dictator had brought about much of the calm that we had been looking for.

Are these good results an argument for the Dictator? To make that flat building really habitable more money should have been spent on sound insulation. There should have been a place for dogs, a playing ground for children, a place for servants, a place for motorcars. To clamp down dictatorial restrictions may ease the situation but it does not go to the root of it. Where the profit motive had led the builders to ignore the social motive, eager to squeeze an income out of the investment, the same sort of mistakes could be made again. A parvenu may lie low till the blackout is over. He does not emerge "house cultivated." Destroy all the dogs, a new generation will follow. Each of these irritations must be recognized by the people who cause them. In this way we have evolved the sibilant w.c., the noiseless portable, the children's nursery.

What are the chances of these amenities, if people are so inexperienced? Well, our laundress had a problem at Christmas, whether to give a friend Louis Bromfield's *The Rains Came* or Pearl Buck's *The Patriot*. (These were in Danish.) Signe's dressmaker was reading Proust. Her hairdresser was going to a class in music on the evening before she went to the symphony orchestra. If the preoccupations are of this order among those who have so little to spend, maybe those who have more to spend, on hunting dogs, on motorcars, on night life and so on, may arrive at being more mellow. As inexperienced spenders, I admit, I was reminded of a young lady who brought a yapping dog into the dining room of a hotel in France. A French naval officer endured it for a while, then he turned to her and with perfect solicitude said, "Your first dog, madame?"

Prosperity is a manure that makes some people grow too rankly, and our little flats were irresistible for just the kind of young people who wanted to make a dash. The others, who crowded children into them, were attracted by the fresh sea air, and so charmingly placed was the building that we found it hard to relinquish it. What made it harder was the care that one of our friends had lavished on our flat. For we had begun housekeeping in Denmark under the wing of a guardian aesthete.

CHAPTER SIXTEEN

Guardian Aesthete

YEARS BEFORE, on one of our first visits to Copenhagen, we were thinking of furnishing in Ireland, and, in the unsystematic way that one goes about these things, we were lazily window-shopping.

At that time it was not clear to us which were the principal streets, since side streets manage for a few houses to keep up the display that better streets do, and we did not know we were rather off the beaten track when we came to a delightful window. There was a set of Swedish furniture in it, a dining room set with high-backed chairs that were at once stately and peasant. They were painted a sealing-wax red. We looked wonderingly at those chairs. The price was not too great. But how to ship them? I had once been idiotic enough to send trunks through the Port of London, and the amount of hocus-pocus that this involved taught me an unforgettable lesson. Might there be a steamer direct to Ireland? No, the difficulties were too great. We went into the shop to have a better look at the adorable table and chairs and ended by buying an ash tray.

It was a small establishment. On a kind of ledge in the back sat the proprietor, a dark young man. We could not know that he was, ten years later, to become our best friend in Denmark.

2

So far, in this casual book, I have striven to show the growth of my faith in Denmark as an organic whole. I haven't tried to discover master principles or central ideas or keymen. Being a true democracy, to my way of thinking, Denmark is swayed by the force we call public opinion, and it is to the degree that this force is operative and competent that it can honestly be called a democracy. People who are lazy and want things spelled out for them love to be told about keymen, and in the countries where the organs of public opinion are enfeebled or undeveloped or just simply don't exist you are obliged to look out for the personages that you can dramatize. A dictator simplifies the story. And the higher-ups in one country, often rather simple people, can grasp at once the opposite number in another country, where the intangible and imponderable elements that blend into "public opinion" are hard to get at. Engineers, accustomed to inert material, and industrialists, in favor of the master-and-man relationship, can easily put themselves in the dictator's shoes. They have a job of work to do, the engineer and the industrialist, and they readily suppose that to guide a commonwealth is just another job of work. After a long experience of venal and slipshod politicians who can't even deliver the goods, a New Order must seem pretty desirable in which there is a Boss, not merely free from the vagaries of public opinion but so in control of his masses that he can go up, up, on top of a private mountain and even on that height, with the kingdoms of the earth beneath him, need only press a button to have 200,000,000 wince. Who'd want to manipulate public opinion, with all its caprices, its indecisions and turmoils, if this other way were open? It is absolutely natural, granted the overwhelming desire to get things done, to prefer autocratic method as against the slow and wearisome method of consultation and consent.

And even when the method of consultation and consent defeats the professionals and produces a Wendell Willkie at a convention, in abject obedience to current opinion, the men who most admire that result still have no faith in the process.

But in this process, this one of consulting the public through one genuinely expressive medium after the other, the part played by keymen is not to be minimized. Grundtvig was a keyman in the Danish folk high schools. Georg Brandes was a keyman in Danish rationalism. You cannot think of Danish letters without noting Hans Christian Andersen. You cannot omit Johannes V. Jensen, Martin Andersen Nexø, if you are to mention contemporary letters, or Kai Nielsen if you are to name sculpture. No Dane could fail to recognize the leaders in Danish shipping, in the history of the North, in science, in painting, in medicine, gymnastics, merchandizing, margarine, the law, in printing, in religious circles, in criticism, in the theater, music, sport, architecture. I could myself recite dozens of names, either of men I had seen or read about or known through their work, whose activity has been essential to the forming of public opinion. There are closely printed books filled with the names of these keymen and the history of their performance. To read six pages of one of these biographical lexicons is to die of indigestion.

Back to the little furniture shop! Up near the ceiling, in the bad air, is this Spanish-looking Dane with coal-black hair and an immobile face, drawing fine little lines with exquisite precision and making notations in fine little writing that he finds perfectly legible. His whole heart and soul are absorbed in central ideas, master principles.

3

The next time I saw this shop it had come out of the side street. To say that it had expanded would be a miserable understatement. It was in the center of the center. It had grown as if liquid air had been blown into it till the original shop had swelled so that only a thin film of plate glass kept it from filling the block. And nowhere was unsold furniture more spaciously at home than in the cubic space devoted to its display. A museum of modern art could not have been more ceremonious with its acquisitions than this gracious shop with its merchandise.

The custodians—the young ladies, I mean, who move among these objects on display suggest that a career for the modern young women should be opened in metropolitan museums. To give oneself to a work of art with a sour-looking attendant three feet away, dangling the handcuffs, has always made me feel at one with the zebra-striped convicts in Florida who are supposed to give of their best with an armed guard standing in glum contemplation. If only the gunmen could keep out of sight while one revels in priceless treasures of art. But in my friend's shop there are no guardians, only these young ladies with their hats off, whom some find so haughty and whom others find so marriageable.

We made up our minds that if we ever furnished a house in Copenhagen we'd buy all our furniture here. And not only furniture but hangings, carpets, pillows, pottery, crockery. All but the cage of lovebirds that made gay one of the inner rooms.

4

We met the owner of this shop at the house of a friend. He was tall, slender, broad-shouldered and streamlined as a fish. He was one of those men whom one meets in profile. He smiled and bowed but he was not present. The intense concentration of which his precise appearance gave a suggestion—in the long head, the long hands, the tenuity—was obviously not arrested by our being there. "I did not notice you," he said afterward. Nothing was more probable. If El Greco had not painted him, Velasquez might have done so, mingling the exotic and the quixotic.

What was really exotic in this dark, elegant figure? Only a fatal passion, the passion for perfection. It might have made him a poet or a painter, but it had seized on him in this more complicated and, as it were, less betraying form—the ordering of civilized interiors, the placing of the background. But it was not the background of the wealthy that engaged him. The interiors that were in his mind were those everyday, homelike, traditional Danish interiors, so often accepted without a moment's disquietude but to him agonizing, devastating.

He had begun, in his youth as one of a minor dynasty, by deciding to study plant life, flowers and trees, and to do this thoroughly he had taken a course at Cornell. But when he had changed his plans, becoming interested in the textiles that are in daily use, the shapes of chairs and tables, the design of carpets, the placing of pictures, he had left Denmark to see what was being done in Europe, and he had spent years in a systematic study of every branch of what is roughly called interior decoration. But it was much more than decoration. It was the actual design of things, the placing of things, the shaping of the interior in its form and substance. He was the man who orders the interior as against the architect, and a good name for him has yet to be invented. You can't suggest oikotect in New York, a home builder. Perhaps he should be called the Designer.

What he planned was to have a shop in which the very best in Europe could be brought together, the best glass, the best modern wall decorations, the best beds, the best everything for the home; and in the succession of broad galleries, with a hall on the street where lectures or concerts or exhibits could be held, he could enable Denmark to make its choice and lend its approval.

To do this in a Europe that was erecting tariff barriers soon became impossible. Denmark could only buy from those countries that bought from Denmark. Nothing could be imported except on quota and by permit. This was called valuta control, and a traffic jam on Fifth Avenue facilitated wild progress compared to it. To obtain anything, even from Sweden, took a major operation. It was simpler in the end to start factories for the making of goods which, however, could be better made, for a variety of reasons, in the countries that had initiated them.

Few things are so stimulating as a continuous revelation of the excellence in contemporary craft. Our friend had built a canal for it. Then he had to make it into a dry dock and devote it to his own constructions. He designed tables, dressing tables, bureaus, writing desks, mirrors, chairs. The signature on this work became increasingly legible.

At first his styles were so distinctive that they were rather at variance with taste in the older establishments. His elm was lighter than their oak. His lines were cleaner. His feeling for the wood was purer. His refusal to cloak the design with ornament was inexorable. After a considerable period, in which public opinion resisted him, there began to be an odd indication here and there that the complete converts, especially among the young, could not be entirely ignored. What he displayed was almost Spartan in its apparent simplicity. He did not ask people to conquer their fear of stimulants. He asked them to go to the cold spring and in their bare feet. And they were so cozy in their Empire beds, in their mahogany suites, in their love of opulent details.

Bit by bit, in the windows of the great department stores, there appeared bare, bald little items of furniture. These had not the apparent simplicity of the other type, they had a real simplicity, a plain carpenter's simplicity. They sold. But at each fresh exhibition in the creative shop there were quick men from outside who stooped and peered, who figured and took measurements.

Within ten years, as apartments multiplied in Copenhagen and the other cities, there was scarcely a piece of furniture that had not been imitated, to say nothing of those that had been directly copied. It amounted, in short, to a conquest of public taste all along the line, if not for the real thing at least for the most plausible substitute. In most of the substitutes there was dominant the desire to combine a "modern" look with mass production. Much of the integrity was sacrificed and in some cases all of it, but a bright popularization was still effective enough to capture the public. And the outcome has been more than a modification of taste. It has been a revolution.

Why had our friend not captured the vast market himself? Why had he scrupled to go in for the plausible simplicities of mass production? For two reasons, I think. He did not ignore the profit motive, since he wished to earn enough to be independent of that subjection which, benignly or malignly, comes into every normal life that does not square its accounts, and he had the success that his lofty experiment demanded. There he stood, right at the footlights, with bouquets in his arm. But, while not ignoring the profit motive, it seemed not to interest him. To conquer the field by going in for mass production was to ensure profit, but at the expense of that other and more inescapable motive, the passion for perfection. By serving this passion, which is a lonely one, he was really in touch with the best in Europe, with the Germans who were doing such lovely things, with the Swedes, with the English. And with his own people, right at hand.

5

We went on a pilgrimage with him to Sweden. With him was a great-great-grandson of the Dutch renaissance, a painter of historical pictures, a man from whom there bubbled a joy in the visual world, a joy that France had cultivated and that Denmark had employed. He was a great burgher to look at, with a round Dutch face out of which there twinkled, melted, scrutinized and peered with irony two of the most penetrating of eyes. Nature had not shot this man as a rocket to illuminate the void. He was burning steadily, like a great fat candle, a blessed candle in the temple of beauty. He'd stand in the Swedish woods bare-headed, with open arms, as if to roll forth a benediction. It was a sunny October. No apple on the tree was riper than himself. He was ready to hug me, as the slower modes of language were not so easy for us. As for furniture, carpets, arts and crafts, "industrial art," he professed no knowledge of such things. He gave his wheezy laugh, threw his arm over my shoulder and waved at the little lake before us, on which the crisp leaves floated before they sank to the bottom where ice would later frame them. This mellow sunlight, this amber, this coruscation —he did not ask for a single potted tree against a white wall, he asked for this profusion; and when we went to the old mill, with ropes of silver water twisting on the black wheel that splashed and labored, he stood in the archway that disclosed it and sang his canticle. Old age might track him down. Despair might invade him. He might crumble in his own esteem. But here, with his eyes to do reverence, the Gods had given him a theme. He and Adolphe Borie of Philadelphia, another painter, could not walk a yard without a vision.

At five in the morning, had I been so inclined, I could have risen to see Swedish glassmakers at work. We were at Orrefors. I waited till seven. These men put tubes to their mouths, like choirboys in an Italian picture, but what they blow is not sound but form. For two thousand years the method has not changed, and before our eyes we saw the molten masses grow clear and shapely, fashioned by an older craftsman whose power was like a surgeon's. He had the dignity of a master, controlling his gestures and his timing.

In a forest we met Strømberg, whose massive glass had light in it, but light as flown with color as bog water, and he himself was soldierly, yet simple and massive. These Swedes were not so plastic as the Danes. They had been carved out of a tougher material, yet possibly more brittle. They were hard at work, at home in this difficult medium, saying "thou" to our friend. We enjoyed an exquisite hospitality, but there was no nonsense in the workshop. These men were driving ahead.

In Stockholm we visited a dozen places that sold the work of craftsmen in furniture, in pottery, in textiles. We saw fine examples of pewter, decorative plaques in green and silver, hundreds of ravishing designs in cotton goods, long elegant tables in fine-grained wood and at last an exhibition where ladies wore peasant costumes and the stalls reminded one of innumerable other exhibitions and innumerable other stalls.

Through all this visit our friend maintained that somber attitude which the passion for perfection induces; he hurried from one scene to the other, like a general at the front; he surveyed at a glance the assemblages of earnest women; he did not condemn, he merely whirled to some other center where the battle was being infallibly lost. Our remarks fell into that cleavage between ourselves and the professional. He was alive to certain excellences, but for the most part the game was over, all was better unexpressed, night had fallen.

Only at Vadstena did he cheer up. We came to the church just as light was failing—you could almost see the day lowering its eyelids—and the church was bare, with bare stone walls on which the light lingered and fell. A gaunt statue of Christ was hung on the bare stones, a very old wooden statue, tense with dejection. The sight of it, so far from the cradle of this religion, elevated by faith on a northern wall and hung to catch the dying sun, filled us with the mystery of that forlorn heroism so remote and so present.

6

Like all keymen, our friend had his purpose in taking us to Sweden. He wanted our little flat to be furnished in our absence. His favorite hour for consulting with us, before we left, had been half-past seven or eight in the morning. He would have preferred half-past six or seven. We returned to a miracle; a commonplace had been transformed into a sober, almost secretive lyric. It had been done with a few things, all of them good.

"It's very nice," said a thickheaded visitor, "but"—and she chuckled—"when are you going to furnish it?"

To place a group of prints on the wall he had laid them on the floor, brooded on them, taken endless time and at last, with a lightning quickness, nailed them on the wall. It was as fixed as if he had been working in glass.

Now what can you do if you have not made this sort of thing your own medium? When he said, "Thus!" I could no more alter it than I'd alter a sunset. But if someone said to me, "Would you not like a Picasso, that wonderful study he has made in packing cases and balloon tires?" I'd say, "NO!" I'd take Guernica, an astoundingly expressive thing, but there are others of his that affect me as blood pudding affects me, which is unpleasantly; and even if they were a gift for which countless amateurs would beg on their knees, I would bow my head and say, "Nay, not for me." I know a dog that eats fish but averts his head in a sickish manner if you offer him bread and butter. I know other dogs that hate fish and love bread and butter. When preferences are formed to this extent and seem to reside in the pit of the stomach should you do anything about them? Our friend had blanched our walls and come near to spinach green in our couch cover, and the carpet was a warm gray. My young soul, my myopic and astigmatic eyes, my self-indulgent nature craved for something less white and green and gray. He smiled at me pityingly. On the right day he'd come with a golden apple and all would be well. But only on one day in Copenhagen, and then only in a certain fountain, does one see the golden apples dancing before one. I could not wait.

7

Every year, in that shop of his, he had an autumn exhibition to which twenty or thirty thousand people would sooner or later come. "Can a man lay a table?" He asked this question of a number of Copenhageners—a brilliant young actor, an opera singer, the leader of the ballet, a widely known newspaperman who'd correspond to a columnist, a musician, a gardener, a theatrical producer, a painter, a poet and so on. And, out of devilishness, he included myself. We were given carte blanche. We were allowed to ask for anything we wanted in Copenhagen—silverware, pottery, liquor bottles, actual food, anything. With this material, and the things in the shop, we were told to do our worst.

The night before the show was to open the entire staff was frantically busy till all hours. He could always count on this. No theater group could have had more passionate eagerness to co-operate with the artist than this staff with this producer. And those stories of the blackmailing trade unions with which American theatrical circles are replete—they could not be paralleled in this community. The Danish unions are not quite so bloodcurdlingly steeped in the profit motive. The gangster pattern, the hoodlum technique, are left to gangsters and hoodlums, out of which you may get a Gestapo. In this particular shop even ex-employees would turn up in an emergency and go on till three in the morning for the sake of a result they could be proud of. They asked to be "exploited."

All of us who knew how to lay a table were, as you might suspect, surrounded by anxious women. Still, we were dictators for that single evening, and the tables took marvelous shape. My own was a revenge on the asceticism that had been forced on me. I didn't have one tablecloth, I had three, green on yellow and yellow on wine color. I had a broad low Strømberg bowl in the center with live goldfish in it, on a little elevation, and around this wide low center I had bunches of grapes and vine leaves, embowering three of Kai Nielsen's nude statuettes; the silver was from Just Andersen, with our own Georgian forks and spoons (invisibly sewn to the tablecloth lest any absentminded beggar should come along); the plates were silvered, the decanters and the glass were richly tinted; and the whole effect, with four tall yellow chairs, would, as someone said, have pleased four cardinals in an earthy mood. It was in good bad taste, and I was horrified to see that it would be copied in dead earnest. There were crowds. "I went into Hackett's room," I heard a friend say, "and there was nothing to see but behinds."

Most of the other tables were refreshingly conceived. The exhibition was a huge success.

8

He did this in his own shop. He'd just as soon have done it without publicity in someone else's shop, and the people who helped him, like many of the people who flocked to see the result, were part of the community that vivifies aesthetic Copenhagen.

The singer, for example, could leave opera to give an evening to the Palestrina Choir. And he had designed every bit of the gorgeous Italianesque pottery on his table. The gardener, whose centerpiece was so subtly simple, had studied with Luther Burbank, and his garden was a place to which we made pilgrimages when a member gave us a ticket. The potter from down in Sjaelland was another to whom we made a visit, an artist who has a piece in the Metropolitan Museum in New York. So with the others. The game amused them, since it was festival, and they are accustomed to make a dinner a festival.

Our Designer invited us, one evening, to join some friends who were to do honor to the potter of Saxbo, Nathalie Krebs. A mysterious "committee," he said, had the celebration in charge. He spoke for the "committee." He acted for the "committee." He invited for the "committee." No other member of it ever materialized.

This turned out to be a banquet of eighty people. But instead of caterers, heavy white linen tablecloths, heavy dishes, heavy speeches, there was a circular table on trestles, paper tablecloths, flowers and leaves and tendrils for decoration, paper plates, beer and marvelous sandwiches, cake and coffee, with a dozen speeches that were quick, light and outspoken. This was in the circular loft, around the oven. And after this feast we went into a smaller room, the sample room, that was lit with hoops of candles, with fruits heaped so decoratively on tables that the look of the clean wood, the sight of the bowls of fruit, the glow of the candles, gave it festivity beyond one's hopes.

He had come out with a furniture van, turned the honored guest out of her working quarters and in a few hours hung the wall coverings, prepared and served this feast. Miss Krebs, still gasping at the surprise, rose to it like a heroine. Her chief workers spoke. Her old professor spoke. Her brother home from years in Manchuria spoke. Several of her ardent collectors spoke. It was a family gathering, in a sense, to which she could respond out of her heart in that dazzling, candid hour of celebration. Within a year she had a triumph in Stockholm, where the special purity and force of her art, the fineness of her glaze, the range and loveliness of her color, brought recognition that was no less welcome for being, as good criticism should be, hard to capture to begin with. But the banquet on paper plates, at the end of the tenth year, was one of those salutations that may even be more coveted, since it was a consensus of the fit and the few, without preamble, without conscription, without publicity. Only a worshiper of perfection could have improvised it.

9

I am rather averse to cliques, whether in them or out of them. All the notion of the Samurai, with which H. G. Wells once dallied but which he abandoned, left out of account the stagnancy of a group that, like a badly devised pool, is not flushed and emptied in a natural order.

If one gets into a clique where one is not oneself, the best thing is to zip out of it. Why keep up with the Joneses? To associate with poets, with dukes, with chimney sweeps, with millionaires, with chorus girls, has the advantage that it aids you to discover where you really belong. When the opening is too wide, when the whole world troops in, when there are so many Joneses that you have a Jones Beach, you do inevitably lose something, which is privacy. You can't be so inclusive that you eat not only the orange but the paper bag as well. How can you be so generously at home that there is no place to be at home in? How can you have a soul flattened by multitude, all entrance and exit, like the Grand Central Station? The emotions must have time to send down root and stay placed.

But when W. B. Yeats said to us that he could not join P. E. N. because it was so "heterogeneous," he raised an objection that has to be raised to life itself; and there are dangers in being homogeneous, as even the Abbey Theater discovered when they froze out Sean O'Casey. Those dangers, when ingress is jealously guarded and egress is excommunication, are probably unavoidable in certain forms of secret society, certain high-minded groupings like the Jesuits, certain tight cliques like the Pre-Raphaelites, certain bunches like Murder, Inc. But in a democratic order the only thing that makes a clique tolerable is its inner, rather than its outer inclusiveness. And that is not a snobbish one.

In Denmark, small as it is, one of my chief delights was to walk in off the street and hear the most recherché, the most subtle, the most trenchant lecture on civilization itself, at the simple cost of paying twenty-five cents. The people who came there were selected but they were self-selected, and if you felt like dropping out you did so. When the leading dramatic critic put on a very highbrow play at the Royal Theater, blending Don Juan with Don Quixote, every other dramatic critic felt free to write at great length about it, for the most part unsparingly. Had there been a clique to protect this distinguished man, there would have been another to denigrate him. But the Danes did not use this spiritual arena for guerrilla warfare. By associating with our aesthetic friend, in like manner, we were not banding ourselves with aesthetes. We were not either including or being included. We were living. We were electing whom to live with, of course, but as our own affair and out of resources that seemed to meet the case. Had we been Danes who felt too burly for this, we'd probably have gone to explore Greenland.

That shop had a fire on the hearth, and when you walked into it in winter it was friendly. At a certain hour the staff had tea, and if you really behaved like a member of the staff you could hardly be thrown out. Our Designer had grouped round himself a band of helpers who glowed for us like that fire. In art there are kinships, as among seagoing folk or medical men or anthropologists.

CHAPTER SEVENTEEN

We Eat and Drink

IN ONE RESPECT was it necessary for me to struggle with the guardian angel whom we had found in our Designer. He was the only Dane I had yet met who was departing from national tradition in a radical respect. He was determined to streamline me!

It is rare in life to meet anyone who is consistent. He was consistent. We had submitted to him on the score of taste in furniture. We had given into him on the arrangement of pictures. In these things he mastered a rhythm that I could not attain. We deferred to him on his preference for Bach. He shuddered when we played poor Tchaikovsky to him, as if we had spread red plush before him in its thickest and softest folds. We had followed him, slavishly as I thought, in his liking for an emaciated landscape, because he sought it as far as possible from human habitation, with no trace of man, without a shrub, or else with one tree that was writhing in solitude. We were ready at seven in the morning or at some thin spectral hour, whenever he gave the command, to be whirled to Sweden or to South Sjaelland. He asked us to go with him to see the sun dance at Whitsun, starting at three, or perhaps he didn't ask us; but we certainly joined him before dawn for early service at

Holmens Kirke on Christmas morning. It was rosy in the sky behind the trees. The air was crinkled with frost. The bells were ringing for Christmas. And in we went to a warm, bright church, a church *en gloire,* where, with a dozen others, we drank in the beauties of a service that had been modulated for a few hundred years.

But for this conformity, for this submission, I demanded recompense. I said, "Christmas service and coffee. No coffee, no Christmas service."

A man who had streamlined our home, streamlined our landscape, a man who ached to streamline my conversation and my books (ha! ha!) was finally, with fiendish resolution, trying to streamline my figure. He proposed a fortnight's starvation. So great would be the improvement, the illumination, he believed, that I'd never be the same. I was sure I'd never be the same. So I held out for coffee at à Porta's. It came at the right instant, steaming and excellent, when we had begun to freeze round the edges. It was one of those good moments when the animal man almost purrs. The best argument for hardship is the moment after it has ceased. So long as you are resilient enough for that, life is a victory. It is only when hardship is too prolonged, too cruel, too inhuman, that resilience is destroyed, and in that period one has to have something more than the animal man to draw on, some ultimate grip on life, some valid intention. I don't think stamp collecting would be enough, but some men, on the point of death, ask for their pink coat and hunting boots.

2

But in Denmark, of all places, the excellence of food is too assured, too understood, for any man to propose starvation to me. In this respect I am unashamed. A New Englander once told me that he dined with a vast churchman who, as he took his twelfth oyster, gurgled, "I eat only to nourish the body." Why this? I gratefully receive and heartily thank. A nation that gets a good mark in the kitchen, that can win praise from every kind of visitor—Hungarian, French, Turkish, American, English—has made a conquest where all are seeking approval. This approval can only be earned by men and women at a certain level of culture. Cooking is more than an indulgence. It is a social art. Pity the country that does not love flowers and does not love cooking.

3

There are fine distinctions I cannot draw. For years, in fact, I scarcely knew they existed. I was an ascetic young man. For many years I asked little of the world but bacon and eggs, but on a certain evening in Boston a light dawned on me. It was during the period when Ireland was fighting for self-government, and at that time I missed no chance of giving a talk on Ireland. That evening I spoke to the Woman's Club, where I was honored by the presence of Judge Julian Mack, and after the lecture he asked myself and a little black fighting cock called Harold Laski and a large, blond, sleepy, benevolent man called Aaron Aaronson to have supper at the Parker House. I was to take the train to New York when it was over.

The judge studied the menu with that intensity of concentration with which a jeweler would have studied a diamond. He sought for the flawless. Meanwhile, like a little angry cock, Harold Laski walked round and round Aaron Aaronson, who watched him through his light eyelashes with benevolent but apprehensive eyes. They were both greatly gifted men, but I felt that unless something was done one or other would be left dead on the field. Aaronson had been up against the Turks in Palestine. He was now up against Laski in Boston. They both had power, but the law of powerful cocks is that only one shall survive in the barnyard. Laski was my black Minorca. I was backing him, but I had yet to learn what the occasion of his ire was. I was greatly taken with this portly, slow-spoken patriot from Palestine.

Like so many cockfights, it never came off. It was not that the police arrived; the waiter arrived. He arrived with the caviar.

Judge Mack looked at it.

"That," he said in a voice that rose a little, "is Beluga caviar. I did not ask for Beluga caviar. I asked for Astrakhan caviar."

If the Parker House could have blushed, it blushed. The waiter crumbled into a little heap. So did I. It had dawned on me that up till that hour I had not known there could be such a difference. I was like a botany student to whom the examiner said, "What's that?" Algy said, "That's grass." The examiner grunted. "What do you call that, then?" Algy smiled. "That's grass too." "Well, Algy," said my father, "what mark did he give you?" Algy, being a good-natured English boy, replied with a sheepish smile, "Oh, Doctor, is it kind to ask?"

The Astrakhan caviar must have been in the vault. It came, it was miraculous. Even Laski, who lived on fish and chips by proletarian preference, moved gracefully back to the fish in that incipiency which is known as caviar. Judge Mack, the most hospitable man I ever knew, beamed with pleasure. The cockfight was averted forever.

I went to the train but not to sleep. I sat up to review a book by a young fellow called Sinclair Lewis. It was *The Job,* and I thought him promising, very promising.

That was the night I made up my mind I was an amateur in more fields than one. I could not write about working girls. I could not cockfight about Palestine. I could not ever know Beluga from Astrakhan.

4

With the proviso that I am neither gourmand nor gourmet I'll confess that Denmark, as against the home of Lea & Perrins, is the place in which I'd rather be hungry. But it is wrong to suggest a comparison. In England, if you can penetrate from the swamps of domesticity to those heights on which the elect are stockaded, you can nourish the body as well as any cardinal. But it is well to be born with a gold fork in your mouth. What is amiss in England is a separation between the classes so drastic that the perfect appointment and luxury of the tops have had no effect on the middles, who eat that excruciating rhubarb and those sour plums with custard and little squares of suet dough, who eat those slivers of unripe melon, a thing called brawn. Brawn! Oxo! Jam roll! Cocoa! How can people play "The Rosary" on their Stradivarius? I have eaten at a glum restaurant in London where the victims were red-nosed with dyspepsia, their fangs lengthening with desperate eagerness to bite into food. The Café Royal, The Ivy, a dozen other admirable places were not so far away, and yet this restaurant, like a house that turns its back to the landscape, went on and on.

"How beautiful!" exclaimed the lovely visitor to the Rogue River Valley.

"What's beautiful?" said the apple man.

"This!" she cried. "The place we're looking at!"

"Is that so?" he said. "I didn't know. I was born here."

But he knew from then on. If only the lovely Englishwomen would now take the alimentary gospel to the English people at large.

5

The first fact about Danish food is the fine conscience about raw materials. Their quality is not a matter of chance. The housewives have a very good notion of what materials ought to be. You have only to see three old ladies in a cheese shop, nibbling small samples with pinched lips, their eyes little points of skepticism, to gather that there is no detail so fine as to be unimportant to the consumer. The shopman does not grow impatient with them. He lives behind the rivulets of water that keeps his window moist for the cheese. He has Christian the Ninth, Holsteinborg, Brie, Swiss, Roquefort, Goat cheese of

We Eat and Drink

that queer mauve color, Primula, cream cheese, Samsø and ten other varieties. He has them in quantity. The minute you open the door and the alarm sounds he steps out, eyes you and moves to the cheese you favor. He wastes no words except in brief salutation and farewell, but he steers you to the right morsel and respects you for knowing it.

These cheeses are not the haphazard products of country people. They have been standardized. They have, if you will, been brought to a common factor. But because they do not have to be shipped long distances or made in immense factories for huge multitudes whose taste is rather crass, they can be transferred from the maker to the consumer with the least sacrifice of essential quality. If you go to shop on Store Kongensgade, with a keen eye to delectation, you can have cheese that almost bleats to be eaten at a certain hour, you can have a boy to whip it home to you in a minute; you can be sure that the entire object of all concerned is to give you a result of which no artist could feel ashamed.

And this artist in the cheese dealer is to be found in the butcher, in the vegetable man, in the florist, in the coffee grinder, in the chocolate maker, in the fruiterer.

Meat of the second class as well as of the first class. Each is marked. You can find it with its label on it and a white coat to sell it to you.

There are hundreds and hundreds of little shops, each of them striving to excel. If you want brioches or small cakes or hard rolls, you can discover almost certainly the precise nuance that you are seeking, because there are artists whose devotion to their métier surpasses their desire to make a sale. With a public so discriminating, with union hours so fixed, with rents and display and service so invariable, the good baker is assured of his good living. The community wishes him to have it, and all it asks in return is that he be a baker to bring comfort and solace to the hungry man. Young boys shoot off on bicycles at the instant the oven has disgorged. From the baker to the customer, if the bread ought to be fresh, there is not a second's delay. You go into a well-run shop, the window has told you exactly what you want, nimble girls bundle it up in white paper, the cash register tells no lie and off you pop. Certain of the famous bakeries are thronged like chapels. The servitors are magisterial. You feel privileged to be allowed to buy. And what you take home is so lasciviously delicious—I think of Wienerbrød—that you determine to swim half a mile the next day in palliation of your excess.

Vegetables in Denmark have not spent days housing themselves in freight cars. They leave the fields in the owner's wagon and come to you with the dew on them. The carrots have still the sap of life in them. They are not dry cellulose. The new potatoes are so thin-skinned, so naïve, that the world has not toughened them. Tomatoes come late, and their Dutch predecessors are not any the better for the voyage, but in the end they are good Northern tomatoes. Peas and beans are as the Lord intended them. Endives, Brussels sprouts, cauliflower, they are at prices not to be matched elsewhere, and they are good.

So are the flowers. There are hundreds of flower shops in Copenhagen. You buy them freely and frequently. The Danes cannot be happy without them, and they are mercifully cheap.

You have grapefruit, Jaffa oranges, bananas, grapes and all the rest, brought in shiploads direct to Copenhagen and at such prices that you can afford them. Fruit in London is more expensive by far, if you compare quality with quality. The Danes do not have to support so many landlords. They do not have to pay such dues. The wholesalers have not so tight a grip on them. They miss, on the other hand, the opportunity to amass wealth so superbly. Whenever I wished to rub shoulders with the wealthy at *peu de frais* I used to stroll through Covent Garden. There were dealers there so exuberant, so bursting with prosperity, to look at them was as good as eating a beefsteak. I rejoiced in them, but I prefer a less magnificent market that lets the public share the plums. As for fruit in Ireland, it was only procurable as Liverpool willed it, and it could be priced by the ounce. An ounce, I admit, would have been cheap.

To inquire what an economy like this in Denmark must have suffered by a derangement of shipping, by an interference with deliveries, by a series of gigantic shocks and breaks with custom, is merely to ask the old question: What good was this? A man smashes a Raadhus clock in order to give you a timepiece satisfactory to the New Order. He is the type of benefactor who leaves a human being bewildered. Has he a new clock to sell? Does he wish you to be his customer?

6

It may be objected—it is in fact often objected—that the Danish restaurant is not hygienic. This, I believe, is a misunderstanding. It is the habit of the Danes to eat lightly at home, where the morning meal is much more like the French than like the Dutch, the English or the American. Men who go to work in their office or factory will often take a few sandwiches with them, which they consume with a bottle of beer. These are sandwiches with a difference, however. There is no lid on them, in the first place. And the bread on which the sandwich reposes is a small slice, either French bread (white bread), rye bread or sour bread; while the meat is not a slab of ham or a slab of mutton, but any one of over a hundred kind of fish, game, egg, meat, vegetable, salad or fruit or macaroni or cheese. The object is not to stultify a man with a thick mass of bread that has a meat filling but to give him delicate and piquant diversity, for which special caterers exist in every town and village, selling tiny quantities of these things. Workingmen, office men, professional men, start off in the morning with their *mad-pakke*. So do admirals and generals. So does the crown prince when he goes shooting. And as for the standard of delectation, Peter Manniche tells a story so good that I'll steal it from him. "Until

1849," he says, "when the free constitution was adopted, the Danish army consisted of peasant soldiers officered largely by aristocrats. Under the democratic provisions of the constitution, the higher ranks were opened to all and, though the army remains the last refuge of class distinction in Denmark, even there the comradely spirit is evident. The story is told of a Danish army captain who, having some sandwiches left after the lunch rest on the training field, offered them to a group of men who were lying at rest in a ditch. 'Would anybody like these sandwiches?' Getting no response to his offer, he repeated it several times when finally a voice spoke up, 'What is in them, Captain?'"

But this lunch on sandwiches so-called is followed by coffee and cake about three. The dinner comes at night: a soup, a meat dish, perhaps applesauce, strawberries, a special kind of red-currant jelly, apple fritters and so on.

If the Dane goes to a restaurant, therefore, he goes for a special occasion. He is then likely to have a hearty meal, and the portions will be big and the sauces will be rich. It is often a celebration.

What the stranger discovers in such good restaurants of the solid kind as à Porta's on Kongens Nytorv is that the main dish he orders from a list of seven or eight is not ready to serve. He may have to wait twenty minutes for it. But when it comes, after this pernicious delay in which he curses à Porta, it is so freshly cooked, so perfectly savory and of such honest material that he forgets his wrath and becomes a carnal, sensuous man immersed in sensation. It may be veal, it may be goulash, it may be kidneys, it may be codfish with mustard sauce, it may be any of a dozen specialties, but the recipe is always artful and there is a chef behind the scenes who cares about these things as an artist should. After your main dish you have a dessert and coffee. It costs you about fifty cents. Can you do better?

You can cut this price in half and still fare superbly. I think of a Woman's Club where you are ashamed to face the bill, it is so small. You can go to a vegetarian restaurant and have a really irreproachable and delectable meal for about eighteen cents. I have been there scores of times. No tips. It is run by the Seventh-Day Adventists.

7

One of the chief features of a prison is the diet. If you want to bring home guilt to a man, if you want to depress him and knead him into dough, so that you can bake him into pretty nearly any shape you desire, you inquire from the sour-faced dietician what is the best way to do it, and then you prescribe for him. If he misbehaves on A, you give him B. If B leaves him cocky, you order D. You can finally run the roller over him till he is so thin that you can tie him into knots and he'll scarcely know himself. His body may not be thin but his disposition is. You have estranged him from himself. You have taken away his pet foods, his preferences, his special sustenances.

Under older methods of social tyranny there were special prohibitions that the Elders went in for. The Scarlet Letter said everything. You subdued man by this method and you subdued woman. But the Soviet discovered that to rule human beings by their stomachs, as was done in prisons, gave you a much firmer grip on them. Make them queue up for hours before the ticket you had grudgingly issued can be converted into the bare scrapings of a meal, and repeat this daily for six months, for a year, for five years, and your citizen at last realizes that life is no longer a place where he can buck up against authority. Life is a prison. The great iron claws of the Master have closed around the stomach. It is no longer your own. Your blood stream is no longer your own. Your children's bones are no longer theirs. If you have an opinion that is undesired, if you are startled into a glance that is undesired, if you have a nose that is undesired, you do not eat, or you eat just what sort of gray bread and skilly the Master cares to issue to you on a ticket.

The warders, the turnkeys, they'll eat, but you won't eat, because you are in prison.

What the Soviet discovered, the Nazis discovered. The stomach is the organ by which to rule mankind. Famine is the best teacher, but artificial famine. Feed the soldiers. At a Jesuit school the boys with the best marks are at the Pig's Table. Put the soldiers at the Pig's Table. But the ordinary man, keep him underfed. Argue that he must drink hay instead of tea, corn instead of coffee. Deplete him.

What crimes have the citizens committed that they must eat skilly and gray bread? The crime is citizenship. Their butter must go into the cannon, they are told. Till the cannon are victorious they are prisoners.

And can they eat then? Well, who knows? What do you mean by victorious?

8

If I complain in the U.S.A of the bread, the soft, spongy, spineless bread that is called Roaming in the Gloaming or Moby Dick or Mother's Day or some other sentimental name that is supposed to enamor me with aerated blotting paper, I can nevertheless find bread that peasants like. On Second Avenue, above Seventy-second Street, there is a shop that sells Italian bread to Italian workingmen. In Vineyard Haven there is a shop that sells Portuguese bread to the Portuguese. I'd travel twenty miles to buy an Italian or a Portuguese loaf in preference to any of these Krispy or Wispy contraptions that are made for people with teeth like rubber sponge. My teeth are tusks. I have been using them for half a century and they are still able to chew. I like to chew. A tough bread is worth chewing. On these grounds, though an alien, I feel entitled to criticize American bread. But even if I do criticize it, even if I do argue that the conditions that favor selling bread over a vast area, storing it and transporting it as wide distribution demands, may not be conditions that favor a pleasant and health-giving bread, at least this species of monopoly is unlike the monopoly of jail keepers. Human beings whose whole diet is determined from on high are like paupers in workhouses, tramps in work camps, convicts in cells. They are worse than waifs, whose deprivation is an ugly accident. These deprivations that are decreed by the New Order are intended. They are a means of asserting mastery, far more than a means of ensuring an economy.

9

Denmark had so ordered itself that everyone could have food and drink. Modest as incomes are, the people ate well at every level of income. It was one of the quiet securities of Denmark.

To wreck this in the name of a New Order is ironic. This New Order has taken away thousands of tons of butter in storage. It has killed the cattle, cut off the supplies of fodder, wrecked the economy. The napkins are left, and the carafes.

CHAPTER EIGHTEEN

Fighting Dane

DENMARK'S standard of life was high up till April 1940. But if men exist who do not respect their neighbor, if the neighbor's standard can be smashed at will, what, as a practical man, is one to say about it? However satisfactory the standard may have been, and I hope I have shown it was really so, the degree to which it was unprotected by arms made it a temptation to an exasperated power. It was vulnerable. And, if it was vulnerable, was it not also culpable? Is it not the duty of a nation to meet any emergency? Must it not band with others if it is not ready to stand alone?

After every disaster this practical question has to be faced. It is no use saying to the doctor, "But no one told me, Doctor!" If you did not look out for yourself, the loss is your own. We are none of us children, to blame a negligent parent. We are none of us imbeciles, to plead helplessness. Any sovereignty that wishes to be respected must be able to maintain itself under all circumstances, at least in theory. A toy state like Luxembourg may, perhaps, be preserved as a curiosity, but Denmark is a full nation, with full rights, full responsibilities.

2

Near the edge of the capital, to the north, there stands an old fort. It was once of importance perhaps. It is now no more protection against an enemy than a railing around a statue is protection against the birds. Possibly because of its commanding position on the water's edge, however, the Conservatives held it for the army. Useless as it was, it had a muscular look, a little bulge of power.

Then the Conservatives went out, and the Social Democrats dismantled it. In the bowl of it on the inside there was a flat bottom that could be flooded in winter, and it made a fine skating rink. We sometimes went up there in winter to see the young ones skating. The high ramparts all around it made an airy promenade, with green banks sloping down to the moat, and the moat itself had the welcome breadth of a river. The tall rushes that bordered it gave that dry, slightly metallic rustle which stirs a far memory of wastelands, silences, the cry of birds. One escaped from the city as one circled the moat.

And on the other side of this moat the Social Democrats made a swimming beach for city dwellers who could not go a long way. You walked through it in summer with swarms, mounds, of half-naked humanity almost under your feet, clustering by the water's edge. As summer enfeebled a few still swam there, and in winter, for sixty seconds by the watch, certain hardy ones, men and women, either broke the ice to enter the water or at any rate plunged into it under the ice-cold sky. The fort was forgotten. It was a free, happy playground, a people's park.

Mind you, the people were not as sightly on the swimming beach as the soldiers in uniform would have been. They did not sunburn so adorably as the girls who use creams and Skol. They turned a raw pink. They had features askew, at times, and bodies askew. They were not idyllic. Mrs de Peyster Vanderboop would not have loved it.

Still, there was a time when Caroline Vanderboop was a suffragist and antimilitarist and on the side of the people, and this would then have been a symbol for her of the successful struggle against militarism. A useless fortification had been condemned, and instead the people were asked to use it in order to enjoy and refresh themselves. A waste space near by had been turned into a lawn with what is termed the taxpayers' money. It was the most passive, the most outspread of defenseless spaces, where only a worm had to fear the predatory bird. Within view, on the lively waters of the Sound, plied the steamers and oil ships and sailing craft. An excursion boat to Klampenborg, where I once saw the stately Premier Stauning waiting for the streetcar, carried adventurers to that ultimate goal, a good cup of coffee. As the breeze swept across Charlottenlund one rejoiced in the amiable serenity of it. One pitied the Conservatives.

3

An army is like a fire escape. When you want it you want it terribly badly. But when you don't want it you are usually earnest in not wanting it. Take away the oppressive thing. Put it in the background. Bury it.

4

And this radical attitude is not only intelligible. It has been developed by events that are too quickly forgotten.

All the world over, until recently, the democrats were forced to remember who the soldiers had been. They had originally been illiterate strong-arm men, dominating the feeble. They had been the counts, the barons, the junkers, the lords and the landlords, with the army as their social weapon as well as their national. The Danes themselves had been faced with these fire-eaters, like the rest of the world. There had been no such violent schism in Denmark as that schism that has never healed in France, between the Dreyfusards and the anti-Dreyfusards. But the army was a great talking point with the Conservatives in Denmark—enough to induce in the Social Democrats their pronounced antimilitarism.

In a pleasant and perceptive volume of about forty years ago, called *Danish Life in Town and Country,* I did not expect to find Jessie Brochner summing this up. But her words are worth quoting:

"When the Conservatives," she says, "during their long tenure of office, appropriated the question of national defense for party purposes, and made it part and parcel of their political program, they did an ill turn to the cause they no doubt meant to serve."

This ill turn, as she explains, alienated "large sections of the nation" who saw vast sums of unvoted money applied to fortifications.

Among those large sections of the nation there were Social Democrats who formed rifle clubs. If the Conservatives intended to have a strong army and a strong foreign policy and meant to deny the people the full franchise, etc., etc., then the answer might best be made in the language the Conservatives were speaking. The Conservatives, in the end, were dislodged without the help of the rifle clubs, and the next step was to weaken the army. The democrats had no other choice. To strengthen it was to strengthen the enemies of Social Democracy as well as limit the funds available for betterment. No Danish demagogue argued for the brand of thing called National Socialism. Every effort was made to avoid bad blood. Every effort was made to bring about a peaceful revision of society on more or less Fabian lines; to get rid of the fires as well as the fire escapes and to develop a Fabian foreign policy. The democrats did not seek to put guns behind their wishes. They went into the League of Nations not because they loved England and France and the Versailles Treaty but because it was the one institution in the world which promised an orderly solution of all the inflammable questions in countries still strong-arm and militaristic.

The postwar mood was the same in democratic Denmark as it came to be in England and the United States. The war had taught the lesson of militarism, of its evils, its criminal waste and cruelty, its poisoning of the human spirit.

We had only to look at the bony children sent from Austria to Denmark to be fattened up to see what the war had done to innocent human beings. At fourteen they had the physical development of the Danish children of eight. Thousands and thousands of these stunted, emaciated urchins were imported in summer, free of duty, and nursed into strength by common Danish housewives who had warm hearts and decent homes. These Danish women did not say, "British blockade." They did not say, "Pan-Germanism, world power or downfall." They said, *stakkels børn,* poor children, *frygtelig krig,* horrible war.

Out of such deep impulses the Social Democrats came to victory in 1924. For the first time in parliamentary history a woman was chosen for a cabinet position in Denmark—Fru Nina Bang, minister of education and a first-rate minister. And at that time former Premier Zahle put his antimilitarism in a nutshell. He "declared that what the Radicals desired was equal rights for men and women, rich and poor. He emphasized the need for cutting down military expenses which now amount to between 50,000,000 kroner and 60,000,000 kroner annually. Dr Zahle wants this amount cut in two. He asks for direct taxation of the greater fortunes and stock companies, and thinks this would help in restoring the krone to its par value." (The *American-Scandinavian Review,* June 1924.)

That's the way the world was wagging in 1924. It all seemed simple. Convinced democrats like Norman Angell argued against war as the supreme irrationality, the great illusion. Stauning, the new premier who had been a cigar sorter, set out to govern Denmark rationally. Steincke, his minister of justice, had a personal interview with every convict in Denmark, as I remember. Bramsnaes, keen about people's schools, was finance minister. Borgbjerg was social minister. Count Carl Moltke was minister for foreign affairs. It was a ministry of good will and good sense.

In that same year the Conservatives in Sweden denounced various parties who "vie with each other in currying favor from an electorate that is disinclined now to make sacrifices for the defences of the realm."

Krupp by this time, I suppose, had moved to Sweden.

5

Did it ever occur to you that so innocent-looking an apparatus as a cash register could go to bed with a machine gun? Yet Marquis W. Childs mentions incidentally that "a powerful international combine, dominated by the National Cash Register Company in the United States and the Krupp interests in Germany, was responsible, co-operative leaders believed, for fixing the price level of cash registers." That's the sort of thing that the "Socialist-colored" Swedes were thinking about, while the Conservatives were thinking of coast defense, fortifications. "In Gøteborg," says the *American-Scandinavian Review,* "the abandonment of the coast fortifications has roused nothing short of desperation."

These things were outside the ken of Caroline de Peyster, our old friend. But she was beginning to prick up her ears at the wonderful news about Swedish matches.

6

Europe,.meanwhile, had begun to develop a germ that needed more than coast defenses to get the better of. And even a Dane, a good loyal Dane, could become infected with it.

It was in the train from Hamburg to Copenhagen that we first met our friend X.

In that quick, apprehensive glance that one usually gives to one's fellow travelers, he was clearly the one who evoked interest. He was then in the forties, I suppose. He was enough of a military man to retain his style even in his well-cut and well-used tweeds. He was lean, of middle height and keen as a hound. But a troubled wildness in his eyes showed him to be occupied with something not immediately present and not flatly obvious.

At the beginning I thought, "This must be an Englishman." It did soon turn out that he had served with a British regiment through the war of 1914–18. Yet his accent and a softness in his manners made it impossible that he should be English. The English, on the spiritual plane, seem to feel it necessary to remain bottled up until the cork is officially drawn. The Danes, on the contrary, make little fuss about protecting themselves from intrusion. And this Dane, complicated as he looked, had none of the languid indifference or frigidity or disdain that might have been anticipated from this elect appearance of his. Especially was I struck, when he spoke Danish to my wife, that his utterance was devoid of that practiced class distinction which is one of the finer insistences of English breeding. Good as the reasons are for the fine Englishman's protecting himself from the coarse and pungent Englishman—that onion—our fellow traveler was ready to entrust himself to us. And I watched him, seeing him open a little, and asked myself, "What is this bloke? Is he a diplomat?" I felt much attracted by him.

When it comes to behavior in a railway compartment I am wary. I have had Germans slam down the window without "by your leave," quite in the best tradition of their international conduct. But I have had Frenchmen do the same. Yet one of these Frenchmen might have been the bearded gent in Somerset Maugham's *Theatre* with whom the heroine finds herself in such intimacy, enchanted by his whiskers and unaware of his trying manners about ventilation in a daytime she was never to share with him. You cannot say of this Frenchman, "detestable on a train." The lady did not find him detestable. Her evidence would also be evidence. The most reserved Englishman, the utter clam and quahaug of Englishmen, starched by a tutor, ironed by a board of governors, might, on a slow train through the Dakotas, suddenly begin to talk to you about his wife. Once an actual English diplomat proffered me hobnailed advice that ran from him as simple and unpremeditated as if we had been cronies in a pub. He was a career man. Had he been born in the U.S.A. he might not have gone to Groton but he would then have gone to St Paul's. And said he to me, "If you can't get her to agree with you," meaning my wife, "kick her in the stomach." At the time I had no wife, and his own wife had an unimpaired front, as I later observed. I do not say that all English career men would talk like this on a train or even on a steamer. Most of those I've met could be better imagined taking out the Sealyham than doing or saying anything in the least violent or willful. They would curb their dog as faithfully as they curb their tongues, and that's faithfully. I quickly gave up the notion that our fellow traveler, whose ideas started to flow, could be a diplomat. He hadn't a silver screw top on the bottle, nor had he to be returned to the shop every time he had to be opened.

The cult of the gentleman, needless to say, must imply a method of subordinating not only the crass but every other sort of intruder on the fine and sensitive order, both of values and indulgences, that the gentleman has organized. Distinction demands distinction. But while inaccessibility has to be stressed so that freedom can be beautifully achieved, the object is your immunity, not the other fellow's exclusion. The end of all things is not to exclude for its own sake. A great, tremulous, so sensitive American author said to the English hostess on the upper landing of her own house, "But you are not going down among the Rabble?" She might invite the literary horde and feed them cake, but to mingle with them, to *contact* them. *Juste ciel!*

7

We had a great jaw with this new friend of ours, all the way to Warnemunde, across the Baltic and half the way to Copenhagen. He had a theory of beauty, and we wrestled with it; but as we talked on, and as we saw more of one another, it was the soldier in him that defined himself.

As a youth he had been sent to a German university. He was rather small and frail, it appeared. His German comrades thought it amusing to set him down. They were not subtle about it, and their sport rather depended on his being a Dane. They rubbed it in. They matched him against superiors, laughed at his defeat and enjoyed his being in a minority of one. The climax of this treatment came at a duel, in which the opponent meant to maim him. Being the son of a military man, however, our friend X was not so much at a disadvantage as had been calculated on, and in the upshot, when he had been goaded beyond endurance, he made up his mind that he would kill his big adversary but decided instead to sever his sword arm. And this he did. An instant change of mood came over the German youth. They wanted him to be dismissed. But he was upheld. He finished his course at the university.

This story made me scrutinize X very closely. He met my examination without wincing. And other stories followed that were in keeping.

When he told me about Manège I tried, as an Irishman, to look wise, but from what I could gather it was the art of horsemanship reduced to still life. You made the horse gallop but you kept him on the same spot.

> *Fast they come, fast they come,*
> *Faster and faster,*
> *Chief, vassal, page and groom,*
> *Tenant and master.*

But always like gallopers on the screen, never passing on, never overtaking. He spoke of it gravely when he turned up in riding boots saying, "Ah, my dear fellow."

He was inventing a gun, a cannon. My judgment on this was, if anything, less expert than my judgment of horsemanship, but he flattered me by telling me about it. His mind was absorbed by this extraordinary gun. The heads of the artillery in a foreign nation were pondering it, and if it had as much merit as the novel he showed me—well, the fragment of a novel, the upper right-hand shoulder of a novel—it was a genius's gun.

But little incidents from the war cropped up. There was the sentry who tried to stop him when he had to disclose a shortage of munitions. He had to break through. He took his revolver from his hip and shot the sentry dead. Yes, my dear fellow, he did. Oh yes! Out of his troubled, rather wonderful eyes he gave me this assurance, and I unfortunately had to believe him. He came to me once when I was in bed with a temperature of 102, and had it been 1002 it could not have made less impression on him. He was then closing in on the artillery chiefs who were to buy his gun. Did they buy it? No. But he had come a few hundred miles to see me and tell me.

When I'd say to him, "Look here, I am a democrat, a pacifist, a plebeian, we are at cross-purposes," he'd shake his head and smile. And then he'd tell me more war stories.

He was in Cork, during the war, and drinking in a pub. His novel, by the way, was about Ireland. He had written a fantastically somber and lovely poem about Ireland. But to relieve the tedium of his visit to this pub he made up his mind to stir up trouble. How to do it? He could not say anything against Ireland, even in earnest and certainly not in jest. He was not like those dear people who say, "I love the Irish but of course I wouldn't trust an Irishman out of my sight," poking you in the eye out of sheer jollity and light humor. He could not hurt these Cork men, so he said to his companion, "Watch out," and he cried out, "To hell with the Pope!" This, he said, was bound to incense them but not to wound their pride. It had the desired effect. Someone took a crack at him. Then it was "Belts, belts, belts, all the way down Silver Street." He came out of it alive, just alive.

8

When I said to people in Copenhagen, You must know X, they shook their heads. His father, yes, but not X. He had made no impression.

When we had first glanced at him, taking a sip before we dared to swallow, he had just that little twirl of personal style which I feel to be unforgettable. But in Denmark he went unnoticed. He walked across Raadhuspladsen, his head whirling with the art of wholesale manslaughter, and beyond seeing that he was an intent, neat man in riding boots, he had no existence. His was a seed that might as well have fallen on glass as fallen on Denmark. It had no soil in which to sprout, no latent Fascism to ferment in, no Nazism, no Stalinism.

I met another Dane who had so completely converted life into a theater of out-and-out assertion, of absolutes, of abstract violences. To associate with such men it is always necessary to give them their head, and not until they demand your head as well is it important to reveal that you have a will of your own; but during the long period in which my sympathy was unqualified—for he seemed to me at once fascinating and pathetic—I also realized how dangerous, how incalculably harmful a man like this could be in a responsive community. Had there been even two hundred Danes to gather round him, to echo him and give him ideas, he could have formulated a new Denmark, a Denmark of dark heroisms and sudden death, a Denmark like a vaulted night in which black forms were threatening, forms to be pierced with a sword of lightning.

Though he had one enemy, the Boche, he may himself have been partly German. But that never seems to handicap leadership. The Irish follow a half Spaniard. The Germans follow a half German. The English follow a half American. Other things being equal, his leadership would have been enhanced by his unfamiliar spiritual tones, his alien discipline. But other things were so far from being equal that he could not make the least headway in Denmark. He could not even make a living.

Sometimes a Dane bobbed up in the newspapers who had a little of the same élan. But whether it was a count or a baron, a man with a historic Conservative name or a frustrated careerist, the material for a cohesion of them, the militarist glue, did not ooze from their countrymen.

Had there been a few million war veterans, denied honor and prestige and pension, cheated of fame, told to eat black bread and wear sacking, you may imagine that a Dane like X could have been listened to, and he would have found burning words on his lips. It is not for lack of these germs that Denmark has avoided a militarist government. It has avoided it because the germs have died of inanition. There was not enough homicide to prepare Denmark for them, not enough desperate infidelity to humane standards, not enough wild dreams, bad nerves, drugs, inverted values and the thirst for glory. The process of derangement that kept America war conscious from 1860 to 1900, with the Bloody Shirt still waving in political campaigns, was so much more extensive in Europe, had so much more food for pugnacity in national differences, had so many richer sources of hatred to draw upon, that the thin squeak of dissidence in *Gone with the Wind* and *The Birth of a Nation* is a howling hurricane in the shattered men of Europe's thirties. Reconstruction! Now whole populations are to be reconstructed, and the carpets of all the magnates are to be made into bags. You cannot sprawl 200,000,000 people into a New Order without derangement, especially when the sources of the New Order go back to mutilated students and slain sentries.

9

At what stage the purpose of democracy ought to be fought for with bombers and tanks depends entirely on circumstances. One of the best men to argue against war, as said before, was Norman Angell, and yet Norman Angell argues for war against dictators with perfect conviction. So does Bertrand Russell. The time has come, in brief, when the system proposed to democrats is so intolerable that they must do or die. By deciding to "do" they risk all the psychic diseases that the last war promoted. By deciding to "do" they decide to kill, with all its pernicious consequences. But what has to "die" if they refuse to kill is something that the democrats have really set out to organize, something compassionate, humble and devoted, a comprehensive human attitude, a kind of religion. It is a rival religion to this one of pride and prejudice. It is also a conformity. But it is not that manège of galloping and standing still that X took pride in. It is not a prowess of the ego, narrowly consulted. It is the ego without any special tonsure and not vaunting its will.

Democracy is no patent device for germ killing. The Danes could not try the Norwegian way. The Norwegians could not try the Swedish way. The Swedes could not try the Finnish way. Each country, taking terrain and resources and neighbors into account, has to resist or submit as the situation presents itself. Denmark attacked by the Faroes would no doubt send out police and then arbitration commissioners. On principle it would give the Faroes independence, just as it gave Iceland independence, not because it is nerveless but because it is social, as opposed to military, in its conception of sovereignty. Confronted by a military autocracy, however, it no more can contend that its principle of foreign policy will work than Michelangelo's Florence could contend it, overwhelmed by the Emperor Charles V. The France on which Florence relied was

Fighting Dane 241

not up to the job, and military autocracies do thrive for a while on the feebleness of republics and the limpness of a militia.

But is the cure for this a society in which X is the leader? Neither Cesare Borgia nor the Medici saved Italy. It is not the adventurers or the bankers or the great artists who'll save Denmark. It is the good will and good sense in the heart's core of the people.

Had the Conservatives been able to give Denmark a few mountains, however, they could have got their army much more easily. The useless fortifications of Copenhagen were no substitute.

CHAPTER NINETEEN

Class Spiral

BUT if what we call a "democracy" has to be fought for, against an autocracy, certain little matters that were not cleared up in the war in Spain had better be mentioned frankly, lest the forces of democracy be themselves divided. If there must be a Class Struggle, as the Marxians state, if there must be a bloody revolution, then the old-fashioned liberals of my type must either pussyfoot, as we did about Spain, or we must commit ourselves to an ideology which, as Lancelot Hogben reports, has made Russia "a vast slum, from one end to the other."

"If we are to meet the 'revolution against' represented by Hitlerism," says Professor Max Lerner, "we must do it militantly and aggressively, with a revolutionary democratic force that challenges Hitler's revolutionary totalitarianism, with a revolutionary affirmative force that challenges Hitler's revolutionary nihilism. We cannot do this merely by defending our culture and our intellectual freedom. If we restrict ourselves to defense, we have three quarters lost the battle already. Scholars, writers and men of letters alike must today not only defend our system; they must also help transform it. In transforming it, the writer can have an important role. But let us not overestimate that role, and let us not ignore the fact that it will be frustrate unless it is linked with revolutionary social energies in labor, in the professions, in responsible business groups, in science, in politics."

That's the stuff for the marines, of course, but if Denmark is in truth a democracy, as I believe, and if it has got there without revolution, then Professor Lerner's hot demand for "a revolutionary democratic force" can only play the devil with understanding between groups who, in the end, must get together unless the Germans are to establish this so-called New Order.

2

My own hunch is that a class struggle is a waste of effort. I believe there ought to be a class spiral. By this I mean one of those double staircases by which those who go up are not stopped by those who go down. You see them in certain French castles. A society that can keep its members in motion, going from the less to the more responsible positions without being impeded, going from the more to the less responsible as quickly and freely as possible, is a society that obeys the spiral motion of life without introducing unnecessary convulsion. It is a system by which the Bottoms go right up. H. G. Wells and Arnold Bennett went from pretty near the bottom in England, with a fierce effort. Mussolini and Hitler did, in their own way, rise from the bottom. So did Felix Frankfurter and Henry Ford, for the matter of that, or hundreds of others who are known to us personally. But the ideal society is one in which the facility for ascent and descent in every kind of career, according to capacity, is so worked out that the private equipment for this facility does not cost society too much and the public equipment, on the other hand, does not cripple individuation. In a young society the best way to conquer poverty is to have cash. In an old society the best way is to have social organization. But if society is organized by the state inordinately, the "strong" democrat can be ousted by a "strong" antidemocrat, and the citizen is a slave. There are such dangers in this that I am amazed at socialists who still argue for centralization and more centralization. This is useful for a military autocracy, but the best friend that democracy has had in Denmark is its power of voluntary association as against the state, to instruct the state and counterbalance it. When Harold Laski was a young man he used to plead for pluralism.

3

This is no argument for the Hard Way. From my own experience of it, it is indubitably hard but it is by no means certainly a "way." The fact that Jenny Kammersgaard did, in fact, swim from Gedser to Warnemunde, the "hard way," is only a feeble argument against the ferryboat. The trip took Jenny thirty-five hours, and she's a whale.

4

What creates this feeling of class struggle is class stupidity, class blindness, class torpidity. But in a country where there is vivid social imagination I contend that the class struggle is a mistake. It is the business of writers, as I see it, to vivify social imagination in the first place, before whetting young egoists into a belief that they are the hope of "democracy" by the royal road of revolution. It is too wasteful. And it releases latent mania in human nature that soon becomes uncontrollable.

But social imagination, such as Denmark unquestionably possesses, is the product of solicitude, of fine breeding, of that slow and exquisite process that produces a civilization. You do not buy this at a cut rate. You do not go up the spiral at one bound. It has been my fate to deal with many youngsters who thought that they could leap out of college into literary criticism so long as they had a fountain pen. They would admit that it might take ten years for a man to become a surgeon, but to become a critic or a social prophet needs no apprenticeship.

Class Spiral

Try to cut your own hair, even! That should teach even a revolutionary humility.

5

It is a minor torture for me to have my hair cut. At one time I was so bored by it that I made up my mind to be revolutionary, to cut my own hair in future, and in the first five minutes I made such brilliant progress that I felt I had got rid of another inherited superstition and I promised myself an emancipated old age. But the hair is laid out in a cunning manner that gives barbers a low advantage. You get rid of the forelocks in no time. It is only as you work around to the back and begin to do the layering that you run into difficulties. The worst difficulty is the cropping of that bunch of senatorial hair which seems to keep warm the oratorical centers of French and American elder statesmen. Haircutting is like etching, once a mistake always a mistake. You can't improve your work by delving deeper. I left my head in tufts and hummocks, so that when I next went to a barber he said, "Do you mind telling me where you had your hair cut last?"

"Down the country," I said.

"I was thinking that," he said. "Was it very far down the country?"

Since then I have placed myself in the hands of the regular profession, and the best barber I had in Copenhagen was the proprietor of the barbershop in a good hotel. He and I like to talk. He talks in Danish. I talk in English. We are both fluent, and neither of us is very intelligible. But one day, as I was speaking to him of France and saying how I loved it, he stopped his scissors in mid-air.

"Have you ever worked for a Frenchman?"

"Not yet," I said.

"I have," he said dryly.

And as I left him I thought how glibly a tourist judges of a people whom he meets downstairs, so to speak, and in a way ceremonially, while all the life in the basement and in the kitchen and in the offices goes on without arousing his curiosity.

Arnold Bennett, a keen observer, crossed the Atlantic on the *Lusitania* and had the run of the ship. He wrote a dozen lucid pages about it—the dining room, the engine room and so on, as prettily described as you could imagine. Some time later I crossed the Atlantic on the *Lusitania*. I went steerage. During the five hours we were herded onto the ship in Liverpool, before the first- and second-class people came on, I had the direct experience of being an underdog. It was instructive. But before the voyage was over I had discovered that I was with the people I genuinely enjoyed. The stewards were warmhearted and helpful. The fellow passengers were unaffected, easy to talk to and extraordinarily satisfying to be with. It was a fascinating contrast of nations, a clash of strong colors, and I was moved and excited and diverted. But what had Arnold Bennett made of it? Not one solitary line did Arnold write about it. He had not happened to notice steerage.

"And how *did* you like it?" said Mr Booth, one of the owners of the Cunard Line. He had written a great work in eighteen volumes about Poverty in London.

"All except the codfish head in the rice pudding," I said.

You can't say things like this. Walter Lippmann was embarrassed. Mr Booth was chagrined. But wasn't I the fellow in whose rice pudding there lay the head of a codfish? Wasn't I the creature who had firsthand knowledge of this little segment of poverty? The thing doesn't bite into your social imagination quite so sharply until you live it. Mr Booth was a highly estimable man. His work on Poverty in London while not ending the phenomenon, described it in fitting terms. But I was fresh from the country-within-a-country that poverty is, and it ruffled him. I do not think he had come over steerage on the *Lusitania*.

There were details that I spared him, since the *Lusitania* was a magnificent ship and I had no wish to make him responsible for every fly that had blown into my eye. But my barber was right: you have to be in the other man's power to judge him for what he is really worth. Under the sunlight of polite and casual tourism you do pass over traits of character and realities of the social system that would otherwise make you measure your words.

6

I have never had a job in Denmark. Whether Illum's is better than Marshall Field's, seen from the basement, I cannot make known. Whether the state railways are better than the Chicago & Alton I cannot proclaim from personal experience. My hunch is that a man of my disposition, sweet as it is, would be irked by employment even in Denmark. The Danes themselves show the most amazing desire to be on their own. They are by no means quarrelsome and they are seldom sulky, but they do not yearn for the master-and-man relationship.

But while I have never been an employee in Denmark, I have lived in a plain workers' quarter in Copenhagen, in a worker's cottage in the country, in the cheapest of hotels, the humblest of boardinghouses. And, matching American experiences with Danish, I believe the spiral works well in Denmark.

There are, I admit, desperate situations in every kind of employment. The consultative method, so useful in government, is only at the beginning in industry. And if an employer clamps you down with iron, you are like a retort shut down so tight that the flame must drive you to an explosion. It needs no psychologist to explain most explosions in this manner, though diplomats sit by with perfect equanimity, watching the flame, seeing the bubbles and wondering how on earth the retort can stand it. Even good men, kind men, can be obtuse to the point that the Class Struggle seems as scientific as Marx argued it to be.

In my first year in America (I sailed in the era of William

McKinley) I ran into the iron law of wages. So I went to the chief of my employers, Judge Philbin. To that honorable and equitable man I said, "You pay me three-fifty a week. Could I have five dollars a week?"

He did not say, "Why, Hornblower, Byrne, Miller and Potter give their office boys seven-fifty. I think it opportune to tell you this. I wish you to be informed of all the facts that may enable us to arrive at a proper judgment."

On the contrary, he looked at me with a pained, almost tragic expression.

"Five dollars?" he said. *"Five dollars a week?"* He shook his head slowly and sadly. I had undermined the basic convictions of his life. "I can do it," he said, "but you must understand that if I do do it, it is very disappointing to me that you ask me to do it." He conveyed to me that if it was not actually in the New Testament it was in all probability in the Koran or the Talmud that office boys at three-fifty stayed at three-fifty until by geological process they were borne up to five dollars. That I had presumed to anticipate this process actually tore his trusting heart. My own heart was a shambles before he got through with me, but, under the stern laws of economic necessity, I kept on mumbling, "I'm afraid, sir, I can't live at all on less."

The little brutes get fifteen to eighteen dollars a week now. I asked one of them the other day to fill my fountain pen. He brought it back with a smile. It was wet. And it was empty. He had not had the brains to fill a fountain pen. When I discovered this, uptown, I understood why office boys have to be kept down.

7

Where there is no social imagination the situation is bad. Where there is a complete lack of social organization as well, the suffering can be so extreme that men must brood on revolution.

When I first lived in Chicago I gave up a job at forty dollars a month. I was commissioned to write a book, on which I was given an advance, the princely sum of one hundred dollars. The book was to tell people how to become both well and beautiful. It was known to me as *Beauty and Health*. The best chapter in it, derived from tomes in the Newbery Library, was "On the Care of the Baby." All of the book was as good as brains without experience could make it. With a loan from my brother I settled down to this task, and I was careful not to waste my pennies. My room on Superior Street cost me a dollar a week.

It was a house with unwashed windows, filmed with slimy dust. So long as it was "for rent" my landlady was allowed to live in it as caretaker, rent free. I was an extra, in a single room upstairs. She lived in the dark basement with her five-year-old boy. The dollar from me was a weekly revenue that meant a lot to her, since it was cash and she had little or none of it.

The house was unheated, and it was the dead of winter. This can be severe in Chicago. The house was unfurnished except for the barest miserable outfit in my room. Bed linen, it could not have been called that. The quilt was alarming. Yet it was so cold in that grimy room, under the grimy coverings, that I hated to step to the grimy floor in the morning. A bath, in the cavern that was called a bathroom, was an event that brought my landlady from the basement with a zinc bucket of steaming water. The towels were gray and torn; the tub itself was filmed with a grayness in which one stood to scrub oneself by the light of a candle. We had no electricity.

My landlady had that leanness one sometimes sees in a stray animal. She had the same hunted, outcast temper, the mood of a creature so baffled and consequently so savage that it was impossible to woo her confidence and scarcely possible to come within talking distance. Whatever had happened to her—she was straight from the country, with her child—was wrapped and hidden like a wound. A gaunt woman with troubled gray eyes, her wisps of hair were in disorder, as unwashed as herself, and her hand clutched at the neck of an upper garment that needed a button. She was willing enough to help, eager to do it, but it was makeshift, haphazard, and when I went out to the palatial meals I could buy for a quarter in a saloon I was glad to forget this rawboned country woman whom life had cornered in a Chicago cellar.

Christmas came. I was spending it by myself. About eleven she knocked on my door and, standing outside, asked me if I'd share dinner with herself and her child. I accepted. It was to be in the middle of the day.

She had cooked dinner, God knows how, in that dingy basement. It was livid corned beef with cabbage, mounds of warmish, greasy cabbage, and big moist lumps of potatoes. There was enough on my plate for four. Her red hands were scrubbed. She loaded my plate again, until I had to stop her. We sat there, inarticulate, munching and mumbling, the small boy devouring me as well as his dinner with red, incredulous eyes. She could not understand how I ate so little. So little! I was still laboring at the mountain of cabbage when I saw there was to be a pudding. She had done her best with it, this prairie refugee who had fled from some home, some man, to find a lair in that vast, roaring, good-natured welter. And even in the fiercest hour of her rebellion she could not deny Christmas Day.

That came to its end. By spring, still alien to one another, we went our ways. Our Christmas dinner was the sole monument to our life under the same roof. A monument of generosity, a mound of cabbage. She had forced herself to offer it to a man.

When one has had even a small sample of poverty—and poverty begins where soap ends—it does help the imagination. I am one of the lesser breed who think of greasy food with aversion, who detest the blubber that would delight the Eskimo, who shrink from rancidity and entrails, though knowing that in the Arctic I might be glad of them. But bad as poverty is, and abominable as its continuation is, the struggle against it is not always won when a privileged class is overthrown. A New Order, a new

Class Spiral

order of the Privileged, is so likely to secure power that the revolution is both costly and unprofitable.

A civilization that is founded on the pursuit of happiness—that's the civilization for me. For that reason I distrust the absolutists. When long-faced men begin to talk to me of "sacrifiss, sacrifiss," I know them as Solemn Covenanters who would be ungrateful to Heaven for fricassee of chicken. Let's postpone delectation, if we must, and be stout fellows if we are, but let's be loyal to delight if we can earn it. Great Stonewall Jackson, refusing to read by any light except the light of God's sun, was no more fanatic about his Bible than the Marxians are about theirs. The fanatic hides under every noble cause and noble impulse, yearning to crucify the flesh and to reach the apex, which is revolution and sacrifice. But these are urges of which economics merely serve the turn. In the sixteenth century exactly the same men were ready for religious war. Some men thirst for Armageddon in every generation.

For this reason I have learned to go slow in condemning any "class." And the longer I lived in Denmark, the more I revised my earlier class assumptions. If these are persisted in, indeed, the Germans can give short shrift to democracy. Democracy can provide and demand class mobility. It cannot demand the proscription of any classes, unless it is willing to be overthrown.

CHAPTER TWENTY

I Find Grandfather

IN DENMARK I found Grandfather. I did not, as a literal fact, find a bearded old Mr Hackett who had been wandering on the Continent since 1850. But I met him in the spirit, for the first time. I had previously met a Hackett in Albany, N.Y., whose father had come with him from Australia. The old gentleman whom I now encountered had had a brother die in Jamaica. He also had had an uncle who was a dignitary in Penang. I myself had a brother who lived for years in China, a sister who was educated in Germany and died in France, another brother who lives in Australia and a third brother who broke my heart by never receiving his decoration from the Portuguese. But it is dear Grandfather of whom I now wish to speak, the late Bartholomew.

Walking along Strøget in Copenhagen, I realized I was short of cash. What was extraordinary was that I had a check in my pocket on a Copenhagen bank. This was a beautifully situated bank, with a churchyard next door whose noble trees rose above the railings, and the pleasure that it gave me to enter a bank so situated has remained with me since. But there was a greater pleasure in store for me, the pleasure of tickled vanity. As I waited for my check to be cashed, floating like an expanded

I Find Grandfather

berry in the sweet soup of deference, a young official with well-marked, handsome features, a fine brow, a high complexion and raven hair appeared at the opening opposite me.

"Do you know a Francis Hackett," he said, "who has written a short history of the Irish nation?"

I sure did.

"I have read it."

He was speaking in English and smiling. He had good teeth. He had, in fact, almost the best teeth I have ever seen.

"Then you've been in Ireland?"

"Never."

"But you speak English. Where did you——"

"At school."

"And how have you happened to——"

"Oh, I have seventy books on Ireland."

His manner apologized for it. I gasped and spluttered. Who in the world would want to read seventy books on Ireland, without stirring from Denmark, sitting under a student's lamp in Copenhagen! This man looked like a poetic athlete, and it soon came out that he had read all of James Stephens, had indeed translated James Stephens into Danish, worshiped James Stephens. I knew James Stephens, that ennobled asp, had been stung by him, had I hope stung him in turn and had once, during a whole long night, sat in a third-class carriage from Holyhead to London while James Stephens gave three Irish shopboys and two or three girls going back to service the fullest evening they had ever had in a railway carriage. On the platform at Euston one of the girls came to me. "Thanks," she said with head cast down but a twinkle hidden, "thanks for the entertainment." She might well have thanked me. I was the man who had held James Stephens' heel in his hand so that Stephens could spring from it to loop the loop, wild and fanciful loops with a divine idiocy in them. But it was not this child of caprice my Dane had translated. It was a poet. The two little butts of horns that spring from that satyr's head, the neat cloven hoofs, the bearded tail—it was not that pagan Stephens with onyx eyes that he most valued, but a poet, a certified member of the Irish union of poets and a union for which James was one of the walking delegates.

"May I take the liberty," said I to the banking official, "of asking how you came to have this amazing interest in a land you've never seen?"

"Esperanto," he said.

"Eh?"

"As a boy I began writing to other Esperantists. There were two who answered me from Ireland. But soon we turned from Esperanto to English. One of them is So, and the other is So-and-So."

I knew So by name. I didn't yet know So-and-So. But in the course of years I was to make his acquaintance. He was Delargy, an Irishman with a living flame in him, whose great energy and passion and organizing ability has been going into collecting Irish folklore in time to save it from that dreadful obliteration in which man's past so molders away that his present is a thing in two dimensions. Delargy has deepened Ireland by framing it and carrying the eye into those remotenesses of fantasy where the Irish folk had their abode during years of penury and enslavement. He has rediscovered what the Irish folk were thinking, for example, in those years when Oliver Cromwell was their Hitler, and this he has done out of old men and women thrown by society on the scrap heap, books in gray paper covers, so to speak, thorn books in the ditch. And it is not Cromwell who is the villain in this retrospect. It is the Irish themselves who are scorned, as if the French in the year 2240 should come on the self-reproach now seething in the heart of France.

Delargy's method, however, had to be learned outside Ireland. It had been learned from Scandinavia. And he and a great Irish scholar came to Copenhagen for one of those international conferences that alleviate the sad lot of the intellectual, teaching

I Find Grandfather

him about his colleagues in far places, teaching him about museums, libraries, Carlsberg, Tuborg, Aalborg and all the other subjects for research and comparative statistics.

Now we come to Grandfather.

"Your grandfather," said Delargy to me, as we sat at lunch with the great Irish scholar and the raven-haired bank *inspektør*.

"I had two of them," I said, "Philip and Bartholomew."

"I am thinking," he said, "of writing a piece about your grandfather. His letters in the Royal Irish Academy show that he, like Oscar Wilde's father, was a man with a true instinct for folklore, nearly a hundred years ago."

I said nothing. For the first time in my life I adverted to Grandfather. He had, then, existed.

2

We are creatures of fierce prejudice. We have memories like dogs, memories of pain and pleasure, feelings so plastic that we are like a pot on the wheel in the first minutes and then hardened in the oven so that our shape can be told by shards for five thousand years.

This paternal grandfather, in whom Delargy wished to give me pride, had been removed from me by my mother.

I remember Grandfather's widow. In fact, Grandmother. She was an old lady who came into our family on a silver tray. She lived in an enclave entirely surrounded by young Hacketts, a fragile old lady on a silver tray. She was one of those gentle, nibbling, persistent old ladies whose will power is incorrigible, a relic of an ancient order, still thinking of the grapes in a hothouse that had gone cold in the years of the Famine. The distillery had subsided about her ears, which she had muffled. She ate herring after the Famine, with salmon in her mind. Clinging to her son, she retreated to a scramble from poverty that only his resolve to be a doctor saved from a disaster and a rout. My father was strong. He went on being a squire, yet learning to be a patriot and in love with medicine. As he clambered out of the pit this gentle mother of his and a gentle sister held to him. They cast their eyes around for a wife for him. Soon there would be another hothouse and a little salmon on the silver tray.

He was out shooting. A farmhouse stood on a plateau, looking out on the soft blue hills. As he walked into the yard a girl with golden hair was milking a cow. He was the young doctor, she had gone to school in Dublin, her father was a "strong farmer," and in that instant, if you please, I was born. Not, however, until a dozen or so had been born before me. These things take time.

My mother was a strong-minded woman, and it was not unknown to her that the old lady on the silver tray would have preferred another solution. With ten little Hacketts romping, screaming, hopping, skipping, in the home of the doctor struggling to bring up a family that would not too much interfere with his snipe and his partridge, his hunting and his cricket, the whole weight of the experiment fell on my mother's broad and willing shoulders, a grim experiment that he took with lightheartedness, gay as a bird. He was gallant, intelligent and devoted. She slugged along, crushed by the burden for which the nuns in Dublin had not given her the slightest technique and pecked at by all the matrons who envied her the charming doctor.

Not being a lady, in their provincial reckoning, my mother had either to rise above them or to combat them. She was harassed by hard work, unsure of herself, aware of subtleties in her husband that were beyond her ken, yet powerful, authoritative and in her way formidable. In spite of his delight in life and his efforts to mellow her, she knew what was inimical, even in the gentle old grandmother. That silver tray on the sideboard was as much a sign of it as three balls signify a pawnbroker.

I was on my mother's side. In those first ten years of feeling life I became a stubborn partisan. If an upper class has silver scales above, it has a plain belly underneath. It was this side of it I saw. My grandmother's complaints (she whimpered like a little greyhound) were caustically and ironically greeted. Her delicacies—ah, that dreadful day when the young ones wedded her precious canister of tea to her precious private jam. It was that incursion, I suppose, that brought the family experiment to a close. But my grandmother was not precisely crushed for all time. She retired to Dublin and lived to be ninety-three.

These social prejudices of mine, born of loyalty to my mother, were already so strong that I revolted against everything the silver tray symbolized. I disowned refined cousins, pious aunts, remote uncles. I disowned Grandfather. I embraced the proletariat and became a member of the Workingmen's Club at the age of eight.

But it was no Oedipus Complex. My mother would have given Oedipus a resounding thump.

3

A class prejudice is easy to fortify. My mother was right to feel wroth at the mincing, preening, tittering provincials, pale decoctions of an English class myth, who took themselves to have more breeding than a farmer's daughter and a higher culture than the deep folk culture of the farm. But strong as my mother's feeling was, and hard as the case was, she was daunted. Her name was Bridget. She signed it B. She gave significance to the sneers and pinpricks of those who were not refined enough to be perceptive but were privileged enough to be cruel. Proud as she was inherently, she resented the privilege denied her and fought for it and exaggerated it. In a word, she thought these enemies more refined and of more substance than they were. By the degree to which they could hurt her and injure her, she believed them superior.

Once, when she was a young thing, she had started home at twilight from the village chapel. She was alone and a bit scared. As she mounted the hill she heard steps behind her and walked faster. The steps came faster. She slowed down and the steps slowed, so she broke into a run, and the steps ran after her. Not till she had reached and crossed the stile did she have courage enough to look back over her shoulder. And there stood a calf, as lonely as herself.

Had she surmounted her class prejudices and really looked at the women who made her uneasy she'd have found most of them calves, some the calves of old cows and some the calves of old deers. But for forty years she preferred to tilt at them and scorn them. She was the victim of her own misgivings.

Those misgivings must have been intertwined with apprehensions for her growing family as well as herself. Far be it from me to make little of them. The least flick of criticism is unbearable to most of us, and as Arnold Bennett once said to me, some of us, even the best of us, don't dare to read even a printed criticism. (I had happened to praise a certain author. Bennett's face clouded. "That man? He wrote—did you not see the thing he wrote about me?")

Violently as we churn with resentments, natural as they are, spurring as they are, the curse of early class prejudice is its unsuspected yet irreversible nature. We all have in us a root of that which sprouts into a persecution mania, and if class prejudice has this sap in it, a bloody revolution can be derived from it. The tragedy is this: however well founded the original anger was, the objects of it may go on wearing the same clothes but they seldom preserve the same animus, while the prejudice fixes sternly on the badge of privilege. Thus certain Irish-Americans go on hating a Britain of their early childhood, a Britain of puffed-up bladders, a Britain of Blimps. To hate this Britain when a new one is itself puncturing the Blimps seems to me a preposterous waste of spiritual effort. It is the privilege, not the privileged, that has to be demolished. It is not the Hapsburgs, the Romanoffs, the Hohenzollerns, the Bourbons, who are worth hating in 1940. You might as well hate

I Find Grandfather

dolmans and bustles. Irish-Americans go on trembling about the Rebellion of '98 when the Hessians have now mastered weapons that can compress '98 into an hour. Hatreds should be brought up-to-date. The objects of them should be dynamic.

4

The Danish nobility could, I suppose, be assimilated to the English nobility, with whom it has many traits in common, but it is relatively not so rich, not so entrenched, not so privileged. Being for the most part a landed nobility, it has been gradually edged off its estates. The cash that has compensated it for the land is not enough to buy privileges elsewhere. To say that it has been expropriated would be too much, but it has been dislodged from its political and economic dominance.

Certain members of it run their estates at a profit, under modern conditions, and they are eminent in their localities. Certain others are high in diplomacy. A fair proportion have other sources of wealth than the land, and they live as the upper class does everywhere. A very large number have had to earn their living in the open market, by starting shops, by plying one craft or another, by practicing law or medicine, by painting or doing sculpture, by writing, by journalism, by going into the advertising business, by developing photographs, dentistry and the rest.

Newcomers like ourselves did not arm ourselves with letters to the kind of Danes who live in society. That is a profession in itself. But in the course of time, by one accident or another, we ran into people. A friend in Persia told a man to look me up, for instance, and at lunch I found myself next an unusually pleasant companion who in turn said, "Come to lunch."

Before we got there, on that cruel day, it was almost as if it had been in Persia. It was a delusively bright day in the early part of the year, and a wind from the north came with such knifing force that our car, a small English Standard, bucked like a nervous bronco, or rather scalloped along on a highway that was quiveringly biffed. I said to the Standard, "Go it." It did its best. But even before we reached the byroad we were late. It took us an hour and a half to land there, and my social consistency by that time had been ruined. I was a pulp.

Yet here, on the edge of a fiord, there stood a house so serene in itself, so self-imposed and self-possessed, that even the desolation of delaying a party of a dozen or fourteen could not shatter my impression of it. I sat next a singularly intelligent woman. She was in a high place at court. She reminded me in certain ways of the finer Jesuits I had known. She looked at me along her clever nose with a delicious discrimination, and she had the physical finesse of a yacht. What, after all, is the nobility for? If there is any law in the world, it is that man, given a chance, will carry aptitude to the limit. He begins with a wild horse. He ends with Saint Simon. He begins with a grunt. He ends with the Memoirs of Saint Simon. He begins with a nightmare. He ends with Simon Stylites. You cannot keep man off a pinnacle if he is allowed to persist and to cultivate himself, and the aristocrat at his best can turn round in an intimacy just as adroitly as a taximan can turn round in a street. A professor often cuts too deep. A politician is too obviously cordial. A soldier is metallic. A sailor is bluff. A journalist is so much at ease in Zion that he perches on the judgment seat. But with the nobility, such as this company revealed it, there was a simple and effortless social veracity leading to such amiable interchange that the effect was to enhance not only existence but one's sense of one's happy presence in it.

Our unpunctuality—oh God, give us a Buick—was an indistinguishable crack in the golden bowl, but only for ourselves. The golden bowl remained, however, and for me it was restored in the room where we had coffee.

If there is to be conversation, let it be in a room on the level of the lawn, with tall windows that lift the room, with furniture so graceful and carpets so gay yet so little assertive that they

I Find Grandfather

linger in memory like certain yellows, and with persons whose voices chime, whose smiles are cordial, whose eagerness is unforced.

The sun came through the long windows. That briskness of the wind, sharp like young teeth, was only a smiling blue outside. We spoke of everything one cares about—of the French, of Europe, of Schnabel, of old photographs on a screen. They seemed to me desirable people, the way sound apples or peaches seem desirable. They were not laid out on a green leaf like a single peach in a window in Piccadilly, a Queen of Sheba among peaches. They were no less consummate for being four or five in a room. We left there no more intimate than we came, but it has for me the quality of one of my dreams. I occasionally dream of a room I have never been in, with charming people in it, some of whom I have known and perhaps loved, and the dream has the merit of slowness and penetrating individuality. This actual visit had a touch of the same enchantment. It was gentle, cool and perfectly culminated, so far as it went, with that slight inconsequence which is inseparable from a flower.

These Danish houses are called manor houses sometimes, and sometimes they are slots, like the German schloss. The word castle is too ponderous for them. I am not sure that the slots, dotted round the country, do so much less for it than the dairies. Without the co-operative dairies hundred of thousands would be miserable, but a slot like this I speak of, a moment of Europe in its prime, intent on the amenities, must be ascertained on some terms as soon as any society is relieved from want. It is, in reality, inconsequent. It is just a flower. To meet, as we did that day, to interchange without the faintest trace of purpose, was at the farthest point from utility that we could possibly arrive. It gave me pleasure, not because it satisfied my curiosity, though this is always a good deal, but because it enabled my curiosity to employ itself on a texture in which the number of stitches to the inch surpassed my hopes.

5

Out of this meeting came three or four others. We went to certain old houses and found beauty in them and charming people who like to talk.

It was different from London. There is a positiveness, a so-called realism, about London for which you'd better be prepared. No one is secure there, not even a king on his throne. It is a city of the most vigorous appetites, the most potent and thrusting adventurers, the most expert gate-crashers and the handsomest rewards. It doesn't do to have a thin skin with these English in London. They are a sturdy, tenacious and somewhat unimaginative folk. If they hurt you, it is extremely important not to give it undue importance. If you are dealing with a real Englishman—not a made-over Welshman or a Scot—the vital point is to break through his obtuseness and his suppressed gout to the warmhearted, resilient and magnanimous creature underneath. Clarence Day wrote a great book about the English when he wrote *Life with Father*. But if the English hurt you, and you resent it and are spiteful, you get nowhere with them. There is a truculence in them that is quickly aroused, and they tend to be intolerant. They are not, as a rule, on such close terms with themselves that they can look at themselves directly. They are at their best when you do something with them rather than talk with them. They like you best if you can shoot, punt, bowl, ride or do tricks. You win their hearts by some schoolboy dexterity. They admire prowess, though they belittle an enemy's prowess so contemptuously that you'd suppose, from talking to them or rather listening to them, that no other nation had ever colonized, had ever built ships, had ever kept faith or had ever appreciated singleness of purpose. They can tell, after a while, how much you are falling for this stuff, and if you don't bat an eye but return these blank checks on your credulity with the words "no funds"

I Find Grandfather

on them, you may be sure, if they think you are congenial, that you'll arrive at a genuine understanding which may even become deep-seated and affectionate. They are the most loyal friends in the world. But only a small proportion have cut through tangles of instinct into those clearings where the full intelligence can play with anything and everything. When the English arrive there they arrive full-bodied and invincible, the most heartening, tolerant, racy and luminous of companions. These are a liberating people, an emancipated people, and for their sake much may be forgiven, the wags and the hags, the boors and the bores.

England, however, is a power country, and the play of the mind in a power country is much restricted among acquaintances. The English are expert at censorship. They do not club down the adversary. They snub him. They boycott him. It is for this reason perhaps that they prefer a platitudinous mediocrity as prime minister to a man who cannot possibly be censored, however boycotted and snubbed.

No one can tell me about free speech in England, except as a legal concept. In practice the English are so conditioned that true freedom in ideas is rather hampered, especially by the fact that the vast majority of the women are undereducated and without intellectual curiosity. Ideas are not systematically marshaled by the state, as in Germany, and in this sense the English possess and love freedom. But if you study the British Broadcasting Corporation's method, you see how many topics are avoided, how many dishes are prepared and how punctiliously correct, to the point of utter fatuity, most of the official offerings are. Rothermere and the Berrys, the big news vendors, are magnates of stupendous power and right thinking. They cramp English intelligence in order to preserve its docility, and if you wish to find sharp intelligence you must go to places where indocility is obligatory and intelligence is perverse.

By good luck we knew an American who had settled in England and had been adopted by it, since she was the most adorable of human beings. She used to say, "The tops and the bottoms here are the best in the world." The part that she did not commend, the part processed by Rothermere and the Berry magnates, was by far the greater part. The "bottoms" had folk culture and would have attracted her anywhere, but the "tops" wished to remain "tops" so ardently that they issued few tickets of admission to their kin the middle of the barrel. "You're an engineer? Oh, I thought you were a gentleman." It is that sort of conditioning which makes the great democracy of England so uninteresting to live with. The engineers, the technicians, the craftsmen, the inventors, snubbed by muddied oafs and boycotted by flanneled fools. Had this not been grappled with early in 1940, England would have gaped open, as France did, to invite the Nazi in. But in spite of Rothermere's pro-Nazi propaganda, carried on for years, the long-maintained docilities are breaking up, and a whole people is being fused in a struggle that should educate not only the in-betweens but also the tops and bottoms.

6

Do you want to be an in-between? A shocking thing was said to me by King, a steward on the *Mauretania,* second class. Said King, "The middle class, sir? I don't belong to it meself, but it's a splendid class, sir." King knew his place, yet in Heaven, who knows, I may be blowing a trombone with King at one side and another King at the other. Who then is to pin a second-class ticket on him or me? We'll be three Kings in Heaven. A rank may be a convenience. It should scarcely be a state of mind. Yet to escape it, whoever you may be, you must not gate-crash Heaven. You must practice the trombone.

7

It would be inconceivable in Denmark that anyone whom you met at lunch would greet you the next day with eyes like

I Find Grandfather

eggs. The English are so afraid of losing their social integrity that they do sincerely think of others as Untouchables. The Danes do not. They are aware, I imagine, of distinctions between man and man. They do not visibly worry about them. They are not troubled by slight incongruities. A major in the army will cycle along Bredgade, his sword in one hand. Were he to do this down Piccadilly, on his way to the court, he'd be classed, yes, *classed,* as a lunatic. To be treated civilly in Copenhagen you need only be civil. To be treated civilly in London it is best to have a Mayfair address. If you stay at Brown's and then marvel at English sweetness, you are still an American. But if you stay at the Regent Palace with Tom, Dick and Harry, then the parasites won't give much heed to you. In England and Ireland there are hundreds who envy you and look up to you if you have money. In Denmark there are fewer parasites. I am not sure, after all, that co-operative dairies are not more aesthetic than castles, since they eliminate parasites.

It is a sad fact that the only real peasants I have seen in Denmark—I mean the sodden, dejected and opaque kind—have been in the neighborhood of big estates, especially those estates that are coming to grief. There is undoubtedly more clear social gain, not only in comfort but in creativeness, in the increase of small holders than in the perpetuation of big owners. Denmark has lost patrons of hospitals, of homes for the old, of artists and poets and scholars. But it has better hospitals, better homes for the old, better foundations and endowments than it ever had under the great landowners. Benevolence to parasites has dwindled. A right to social help has taken its place. And while a small proportion of the ex-parasites feel it laid on them to be uncivil, the nobles move steadily into a position where, on their own merit, they are valued and valuable.

In the meantime the social art as such, the art of cultivated personality and of appreciated personality, is at its best in that particular circle. Our glimpses of it aroused no prejudice in me once I had found it possible to tolerate Grandfather.

CHAPTER TWENTY-ONE

Noble Lady

ONE of the solaces of Denmark, as I have suggested, is its social simplicity. You are not oppressed by caste, either in its implacable integrity or in the shattered state where you are cut to ribbons by fragments of it. This is so singular, considering the "revolution" we hear about, that a little more should be said about it.

Since 1918 the masses have furnished most of the high rulers in Europe. It is coachmen, cooks, servant girls, blacksmiths and so forth who have bred the men recently on top. What has happened in Hollywood, in the film world, has happened in Europe in that other fantastic realm, the realm of postwar politics. It is so new a business that it has been grabbed by the New Men. At the head of affairs in Russia, in Germany, in Italy, in Turkey, in France, in little Ireland, you observe the children of outsiders and very often of manual workers, of the newly literate artisans. It is not the court cards that have won the trick. It is the two-spots, those dear little, kind little two-spots who are supposed to be smiling at you meekly when they are showing two rows of shark's teeth. Two-spots like Mussolini, like Stalin, like Hitler.

These New Men, these Parvenu Men, have agreed on a formula of simplicity and frugality to reassure the workers.

They may plaster themselves with medals and hang medals on others, they may marry their daughters to the titled nobility, they may strut in uniforms, review troops, grab castles, have strings of motors and airplanes and take royal salutes, but the convention is maintained that they are untainted by wealth, that they are still putting away the crown, that they are always men of the people, comrades, antiplutocrat. Under the apparatus they have borrowed, under the gorgeousness they revel in and the lavishness the state affords them—renouncing wealth and luxury as they do—they are in reality quite incapable of resisting privilege. They are ravenous for it. They pick and choose among the costumes and treasures of the class they have ousted.

Yet in the North, where the Social Democrats have put the children of workers in power, you see nothing of this. Denmark, it cannot be denied, was ruled by men drawn from a relatively small class and looking on themselves as superior, until comparatively recently, yet between these men and the workers there is no bitter animosity. The workers neither ape them nor try to supersede them.

How is this? And have the nobles, like the workers, come to be socialized?

2

By sheer accident we met a Dane who threw light on this for us. She was a person whom we came to know so well and to admire so much that the accident has to be set forth in some detail.

After we had settled into our flat we were eager to escape from it. There was no snow in Denmark, so we decided to have a white Christmas in Sweden.

During the previous summer, with our two friends the

Painter and the Designer, we had been in the south of Sweden, and one afternoon, under the benevolent despotism of the Designer, we climbed up a broken road to have a cup of coffee. Our inn, which had been a small manor house, was perched on a ridge over a bay. What made it a magical choice was the green plateau on which we found our table. It was like an immense balcony in a theater, but a balcony so vast that all the little groups on it were set far apart, islanded in green, and out beyond us, with a fringe of birches on one side and a fringe of pine trees on the other, was the lustrous water as the stage, with a few little figures promenading on the edge of the balcony and on the stage itself a tiny sailboat. It was a spectacle. A quiet waitress, with small hands and small feet, came toward us as gracefully as a Chinese. She smiled and served us coffee. We took cakes, those minor infidelities, and looked at the great mirrored clouds that lifted their bulbous heads.

"This," said Signe crisply, "is shamefully good coffee!"

It was so good that we looked into the inn itself. The dining room was in robin's-egg blue with white woodwork. The room inside, with its books and portraits and old furniture, had quite the feeling of a manor. We fell in love with it.

And so, with the roads still open in spite of the snow, we motored up to it for Christmas.

3

The Lutheran church in the town was already dark at three on the afternoon of Christmas Eve. And it was filled. We managed to find places in a side aisle. The white pillar in front of us was circled by candles, a cincture of flame. Candles burned in a row on the endpiece of every pew. The church was a blaze of light, and the white walls of the church were honeyed with it.

The countrymen's heavy dark clothes brought their white collars into relief. They had stiff faces, stern faces. The housewives sat shoulder to shoulder with them, and yet each of them was uncompromisingly individual, marked by the unsparing struggle of life. They were massive people. But above their voices, when they sang hymns, rose the fresh girls' voices, still virginal. Then the pastor, with a fine-drawn face, slowly mounted the wooden pulpit and gave a pondered sermon. He spoke of the evil times we lived in, of the hatred in the world and the base lust for power. Tight-packed in the church, the congregation took it as he gave it, slowly, ponderingly.

The feeling of Christmas met us in the air when we went out. Like a dark stream through a virgin snowfield went those honest, dreadful words of fate impending, but we walked through the churchyard into the sparkling cold. Voices were gay. We threaded through the cars and up the silent hill. It would be a happy Christmas.

4

"Do you ski?" she said to us, smiling.

No, we didn't ski.

Her face was small and pointed, with large eyes, hazel eyes, and her lips rippled. She was one of those persons into whose eyes you could peer to the depths, and there was a discovery to make: there was reserve in them but no malice. From the very first you could see that she was capable of reserve and incapable of malice. But at the moment she was a Salvation Army Nell engaged in missionary work. Her mission was to make us ski, and in the most dulcet tones she was explaining it to us.

But the *clothes?*

She was in blue, a blue windbreak with a hood and blue trousers.

"But"—she was in her element explaining to us—"it is perfectly simple. I will show you." She pulled up her windbreak to show the trousers. "Here"—she pulled out a little white—"is the woolen underthing. But that is not all. Wait." She struggled. "I cannot show you, but there is another thing, a fine, fine cambric, and it is a windbreak." So, as she stood there, a small figure in blue, we studied the manner in which she was upholstered for skiing. She explained everything.

"But now," she said decisively, "it is time for lunch. I cannot keep Mother."

I was too old to learn skiing. That was my defense when we resumed later. But why? We compared ages. We were the same age. If she could, I could. As for Signe, she was an infant.

It is not every woman of my age who can wear trousers, and it is not every woman who can draw a hood over her head that is lined with lamb's wool. But she was small, her bones were small and her shoulders gracefully modeled. Flushed from her rapid descents down the hill and powdered with snow and lamb's wool, she was radiant. There were only a dozen or so in the inn for Christmas and most of them subdued. It was clear it would be a good Christmas; we were all going to be subdued together.

Weaving through us was the smiling waitress from summertime. She never hurried. She never failed. And the coffee was better than ever.

All the dishes, hot and cold, were at a central table for lunch and dinner. We helped ourselves, rotating round the table. By the time you had found 3, 5 and 7 irresistible you were awake to the awkward fact that 9 and 11 were also irresistible. On the return visit 2, 4 and 6 knocked you out and so did 8, 10 and 12. All you had omitted was No. 1. Up till then you had shown character.

5

In the evenings we passed from skiing to Geneva. This lady had been at Geneva more than once. The peace of Europe was, more than anything, the one concern of her life, but she was just as eager to do something about it as to make us ski, and all her judgments of people were reserved until she knew how they would serve this main purpose. To talk of it, aware she was amateur, aware she would not be ridiculed, enabled her to disclose the single-mindedness of the born ideologist, but instead of the consecrated ideologist to whom people are pawns, people for her were the most astonishingly real phenomena. She saw them in the body, to the last detail of their features and their habits, and with a special light appreciation of their more comic aspect. She saw them in their habit of mind, originally and vivaciously. And she saw them in their entourage, whether they were at the top, at the bottom or in the middle. This was not a gossip. This was a historian, at first a reserved historian and always, as I have said, without malice. And her range included not only the present but generations. She did not see people as trees walking. She saw them as trees rooted, as banyan trees if you like, up and down and up again. And people with paraphernalia, with houses, objets d'art, darling possessions, castles. But even more than that, and with a perfect absence of pudeur, she saw them as creatures in a moral drama, sometimes afflicted with a squint native to certain stock, sometimes wildly ungoverned, sometimes inherently romantic, but moving through scenes where the dangerous or the subversive could at any moment convert a polite balance into a catastrophe. It was never her desire to make a good story at the expense of veracity. The good story, for her, depended on veracity. It was her special quality to have a powerful sense of life but no hidden motive and no artifice.

Her mother was what people label a Great Lady. She too was a limpid person, in no way inaccessible and with a voice of such lovely modulation that to hear it was to know she was predestined to Heaven. It is not a place I'd feel at home in, but I believe I'd like the tones of their voices. Hell is a scream.

By the time we returned to Denmark enough had been said to make it impossible not to go on. And, in any event, the only way to get one's innings with her was to start new innings.

6

Perhaps it was the accident that we had gone to church the previous day and come home alive with the sermon, but we had satisfied some expectation in her, reassured some nerve and passed through to her inner confidence.

Even before she left the inn, a friend of hers came with his wife. He was a diplomat. He was strong, mature, clear-minded. Before long he was to wear himself out in a difficult mission and to die before he had rested from it.

Not by wealth, certainly, was she protecting herself or her rank from the common concussions. If she wished to see us, three miles away in town, she came on her bicycle and always, like so many Danes, bearing a gift, either a book or some cakes or some flowers. She had been prepared for the fact that we had plucked our furniture's eyebrows and cut its hair, but she accepted it with that little heightening of veracity which is permitted in the name of kindness. Otherwise we'd just kill babies the minute we saw them. Not yours, perhaps, but most babies. And at a certain stage a home is a baby.

It was not precisely because she was a pacifist that I was impressed but because she, whose husband had been a hussar, whose son had been in the guards, whose brother was a born cavalryman and whose friends and relations and equals were all either in the army or diplomacy, had, by some sort of spiritual osmosis, pushed out of the noble tradition into a new one, a new and not less noble tradition. Her grandfather, or her great-grandfather, had done the same sort of thing. He was a physiocrat. Her father had done it. He was a radical in his day. And by an urgency in her blood rather than in her brain she was driven to question the very pillars that supported her, to reduce them if possible to one pillar on which she'd be left an anchoress and in the desert. This unworldliness, however, she did not yield to. Only in one thing, and that was her squat little hats, did she betray this passion for renunciation. Otherwise, loyal to her order, she flinched at no demand that did not ask her to be unprincipled.

And, belonging to an order which is European, her thinking was not meager. Russia, I mean, was of concern to her through scores of Russians whose fate she had alleviated. Finland was real to her. So was Poland. Germany was not only next door, it was a Power that had always been next door. France was known at firsthand and through intimates. So was Holland. So was England. Sweden and Norway were familiar. She could speak Italian, German, French, English and so on. Brazil was quite close to her because of friends. And in the endless meeting of wayfaring Europeans who had once been at home in Copenhagen, in the continuous conversation she engaged in, she was in and of herself a magnet not merely of gossip or of ideas but of the force that has its outcome in politics.

Had it been her own order she strove for, one could only smile. Those aristocrats with woebegone looks who set out the beggar's bowl, hoping for Mussolini or Hitler to drop his favor in, are scarcely an enticing group. The totalitarian state may employ such people, but it has no gains to split with them. The order she strove for was another order, a moral order in Europe, and if one were to smile at this as naïve, since Germany and Russia are so likely to continue the present dispute on terms that leave out the whole of her moral preconceptions, I can only enumerate the things I found her to care for. These may go, indeed. The pilgrimages of the twelfth century have gone. The moralities have given way to more vivid secular drama. The burning of witches has gone. The whole mumbo jumbo of medical science has changed. The ideas of personal service, of legal retainers, of good men and true, have vanished. You could construct a whole moral and social system of the twelfth and thirteenth centuries that has as completely disappeared as the Latinity to which Erasmus and Thomas More were clinging as the *sine qua non* of civilized communication in Christendom.

But what she clung to, as totally valid against the New Order, was a spiritual amenity as certain to have been found in the Bastille as in the France where it came up again, like grass between the stones, watered by the aristocrats' blood. That amenity cannot be guillotined. While pilgrimages and moralities and incantations and servitude might all be washed off the slate, the impulses behind them remained in just such a person as herself. She took us to see the plot where she was to be buried, between two humble folk; she hurried from us another time for the funeral of an old retainer; she heard with amusement of those midsummer dances we had voyaged to see at St John's Eve in Sweden, and she herself went on a pilgrimage at the call of a separated friend. What "revolution" in Europe can make an order binding that meets opposition with annihilation? The Huguenots were not annihilated. The famine-stricken Irish, who were to be as rare in Ireland, one hopeful prayed, as a Red Indian in Manhattan, have not been annihilated by half, though the sentiment is still heartfelt in many circles. Even Southern Democrats, who share the sentiment, do not want to see this massacre till after election. If the history of Europe teaches anything, it is that extermination doesn't exterminate, that penal laws defeat themselves, that boundaries are fluid, that loyalties are transient, that scoundrels are either tamed or doomed. The age of the machine has liberated man from innumerable bondages and limitations. It has given him new eyes, new ears, new legs, new hands. But mobile as he is, facile as he is, docile as he is, labile as he is, he still is born of woman, he still wants to dance on St John's Eve, he still has to have friends, he still wants a friend near him when he comes to die, he still has to keep accounts with himself in regard to the others—that is to say, the innocent, the injured, the alien. The young are glib in calling this war a revolution. All revolutions have to be judged by the counterrevolutions they provoke, just as all disciplines have to be judged by the resulting breach of those disciplines. And what inevitably attracted me to this member of the aristocratic order was the driving persistence with which she pursued the Danish solution by reconciliation, by good will and by consent.

Do I hear the word "appeasement"?

"We had a German manager," said a Dane to me, "a branch manager for our product, which is sold all over the world. And one day, when we asked him to come up to see the directors, he wrote back that, as a German, he had to be considered the head of the concern in Germany, and if we had anything to say we must come to him.

"We told him he must come. And at last he came, with his lawyer. He was really a good fellow. We asked him to my house to dinner, and we made no effort to persuade him, but we talked the whole long evening. His lawyer told him he hadn't a leg to stand on, and at last he came round.

"I heard from him not so long ago. He said he had to go over into Switzerland for a day, to breathe a breath of freedom."

If by that you mean "appeasement," the Danes are appeasers. But the toughness, the patience, the dogged tenacity with which the Danes argue their point do not make the prospect particularly happy for the Germans, since the time always comes when the Germans, also born of woman, etc., etc., have to try something besides the third degree.

A "revolution," in any event, is either one of two things: a fundamental change in the social system, like the Industrial Revolution, or an internal revolt by the subjects, like the American Revolution. This war, so far, has seen no honest revolt by the subjects of any nation that has been attacked, though it has seen creep-ups like Quisling and the rest, who have been bolstered into place after attempts have been made to murder the established ruler, as in Norway. What, then, of a fundamental change in the social system, a change to totality? This, of course, would be a most desirable doctrine to spread, since one bunch of totalities could do business with other totalities, after the "revolution." But the issue is falsified and poisoned by this suggestion that a revolution has started and that our society is on the skids. The society that has crumbled is Russian and German society. It has slithered from a consultative society into a society that doesn't argue with you but tells you. The murder gang, the concentration camp and the "correct but arrogant" army of occupation are the three necessary preliminaries to the New Order, which is a social receivership and not a society at all. The revolution that German propaganda talks about is nonexistent. But the shake-up in democracies that themselves have been evolving a genuine new order can very well be accelerated. And that shake-up, if the democracies are wise, ought to follow on Danish lines. It ought to reconcile, within its own borders, the differences that embroil one group with another, not by planning for "appeasement" with a totality expressly inimical to it and thereby splitting itself in two, but by saying, an international system based on the violation of neutralities, on the employment of murder gangs, concentration camps and armies of occupation is clearly not an international system, and until the process of social consent is restored appeasement is treachery. It is treachery to the slugged and beaten millions of minorities. It is treachery to the blackmailed and the violated. It is treachery to the gagged and bound. It is confederacy with the gangsters on the familiar basis of submission to extortion in the name of business as usual.

There are those who, when themselves outraged by kidnapers, ask for every penalty the law can give them. It is strange they can be willing to see whole nations kidnaped and expect those nations to pursue appeasement. All those nations ask for is to be given back to their own direction, to be given back while there is still life in them and while they can make their voices heard. How deaf the inner man must be who cannot hear that cry.

And how absurd, when the nobility has become a citizenry, to talk of it as alien to a democratic experiment.

7

She had a better dentist than we had, since ours fell ill. She had a better shop for ski clothes. But we had a better doctor of sorts. She had a better inn in the country, but we had a better restaurant of a kind. We had friends whom she could share. And so had she. We went to her ancestral home and to her flat and on odd excursions.

She was, at heart, rather indifferent to music.

Her staying power as a friend did not raise her above the irritabilities that all missionaries are subject to. And in the fineness of her being, not to be seen in her hands but in the articulation of her limbs, in the quick freshness of her laugh, in the poise of her head, there was also the danger of disharmony. The exquisite are more easily jangled, especially when so much in exquisiteness is shaped by a code, for a group and a manner of living. But her true manner of living and her inner code were far more gratified by the aliens than by many of the habitual. And yet her reserve saved her from the dullness of liabilities to those so obviously in transit. We were not casual nor were we greedy. The perfection of knowing her was to be spiritually related. It rather upset one supervisory matron who, being alien herself, feared for the European order. But the European order was safe in the old hands, as safe as wind and weather permitted.

Hers was the kind of home where Hans Christian Andersen had had two rooms. It was one of his pleasantest havens, and the Great Lady actually had known him. Her home, indeed, was in the lap of the land, where manor houses and castles were linked one to the other in friendship, in common life, in intimacies. The carp were still in the moat, and in the quietude of the grounds there was that hovering magic, that spell of the past, that enclosure of more than private earth, that welling of memory and of beauty. Who lingers in those old avenues? Who has left his wistfulness in those woods? The drooping trees, the far islands in the lagoon, the dwelling silence, enrich and sadden the inheritors. We left there no less intimate.

Denmark, through such as she, absorbs into itself the poetry of this noble order.

CHAPTER TWENTY-TWO

"Danmark" Ahoy!

JUST by living in it we began to lose the broader vision of Denmark. It was our immediate world—the Designer, Harald, Frithjof, the Noble Lady, the Painter—that stood before us with each step we climbed. Not till we reached a plateau could we stop to survey.

That plateau came in December 1939, when we decided to sail for America.

On giving up our little place in Hellerup, we had moved to a hotel. This was a haven. It was a hotel on the top floor of an old palace, and it had only ten rooms in it. We had three of them, under the roof. Up from the courtyard rose a tall elm to a level with my bedroom. Across this courtyard was a factory that purred steadily until four P.M. Then it closed down and quiet fell on us. All day we could work undisturbed or, when the time came, could go down into the old Copenhagen that has dignity and reverie. We had two such kind maids in the hotel, one from Jutland, the other from the Faroes, that it was like living in a home. The Faroe girl had that china whiteness with pink roses that one sees in an eighteenth-century painting. She came from her islands of 25,000 population, very ceremonious and yet eager. The other, good Enemark, was brunette, vigorous, fresh as a salt breeze, with a prompt heart and a lively tongue. She accelerated the universe, which still had the power to excite and surprise and touch her. She had all sorts of duties in the rest of the palace, where weddings were celebrated by banquets and so on, but she had energy for anything. She was one of those brave soldiers of the people who keep marching no matter what. She had some deep-down faith in her, could laugh and yet serve as a matter of course, tireless and vigilant.

The steamers that called for the bridge at night would sometimes fill the air with noble booms of sound. Otherwise it was very still. We ran to the windows when we heard flying machines, but they were always patrols or the regular passenger planes. Why should anyone invade Denmark?

By December I had finished my play on Queen Anne Boleyn. From New York I gathered that producers of plays hate to invest their money in the work of untried dramatists, so we booked our passage by the steamer *Drottningholm*. I wanted to learn about producers.

2

This Denmark I had "chosen," could I still account for it? Day by day it was changing. There were breaks with the past, friends in hospital, friends in trouble. At times these misfortunes, however lightly one took them since they were not one's own, contrived to dim the sky so that one felt permanently dingy. Even a glass of snaps was no great alleviation. Every day someone seemed to be losing his hair or his teeth or to be just plain dying. And, on top of this, the Germans! They had crumpled up the Czechs. They had savaged Poland. Was Daladier big enough to meet this? Was Chamberlain possessed of any imagination? I found myself completely at one with the English in this fight for what seemed to me freedom. But it was not being publicly focused for Denmark; the English were full of illusions and still muddled.

By "muddled" I mean that England had sent out Runciman and then listened to him when he was the type of appeaser who ignores inconvenient spiritual and political issues. Rothermere, again, had been prowling around Denmark at the time of Munich. He had misrepresented real European issues for many years. And miniscule Duff-Cooper had been in Copenhagen. These men were the fixed charges, apparently, that England felt had to be met by democracy before any understanding could be reached. Democracy had to face these debits, these obligations. Well, England is a grand old concern. It had survived F. E. Smith. It had survived the glass-eyed Sir John Simon. It probably could survive anything. By some sort of instinct I found myself wanting to be with Englishmen. To them Runciman, Rothermere, Duff-Cooper, John Simon were not thin slabs of linotype but actual human creatures, possibly better than their deeds and their words. Certainly the words of some of my Englishmen were often wholly ludicrous. But they were sane, they were fighting men, they were passionately aroused. Strong and silent, indeed! They shouted me down, these silent Englishmen in Copenhagen. But when green-blooded German theorists said the English were degenerate I always laughed. Degeneracy, for me, is decided by murder and torture in a society, by the imprisonment of a Schuschnigg, by the theft which calls itself "confiscation," by the treachery of pouncing on neutrals. The English had been culpable in India, but what chance would a Gandhi have in Berlin, a Polish Gandhi, a Jewish Gandhi? The Germans had no place in their cosmos for that. England had. England is experienced. Germany, when it comes to power, is spiritually unripe.

Danish ripeness was socially evident. Think, after all, what it had been obliged to confront. From the time of its defeat by Germany in 1864 it had been called on to solve the whole question of the peasant and his tenure of the land. By a steady and unselfish policy, one step at a time, it had given the peasant social training or rather helped him to give himself social training, it had given him private ownership of the land but on terms of a social development ensured to it by co-operation and co-operative marketing. This was not Marxian. Denmark had to clear its mind about Marxianism and had done so. Its Communists might find supporters among the *intelligentsia,* since the unemployed were a constant reproach to the existing system, but the Communists could make no headway in the countryside and little in the towns. Soviet Russia was too near.

By the élan and the versatility of the rationalists, besides, Denmark after 1864 had tamed the Church and given full play to science and free thought. This had been one of its most fruitful developments. When a great resource was opened to it such as the Carlsberg Foundation the University was full of fertile minds, so that scholarship and the critical sense reached a level that no mere pietist could challenge. Niels Bohr was a fact. So was Madsen. So was Krogh. This went with a dispossession of the nobility in the field of government. The Social Democrats had gone to school to first-rate teachers. They took over power with greater firmness than the corresponding class in England. They were not merely the victors in trade-union circles. They had ideas. They had a map of the universe in their heads. They were not pure evangelists. The work that the Fabians had attempted in England had, by a parallel process, been more effective in Denmark, since the entire national culture was itself more Fabian. The vested interests had no such hard shell to crack, and the cracking did not have to break down a police. It was done with the ballot, by journalists, by professors, by men of ideas. Johannes V. Jensen added a few thousand years to Denmark's large awareness of itself. One of his books became a Bible.

By fundamental legislation, by a resolute superintendence of the profit motive, by indefatigable social work, Denmark made definite advance in dealing with poverty. Old-age pensions came very early. Insurance was grasped as a social idea and well inflected to suit Danish needs. Drunkenness was eliminated since

1900. Disease was lessened. In such a region as personal relationships the divorce laws, the laws concerning abortion, the laws concerning illegitimacy showed rationality at its best. The opposition on these questions, stripped of the old magniloquence of the Church, was seldom impressive, yet it was not treated hilariously. The Danes have no complacence of this sort. They are not "naturalists." Nor are they jovial adolescents toting a hip flask.

One circumstance that made it easier for Denmark to effect these changes was its religious and racial uniformity. No Danish La Guardia would have had to wriggle out of appointing a man like Bertrand Russell for fear of the Catholic vote. The radio does not have to be so timid as the British Broadcasting Corporation. Denmark, in this respect, has been singularly fortunate. Its minorities have been feeble minorities, and it could give them great latitude while still going its own way. That way, for half a century, has been increasingly "liberal," pursued with gentleness and persuasiveness. The astonishing fact that Stauning has held office for a decade and a half, with a majority in the lower house of only two or three, shows that it is not only in Greenland that a kajak is navigable.

From my vantage point I remained impressed. Though we had not been inside more than forty or fifty homes, though we lived withdrawn as plodding writers must, though we had no "circle" to speak of, it was impossible not to be weighing the evidence for and against Denmark every day. A single visit to the Arsenal, to see sixteenth-century armor, was enough to enchant one with its scrupulous historic sense. A visit to Police Headquarters revived one's confidence in new architecture, with its refusal to persist with Christian IV, its willingness to use humble material with a noble rhetoric. All these experiments, the new bridge, for example, over Lillebelt, permitted one to believe that complacency had not closed down. Denmark was not yet a folke-museum.

But a new inquietude was capturing the country. Europe was

in turmoil, and a new dramatist with a vivid and vehement gift for contrast was drawing Denmark to his peep show. He was openly referring to Hitler, to the Tyrant, to Mussolini.

This met Danish inquietude. The Tyrant was at Warnemunde, at Sild, at Paddeborg. The Tyrant had scores of Germans in Copenhagen to phone to Berlin hour by hour, relaying what a political expert was writing, what a socialist minister was declaring, what a cartoonist was drawing, when the freighters were passing, where the officers were living.

Denmark was determined to behave correctly. But would it be a case of Androcles and the lion? Was Denmark to end in the arena? Was Shaw's adorable fable to prove true, or would favor shift, as with Shaw himself, from Androcles to the beast with an inflamed temper? For a small sovereignty the whole problem of sovereignty was now being opened. The French design for the Continent, based on a Little Entente, had visibly crumbled. The League of Nations had dissolved ignominiously. Germany had burst from its lair. What small sovereignty could hold against its dynamic policy? Was it not the end of small perfections, local experiments?

Or could Denmark beg off? Could it fit in with the plans of the Tyrant? Could it evade? That was the most dangerous of temptations, and the ideologists of Berlin understood how to tempt the Danish businessman, the Danish aristocrat.

3

I spoke earlier of tales that Delargy had collected from the Irish folk. Here is one that he told to us in our garden in Wicklow:

It was in the time of Cromwell. Cromwell was leading his army up an Irish valley at the fall of night, and on the side of the hill he saw a house with a bright light in it.

"Go up there," he said to his lieutenant. "Find out what that's for."

The lieutenant came back. "The man of the house is dead," he told Cromwell, "and now they're waking him."

"Is that so?" said Cromwell. "Go up now. Tell them I'll give them fifty pounds for the corpse."

He did as he was told.

"What did they say to you?" asked Cromwell again.

"They were horrified at us," said the lieutenant. "Is it sell the corpse of their own father, they said."

"Go up again," said Cromwell. "Say I'll give a hundred pounds for the corpse. And show them the money."

When the lieutenant came back Cromwell was ready for him. "What did they say this time?"

"They asked me what kind of a heathen I was, to come into the house of the dead and make such an offer. They told me to respect the dead and leave them in peace or it would be worse for me."

"Is that so?" said Cromwell. "Go back. Say I'll give five hundred pounds for the corpse."

"They'll kill me, sir," said the lieutenant.

"Do as I bid you, sir," said Cromwell.

When he returned Cromwell said, "And now what have you to tell me?"

"One of them said, 'He must want the corpse terrible bad to offer so much as that. Isn't Father dead anyway? What harm can it do him now! Let him have his way for the five hundred pounds.'"

"Did they take it?"

"They did, sir."

"Ha!" said Cromwell to his lieutenant, "now I know that I can conquer Ireland." And he took the army on up the narrow valley.

4

No Danish businessman, no Danish aristocrat had been seduced. When we left in December no one was selling Denmark as a corpse. Neutrality was assured by treaty. It was being respected. England had paid compensation for bombs dropped by accident at Esbjerg. Germany was equally punctilious. It seemed then that unless events were peculiarly untoward Denmark could count on peace, as it had between 1914 and 1918.

We said our farewells. Our dear friends seemed sorry to have us go. The Designer had planned a house for us in beautiful detail. I had, with native modesty, urged a bungalow. Not a suspicion of the bungalow remained in it. He had seen a house, in his mind's eye, of such composure and distinction and finality that we could at last receive our world, our particular world, on the terms he supposed worthy of it, and if we could only yield to the profit motive in the right time and place, the new house would be realizable and in full sight of the Sound. We looked at the design and at the Designer and said a reluctant good-by.

The war became slightly more real after we left the Swedish harbor. The waters were mined. We anchored at night and we kept within the Norwegian three-mile limit.

For several days we continued up the coast. December though it was, the air was mild. The day was extremely brief. Hardly had the night been withdrawn, between nine and ten in the morning, than it began to fall after two.

It was no longer the receptive plain of Denmark we had to look at. We sailed under the mountains of Norway. I had heard of these mountains from summer tourists, but we were cleaving waters that had their reflections in them, and it was the solemnity of winter that brought me on deck and held me spellbound. The ship came to be a moving platform between these ominous and tremendous presences. I went to the top deck so that I could pass quickly from one side to the other. With slashes of green and dull rusted brown, these black masses lifted to heights on which the snow had lodged. They were profiles of a North that had no longer the habit of men and cities but that raised themselves to confront the universe itself, peaks so serene yet so incalculably remote that it was as if they alone contemplated eternity and infinity. It was no passing moment of awe in their presence. One stood among them for hour after hour. They mounted on either side and in front, so that the ship appeared to be locked in their midst, like a fugitive trapped, and only as we advanced against the face of a mountain did these slow barriers recede to permit our passage. They were not "scenery." They were majestic beings. They continued before us with rhythms so exalted and so somber that we could not escape them. To leave them, in their surprise of form and magnitude, was impossible. They stood to communicate tidings from a world hitherto unknown, tidings of reserve, of implacable gravity. They brooded on man.

At any moment we might, by unhappy accident, run into a floating mine.

"I remember once," a Danish passenger would say to you, "a mine was sighted, and before we could alter our course we had gone over the blooming thing. We exploded it with gunfire."

The sublimity of this coast, our steady pace, the placidity of the day, made us feel that mines were no danger. Man could not affront these mountains.

A German boat passed us, quite near.

We saw tiny settlements at the foot of these lonelinesses. In one harbor a girl rowing a boat glided from us as if on glass, far down below. We waved. Then wakes of glass curled her boat around and she had to row manfully.

Further north there were heights more stupendous, but we only reached Aalesund. Our captain at last thought we should go west, so we turned for America, steering between the Faroes and Iceland.

5

We were in Florida when the radio told us that Germany had broken her word. The neutrality of Denmark had been violated. This happened on April 9, 1940.

We did not then know that the bombing planes came over

Copenhagen as an ultimatum was delivered. During that brief hour the hatches of coal ships in the Free Harbor were opened and the German troops that had been concealed in these merchant ships poured into the sleeping city. Every important Danish officer was arrested in his own home and held by German agents. German troops took over the French and English embassies. They invaded the palace, were resisted and were then admitted as the ultimatum had been accepted. Thousands upon thousands of German troops were entrained, going to destinations that had been designed for them soon after Hitler had come into power. This move had been long contemplated and arranged for, though the German minister gave his word of honor that no move would be made. A military power was applying its technique to a small democracy. What weapons had the democracy to retort with? Treaties? Agreements? Proofs of neutrality? These were of no interest. Denmark had flying fields. Denmark was convenient for attacking Norway. Denmark was convenient for holding the Baltic. Denmark was a larder.

6

Democracies, then, are the playthings of tyrants if they are not ready to defend themselves. It is not a mere accident of juxtaposition. It is a conflict of conceptions. The tyrant cannot admit the success of an Order that is not his Order. He must break down successful democracy, as such.

7

In the month of May we visited Jacksonville in Florida. In the harbor there lay anchored a sailing ship. It flew the Danish flag. It bore the name DANMARK.

This was the training ship for the Danish merchant marine, and we had to wait, before rowing out to her, till the cadets had loaded vegetables into the boat. These were fresh vegetables that a friend sent every day. Who was she? Just a friend. She had never visited the vessel. Ever since the *Danmark* had come to rest at Jacksonville there was no kindness too great for the people to show to her. The captain had to be stern, lest his entire crew of cadets be spoiled by kindness. When we came on board and peeped aft we saw some of them resting after a morning's work. They were so exhausted that it was evident they had not yet relaxed a moment of discipline, but the minute I saw the mildness of their glance, its absolute directness and frankness, I could say to myself, "This is Denmark."

The little ship—for in the world of mechanized shipping this was a little ship—had the extraordinarily clear presence, the snug and compact and ordered personality of a clean sailing vessel. The woodwork is unornamented and definite. The planks are scraped and scrubbed. The spars cut into the high sky with an edge like music. The masts spring upward with the audacity of a function that is stripped of every disguise, a pure, naked confrontation of a task on which life itself is staked and trusted. At one glance, on board the *Danmark,* the organism spoke for itself. And then the captain was there to shake hands with us, Captain Knud Hansen.

He was a relatively young man. Where he might have been jovial in carefree times he was now almost like a captain on the bridge, wary, eye-tense, controlled. A quick hospitable smile, and then he resumed that Watch which was becoming habitual with him, a watch during all his hours awake, a watch over his ship's actual destiny.

His task was to equip young men for the merchant marine. They would have to spend seven or eight years, these lads, before they could hope to have their certificates as mates. First, a year before the mast, a year on board with himself. Then three years on steam or motor ships. After four years of practical sailoring they would be ready for a training in the navigation school on land. There they would spend the time necessary to master navigation, with six or eight months in addition to become radio telegraphers. After that they would go in the navy, to serve their time as conscripts, and from the navy perhaps into the marine as officers.

With such a course laid out for them and for himself, the *Danmark* was free to circle the world. But now! Now, after April 9, he had no longer the right to travel on the high seas. He flew a flag that was under alien suspicion. For the first time in those centuries that had passed since Dannebrog was grasped by Danes in Esthonia and carried to victory, June 15, 1219, he could no longer assert it as a free flag. Denmark was under "protection."

Here it was at anchor, this trim vessel with its hundred young men on board ready to pursue the hard training that would make them men, ready to develop themselves for the work that the Danish merchant marine would require of them, essential to its existence, and instead of being allowed to do the job they were cut off from their government, from their base, from their function, crippled in their exercise as free men.

"They heap kindness on us," he said, speaking of the people in Florida. But still!

He and his second in command have only the cadets to aid them in sailing the ship. He told of going up the Hudson with them. She stood right up to Brooklyn Bridge before she tacked. She crossed to the Jersey side until her bow was almost over a wharf and then carried right up the river. He smiled at this recollection with a tight and grudging smile. No, he could not be happy. Not till he took her out to sea, stripped for work, could this man be himself again, with these keen youngsters obeying him.

After lunch we walked aft, and it was Denmark everywhere. But why a sailing ship? Why an outmoded service?

"Because," said Captain Hansen, "here's the best and the only chance to foster the abilities we think a man has to possess to be put in charge of millions of value, not to speak of passengers, not to speak of the crew or the vessel.

"Why," he said, "a sailing ship? Because character is the thing to strengthen. Here you can train men who'll be responsible. Here you'll test courage, initiative, self-help." He paused. "You can see yourselves we could not run the ship without order, quickness, discipline, cleanliness . . ."

He was quite unashamed to speak of these things. He was a stubborn, grim man, thinking of the human responsibility he had and the obstacle that had come athwart it.

Signe and I looked at one another. For us, and for the American commander of the navy and his wife who had accompanied us, Denmark and the *Danmark* were interchangeable. Then, rather timidly, Signe turned to the captain.

"But, Captain," she said, "what—what can you expect of the future?"

The future?

"It's very difficult for me to say," he answered without a smile. "If lies, injustice and violence are to conquer, what is left then to live for or make plans for? On what foundation can you build?"

We left him at that.

As we sailed out of Jacksonville there lay the *Danmark*, anchored in the friendly harbor.

Martha's Vineyard, Mass.
August 27, 1940.